Embracing Change and Developing Leadership

IN THE EARLY YEARS SECTOR

This book champions the unique knowledge, skills and behaviours of early years (EY) practitioners, and shows how they can exercise individuality in response to the diverse needs of children and their families.

Fully mapped to the requirements of the new Early Years Lead Practitioner HTQ, this practical guide offers a reflective and challenging stance to critically evaluate the intentions that underpin EY policy and practice, and considers how to reimagine practice in challenging times to remain aligned with child-centred values. Structured to inspire, chapters delve into six key themes: the educator and developer of children, the custodian, the planner, the advocate, the collaborator and the innovator. It includes critical questions, reflective exercises and case studies, enabling readers to directly apply their knowledge to practice and use this text as a comprehensive, one-stop guide.

Embracing Change and Developing Leadership in the Early Years Sector is a contemporary guide for early years practitioners and students. It is an essential resource for the new Early Years Lead Practitioner HTQ qualification.

Michelle Malomo is a Senior Lecturer in the Department for Children and Families within the School of Education at the University of Worcester, UK, lecturing on the Foundation Degree in Early Years (0–8, Professional Practice) and the top-up degree in Integrated Working with Children and Families.

Emma Laurence is a Lecturer in the Department for Children and Families at the University of Worcester, UK. She is course leader for the BA (Hons) Early Childhood and is also studying there for a PhD in Educational Leadership.

Embracing Change and Developing

LEADERSHIP IN THE EARLY YEARS SECTOR

Edited by Michelle Malomo and Emma Laurence

Routledge
Taylor & Francis Group

LONDON AND NEW YORK

Cover images: AdobeStock

First published 2026
by Routledge
4 Park Square, Milton Park, Abingdon, Oxon OX14 4RN

and by Routledge
605 Third Avenue, New York, NY 10158

Routledge is an imprint of the Taylor & Francis Group, an informa business

British Library Cataloguing-in-Publication Data
A catalogue record for this book is available from the British Library

ISBN: 978-1-041055-34-1 (hbk)
ISBN: 978-1-916925-78-6 (pbk)
ISBN: 978-1-041055-35-8 (ebk)

DOI: 10.4324/9781041055358

Typeset in Franklin Gothic Book
by Newgen Publishing UK

Dedications

There are some key ingredients in my philosophy for practice which have been gifted to me by loved ones.

Ben, your profound sense of justice and desire for a fairer world, Nonie, your steadiness and grace, Aurora, your sincere compassion, Ezra, your complete disregard for "because that's just the way it is" and Phinby your endless imagination. When I grow up, I want to be like you.

Emma Laurence

Dad, your passion for children and their families has been incredibly influential in my life. Your work with children and families at the margins of society lives on. We miss you, Dad.

Kelston, you too have inherited this passion, and I am proud to call you my brother.

Michelle Malomo

Contents

About the editors

Emma Laurence is currently a Lecturer in the Department for Children and Families at the University of Worcester and course leader of the BA (Hons) Early Childhood in Society. Alongside this she is studying for a PhD in Educational Leadership. Her current research centres on the ways that cluster groups of headteachers can provide a unique source of support. Prior to this, she studied both the BA (Hons) in Early Childhood and the MA in Education before completing her PGCE with TeachFirst and then her PG Certificate in Learning and Teaching in HE. Emma's experience spans EY settings, primary schools and now teaching in Higher Education. Her interests are in human development both individually and communally, meaning her work spans education and care across all ages and well beyond the school environment. Social Pedagogy is a key area of focus for Emma who is currently a trustee of the Social Pedagogy Professional Association and a member of the Social Pedagogy Research Group at the University of Worcester.

Michelle Malomo is currently a Senior Lecturer and partnership coordinator for the FdA in the early years (0–8) (HTQ) at the University of Worcester. She is also a Senior fellow of the Higher Education Academy. Having worked as a manager of an early years setting, she developed a passion for supporting early years practitioners to develop their practice and gain work-based qualifications. Michelle also has a passion for the power and value of play as a therapeutic approach for children and young people's well-being. Alongside this she is an advocate for Universal Design for Learning (UDL) and is an active member of the Universal design for learning research group at the university. She also co-leads a Community of Practice (COP) for Study Skills within the University of Worcester that focuses upon the importance of study skills for students in higher education. Outside of work Michelle volunteers as a children/youth worker.

About the authors

Janet Harvell

Janet Harvell is a Senior Lecturer at the University of Worcester. A qualified teacher, Janet has worked in the early years sector for the last 35 years. Having lived and worked abroad, her research interests are focused on international approaches, and this has included research in China and involvement in a collaborative learning and teaching project linked to refugee children and their families in Calais. More recently she has become engaged with charities working towards eliminating the use of single-use plastic and promoting the adoption of eco-friendly practices.

Angela Hodgkins

Dr Angela Hodgkins is a Senior Lecturer at the University of Worcester and is course leader for the BA (Hons) Integrated Working with Children and Families. Angela's professional back-ground is in the early years; she qualified as an NNEB nursery nurse in 1984 and has had a wide and varied career in working with young children. Angela is also a qualified counsellor. Recently, she completed a PhD where she researched early years practitioners' perception of empathy within their practice. Her research interests are in empathy, compassion and the well-being of practitioners.

Amanda McCully

Amanda McCully is an Associate Lecturer at the University of Worcester and course leader for the FdA early years at the Heart of Worcestershire Partner College. Amanda is a qualified teacher/lecturer who has worked with a wide range of age groups in schools and colleges. She has been involved in the teaching and course development of the University of Worcester FdA Degree in early years since its first delivery in the early 2000s. She is interested in the intersection of equity, education and learner self-belief, and also indigenous approaches to caring for the planet.

Sarah Phillips

Sarah Phillips is an Associate Lecturer at the University of Worcester and course leader and lecturer at a Partner College. A qualified Primary School Headteacher with over 35 years' experience in education and early years, Sarah brings a wealth of experiences from a wide variety of the sector to her teaching and practice. Her mantra is that the next generation of children deserve the best we can provide.

Alison Prowle

Dr Alison Prowle is a Senior Lecturer at the University of Worcester. Alison is a qualified teacher and spent a number of years working in the primary and secondary phases, before managing a Surestart programme in South Wales. Subsequently, Alison worked extensively in community development and managed preventative services for children and families in a Welsh Local Authority. Since joining the University of Worcester, Alison has specialised in children's adverse life experiences and trauma-informed work. She is passionate about supporting improved life chances for children in adversity and has undertaken extensive research with refugee and asylum seekers, care experienced families, and families in poverty.

Olivia Storey

Olivia Storey is a Lecturer at the University of Worcester, focusing on health and well-being, collaborative learning, and reflective practice. Her career began during her psychology degree, where she gained hands-on experience in early years settings. She worked as a Teaching Assistant in a mainstream school and volunteered at a special school and autistic unit, addressing holistic needs. Later, as a Family Support Worker, she supported families, including newborns, through structured sessions. As a youth worker, Olivia planned and delivered programmes promoting equality and participation. She qualified as a lecturer in 2008 and taught in Further Education colleges for over 13 years, covering subjects in health and social care, education, and early years.

Samantha Sutton-Tsang

Samantha Sutton-Tsang is a Senior Fellow of the Higher Education Academy and a Senior Lecturer and course leader for the FdA early years at the University of Worcester. With extensive experience in early childhood education, Samantha is dedicated to fostering innovative teaching practices and supporting professional development. Her work emphasises the integration of technology in education and the promotion of high-quality early years practice through research.

Acknowledgements

There are a huge number of people, without whom this book would not have been possible. The Department for Children and Families at the University of Worcester and in particular the Partnership Team have been a driving force for positive change in the sector for decades. This team has championed the significant role of the early years practitioner and supported the development of a huge number of student practitioners from a diverse range of backgrounds. You have all been a rich well of support and inspiration for us and a key factor in the successful completion of this book.

We would like to acknowledge the generous contribution of all of our chapter authors. Your time, commitment and your knowledge and expertise have been the bedrock of this book, and we are delighted that our readers will benefit from the wealth of experience and passion you offer. We would like to acknowledge the generosity of Alison Prowle and Angela Hodgkins who happily offered their framework for strength-based practice for free (see Figure 10.1, Chapter 10). The creation of this book could not have been possible without the guidance of Julia Morris and Lily Harrison, thank you. Thank you also to Annamarie Kino for helping to get this text across the finish line.

And finally, thank you to our families who have provided endless cups of tea and words of encouragement.

Introduction

This book argues that the early years sector needs to re-evaluate what it means to flourish as a human being and how best this can be nurtured in the youngest members of our society. We see an opportunity to re-write the vision for children in our society and establish what the key values are at its core and what kind of leaders are best placed to drive this forward. This book offers hope against a backdrop of continuous change in social policy. It champions the unique knowledge, skills and behaviour of the EY practitioner as they lead practice and identifies how to exercise individuality in response to the diverse needs of children and their families in today's society.

This book will encourage you to reimagine how childhood could be. It asks you to purposefully daydream about a world which places children at its centre and nurtures playful interactions between children and families. Rather than simply critiquing practice we want to begin a conversation about how it could be otherwise and to inspire action which aligns with these visions. The EY sector has faced significant challenges over the last number of years and existing inequalities in society have been exacerbated. However, there are also reasons to be hopeful. We consider there to be an opportunity to reconstruct practice: to consider why we do things the way we do them and whether they could be done better. There is a genuine desire for aspirational practice which is above and beyond the statutory and we can see this in our students. Many of our students arrive with a passion to support children and families and quickly become an agent for change in the sector. The book embodies this aspirational practice and professional strength in the face of change and provides an invitation to join us in reimagining possibilities for practice and provision.

This book is for leaders of practice in the early years sector, whether you're new to the sector, or have watched it change over recent decades. This book particularly supports student practitioners who are studying at undergraduate level. The book is mapped to the 16 duties required of the early years lead practitioner, as identified by the Institute for Apprenticeships and Technical Education (IfATE). It equips individuals with the knowledge, skills and

DOI: 10.4324/9781041055358-1

behaviours (KSBs) to lead practice. These KSBs have been developed by professionals in the sector and underpin a range of level 5 qualifications within the early years. It is these building blocks which provide the DNA of the early years leader. This book supports your development towards these KSBs and each chapter is mapped to identify this. However, the content of each chapter has a narrative of exploring practice which goes beyond these expectations. The purpose of this is to empower you to not only embody the KSBs required to become an early years lead practitioner but to also support you in creating meaningful change in the lives of children and families. A full list of the duties and their corresponding KSBs follows this introduction chapter.

The book has been structured into six themes which reflect the attributes needed when leading practice within the sector. These are:

*   the educator/developer
*   the custodian
*   the planner
*   the collaborator
*   the advocate
*   the innovator.

You will see that the book is organised within these themes and that the knowledge, skills and behaviours are clearly mapped at the start of each chapter.

Theme 1: The educator and developer of children

1: The child at the centre of their development

This chapter focuses on the holistic development of the child and the professional's role in supporting this. Using a child-centred framework, practitioners will explore key theories of child development, both classic and contemporary, which underpin practice and contribute to a growing knowledge and understanding of how children learn and develop. Developing skills in observing children will be identified as a key tenet of child-centred practice in this area. The importance of relationships between the child and primary carers is a key component which runs throughout this chapter.

2: Supporting children to be healthy and well

This chapter will consider a holistic and context-sensitive approach to well-being which identifies the role of children's social worlds in supporting health and well-being. It will critically explore contemporary issues facing children and families in terms of being well, such as the impact of social policy and rising concerns about children's mental health. This chapter examines health and well-being across the life-course but with specific emphasis on prenatal and postnatal phases and early and mid-childhood. It will consider a range of definitions and understandings of health and well-being, exploring how these are impacted by cultural and social determinants. It will explore how practitioners and families can best support children's health and well-being.

Theme 2: The custodian

3: Understanding, applying and managing legislation and regulatory frameworks

Social policy impacts on children and families in all areas of their lives. It can empower or disempower young children and their families through its impact on the level of provision, access and suitability of services for children with differing needs. This chapter considers current legislation, professional guidance and national and local policy initiatives, supporting you to analyse critically so that you may lead practice in relating these to the needs of children and families. Within the chapter, there is a focus on the rights of children, inequality and social justice in order to evaluate policy, practice and provision through examination of a rights-based perspective. This will provide you with an informed awareness of how policy impacts on your leadership of practice and the quality of provision.

4: Leading practice to reflect current and emerging social policy

Building on Chapter 3, this chapter identifies effective individuals and teams as being essential to organising, evaluating and supporting work with young children and their families. It considers the role of leadership and management in supporting positive change for children and families. A range of theoretical frameworks and models of leadership will be explored throughout this chapter with opportunities for self-evaluation as a developing leader of practice.

Theme 3: The planner

5: Its child's play – playful curricula and spaces

This chapter will focus on developing practitioner's skills in implementing and developing practice that reflects a playful pedagogy in the current social policy climate. Throughout the chapter, an emerging critical understanding of the inter-relationships between political, economic, cultural and ideological contexts in children's lives will also be explored. Your emerging thinking will be captured through reflective activities throughout the chapter to support development of practice within this area.

6: Facilitating child-centred practice

Having developed a play-centric pedagogy within Chapter 5, this chapter builds upon this and asks practitioners to reimagine a child-centred and therapeutic approach to pedagogy and provision design. What would early childhood provision look like if it were bespoke for each child's uniqueness? This chapter forges a bridge between these reimaginations and real-world practice so that practitioners can locate pockets of practice which embed these ideals.

Theme 4: The advocate

7: Let's get it right – safeguarding

This chapter engages with the statutory guidance to safeguard children's welfare in the early years sector and integrated working efforts to protect children from harm. It encourages you to critically evaluate Munro's claim that we need to learn how to do the right thing (protect children) rather than learn only how to do things right (complying with procedure). It will make reference to thresholds for statutory intervention, current literature, and sector-specific regulatory and inspection frameworks. Practitioners are encouraged to engage critically in the formation of cultures of vigilance within the sector in order to support your practice in this area.

8: Childhood: it's their world – a global and sustainable approach

This chapter gives practitioners the opportunity to consider what it means to be a child, and a citizen of the world, from a global perspective. Contemporary theory and international/global approaches will be explored. There will be an opportunity to explore the impact that different cultures can have on children and their early childhood experiences and how different cultural practices challenge traditional (Western) theories of child development. You will be encouraged to develop an awareness of some of the challenges faced by many children globally, including the rights of refugees/displaced people. You will be encouraged to investigate how international approaches have influenced pedagogy and consider your own practice in light of developing understanding.

Theme 5: The collaborator

9: Leading change: practice within organisations

Having identified yourself as a leader of practice within Chapters Three and Four, this chapter identifies the importance of the relationships within the team to support not only children and families but also one another in this line of work. Throughout this chapter models of teamwork, social capital and capacity building within organisations will be highlighted, as well as the impact of these in creating a shared vision for practice, making sense of policy, and ultimately, driving quality improvement.

10: Collaboration – the power of multi-agency working

The ethos and underpinning theory for the chapter is that of strength-based working. It represents a shift away from approaches which focus on problems and difficulties, and instead it looks for strengths to support and empower families. This chapter will encompass an understanding of the theoretical and policy frameworks which influence professional collaboration. It examines how integrated working requires effective leadership at all levels. The chapter encourages practitioners to think about the key features, benefits and challenges of integrated working to support families who need extra help. An important aspect of the chapter is the critical appraisal of the role of leadership in joint working for children, young people, parents/carers, and families. The chapter will encourage you to critically reflect upon your own practice, dispositions, and skills in relation to joint working and leadership.

Theme 6: The innovator

11: Innovative, appreciative and impactful research for practice

This chapter identifies significant links between research and quality improvement. By taking an appreciative approach, it aims to support practitioners in evaluating practice and initiating small changes within their settings, based upon engagement with theory and research. It empowers practitioners to understand practice-/work-based enquiry. Within this chapter, there is a strong emphasis on improving quality and ensuring that conducting research is purposeful either to the setting, to children's experiences or your own professional development.

It is our hope that this text will support you as you lead practice and will offer inspiration as well as a practical guide to developing best practice.

Knowledge, skills and behaviours index

The table below outlines the duties of the early years lead practitioner as defined by the Institute for Apprenticeships and Technical Education (IfATE). Each of the duties has then been mapped to the corresponding knowledge, skills and behaviours needed in order to perform it. Following on from this mapping index, we have included a list of what each knowledge, skill and behaviour criteria are. The aim of this is to support you in understanding and in turn demonstrating these within your practice.

Duty 1 Promote the health and well-being of all children, self-regulation and resilience through learning rich environments, opportunities for challenging play and a healthy attitude towards risk taking.	**Knowledge:** 1 2 3 4 6 7 8 9 11 14 15 16 17 18 19 20 21
	Skills: 1 2 4 6 10 15 16 17 18 19 21 22 23
	Behaviours: 1 2 3 4 5 6 8
Duty 2 Provide playful, sensitive interaction opportunities that reflect children's needs, interests and motivations in order to facilitate and extend deep level learning.	**Knowledge:** 1 2 3 7 8 9 10 11 12 13 14 15 17 18 19
	Skills: 1 2 3 4 5 6 7 8 9 10 12 13 14 15 18 23
	Behaviours: 1 3 4 6 7 8
Duty 3 Participate in and lead daily routines and practice, including children's personal care, play and maintaining the physical environment.	**Knowledge:** 1 2 3 4 7 9 10 11 15 17 20
	Skills: 3 4 6 7 8 9 10 17 19 23
	Behaviours: 3 4 5 6 7 8
Duty 4 To be an effective key person and advocate for the child, supporting the child's developmental, emotional and daily needs within a secure and caring relationship. To ensure the effectiveness of the key person approach across the aspect or environment for which they are responsible.	**Knowledge:** 1 2 3 4 6 7 8 9 10 11 12 13 14 15 16 17 19 20 21
	Skills: 1 2 3 4 5 6 7 8 9 10 11 12 15 16 17 18 19 20 21 22 23 25
	Behaviours: 1 2 3 4 5 6 7 8 9
Duty 5 To take the lead and provide support in disseminating best practice in the use of observation, assessments and planning to meet children's needs and extend their holistic development within the aspect or environment for which they are responsible.	**Knowledge:** 1 2 3 6 7 8 9 10 11 12 13 15 18 19 21
	Skills: 1 2 3 4 5 6 7 8 9 12 13 14 15 16 18 20 23
	Behaviours: 1 2 3 4 5 6 7 8 9

Duty 6 Promote, demonstrate and facilitate a clear understanding of diversity and equality to support all children, including those with additional needs, those of high ability, those with English as an additional language and those with disabilities. To be able to use and evaluate distinctive approaches which engage and support inclusivity of all children within their social and cultural context.

Knowledge: 1 2 3 4 5 6 7 8 11 13 14 15 16 17 18 19 20 21 22

Skills: 1 2 3 4 5 6 8 10 11 12 13 15 16 18 19 20 21 22 23 25

Behaviours: 1 2 3 4 5 6 7 8 9

Duty 7 Ensure full compliance with all safeguarding legislation, policies and strategies at a national, local and setting based level is promoted, implemented and embedded respectfully within practice, providing appropriate support to colleagues as, or supporting, the Designated Safeguarding Lead.

Knowledge: 1 3 4 5 6 7 8 16 17 18 19 20 21 22

Skills: 2 10 11 16 18 20 21 22 23 24 25

Behaviours: 1 2 3 5 6 9

Duty 8 Demonstrate leaderful practice through the effective deployment of resources and practitioners keeping the child's voice and needs central to practice.

Knowledge: 1 2 3 4 8 9 10 11 12 13 15 16 17 18 19

Skills: 2 3 5 10 14 15 17 18 21 22 23 25

Behaviours: 1 2 3 5 6 7 8 9

Duty 9 Reflect and build on practice through ongoing professional enquiry and action research to contribute to the pedagogical approach of their setting. To be accountable for day-to-day practice, longer-term planning, management and training within the specific aspect or environment for which they are responsible.

Knowledge: 2 3 4 6 7 8 9 10 11 12 13 15 16 17 18

Skills: 1 2 3 4 5 6 7 9 10 14 15 18 19 21 23

Behaviours: 1 2 3 4 5 6 7 8 9

Duty 10 Establish engaging, inclusive and collaborative relationships and participate in multiagency meetings. Enable and facilitate practitioners to develop professional relationships with parents, carers and multi-agencies to meet the individual needs of the children.	**Knowledge:** 1 2 3 5 7 8 14 15 16 17 18 19
	Skills: 2 4 11 13 17 18 20 21 22 23 24 25
	Behaviours: 1 2 3 5 6 9
Duty 11 Commit to becoming a reflective practitioner, enhancing skills and knowledge to improve pedagogical practice. Guide and support the development of the reflective practice of others.	**Knowledge:** 1 3 4 5 7 9 10 11 13 17 18 19 20
	Skills: 14 15 21
	Behaviours: 1 2 5 6 9
Duty 12 Initiate continuing professional development opportunities in response to identification of strengths and weaknesses both personally and within your team. Provide constructive feedback on points of practice on an informal day-to-day basis and contribute to formal performance management as necessary.	**Knowledge:** 11 17 18 19 20
	Skills: 15 16 21 22 23
	Behaviours: 2 3 5 6 9
Duty 13 Ensure compliance with all Health and Safety legislation, policies and strategies at a national, local and setting based level.	**Knowledge:** 10 15 16 19 20 22
	Skills: 2 5 10 17 19
	Behaviours: 1 5
Duty 14 Maintain effective administrative systems including development records, assessment, report writing and record keeping, such as risk assessments and safeguarding concerns.	**Knowledge:** 1 2 3 5 8 11 12 13 14 16 19 20 21
	Skills: 1 3 4 11 12 13 16 18 19 20 23 24
	Behaviours: 1 5 6

Duty 15 Work in collaborative partnership with parents and carers in the planning, implementation and review of strategies in place to support children's experience, holistic development, learning and progress.	**Knowledge:** 2 3 4 7 8 10 13 14 15 16 21
	Skills: 1 4 5 6 8 9 11 12 14 18 19 23 24 25 26
	Behaviours: 1 3 4 7 8 9
Duty 16 To lead and manage across the area, aspect or environment for which they are responsible.	**Knowledge:** 1 2 5 7 16 17 19 20 21
	Skills: 2 4 10 11 13 14 15 16 18 20 21 22 23 24 25 26
	Behaviours: 1 2 3 5 6 8 9

Knowledge

K1: Ethical and rights-based approaches to support the child, listening to the child's authentic voice within their social and cultural context enabling advocacy for the child and their individual journey, developing high-quality childcare environments that are continuously evaluated.

K2: How individual children learn and develop from conception to 8 years in relation to typical and atypical neurological, cognitive, social, emotional, behavioural, communication and physical development within the social cultural context and the impact of this on their future.

K3: Factors that have an impact upon health, well-being and early learning that can affect children from conception to 8 years.

K4: Current and contemporary schools of thought to enable respectful and nurturing personal care.

K5: Local and national child protection and safeguarding statutory and non-statutory frameworks, policies and procedures in practice, how to identify when a child is at risk, and how to challenge in order to protect them. This includes understanding the role of the designated lead for safeguarding and assimilating findings of serious case reviews.

K6: Theories of self-regulation, resilience and well-being and the impact of adverse early childhood experiences.

K7: Current and emerging theories of attachment and how these relate to promoting relationships effectively such as the key person approach.

K8: The importance of the social cultural context on the learning and development of the child and the influence parents, families and carers have within the home learning environment and the complexities of the family situation.

K9: The importance of play and the theoretical perspectives of play and its impact on a child's learning and development.

K10: How to stimulate children's creativity and curiosity and why and how this enables enquiry-based active learning.

K11: A wide range of underpinning theories from physiological, neurological, developmental and education and how these can be incorporated to develop own pedagogy.

K12: The intent, implementation and impact of all provided experiences and opportunities for children informed by the setting's curriculum and pedagogy.

K13: How planning cycles inform and improve practice and the principles of individual needs-based assessment for effective early intervention for all children responsive to typical and atypical needs and development.

K14: Potential effects of transitions and schools of thought on how to successfully support children and their families.

K15: The importance and impact of design, resources and interactions within indoor and outdoor environments to enable learning and development.

K16: How to promote inclusion, equality and diversity in the sector and why it is essential.

K17: Current and contemporary theoretical perspectives and approaches to leadership and how to support others through leaderful practice.

K18: Principles of reflection in influencing early years practice with a commitment to life-long learning including continual professional development and action research.

K19: How to maintain accurate and coherent records and reports for the purpose of sharing information and communicating effectively in both oral and written English.

K20: The current and relevant policy, statutory guidance and legal requirements as appropriate to the sector within local, national, historical and global contexts.

K21: Strategies to effect collaborative approaches to working with parents, colleagues, professional bodies and multi agencies.

K22: The implementation of effective policy, procedure and practice to meet the requirements of statutory and non-statutory frameworks and guidance for provision in early years including SEND.

🌱 Skills

S1: Analyse and articulate how all children's individual learning can be affected by their current developmental capabilities, characteristics and individual circumstances taking into account all factors contributing to typical and atypical development.

S2: Promote equality of opportunity and anti-discriminatory practice.

S3: Observe, assess, plan, facilitate and participate in play opportunities which include current curriculum requirements.

S4: Ensure plans fully reflect the individual development needs and circumstances of children and actively participate in the provision of consistent care, responding quickly to the needs of the individual child.

S5: Provide a dynamic, evolving, and enabling environment that reflects the current interests, motivations, and play of individual and groups of children.

S6: Encourage all children's participation, ensuring a sensitive, respectful, and effective balance within the adult and child dynamic to facilitate play opportunities.

S7: Engage in effective strategies to develop and extend children's learning and thinking, including sustained shared thinking.

S8: Support and promote children's diverse speech, language, and communication development, determining and adapting appropriate responses and interventions to support verbal and nonverbal interactions, and engagement with written communication.

S9: Support children to engage in a range of learning contexts such as individual, small groups and larger groups as appropriate for their play and support confidence within social experiences.

S10: Ensure staff are deployed effectively to suit and enhance the learning environment, prioritising the safety and well-being of all children.

S11: Advocate for the child, cultivating professional partnerships with parents/carers, colleagues and other professionals, presenting their understanding of the child's journey within multidisciplinary teams to holistically support the child's individual needs.

S12: Demonstrate the importance of the home learning environment, developing an effective and collaborative partnership to enhance opportunities for the child.

S13: Make use of formative and summative assessment, tracking children's progress to plan for future learning possibilities including early interventions based on individual developmental needs.

S14: Take responsibility for supporting the key person in articulating children's progress and planning future learning possibilities.

S15: Use current and contemporary knowledge, research, theories and approaches to develop, enhance and articulate their own pedagogical approach and practice.

S16: Use reflection to develop themselves both professionally and personally to enhance their practice.

S17: Plan, carry out and guide appropriate physical care routines for individual children.

S18: Promote, model and support children and families to develop a healthy approach to making choices relating to personal care including eating, sleeping and physical activity.

S19: Develop, model and implement strategies to support the emotional, psychological, physical and cultural needs of all children within the setting.

S20: Identify and act upon own responsibilities in relation to health and safety, prevention and control of infection, carrying out risk assessments and risk management processes in line with policies and procedures.

S21: Ensure the security and confidentiality of data, records and information in line with current legislation.

S22: Be a leaderful practitioner to support, mentor, coach, train and guide colleagues in a range of settings, providing inspiration and motivation to engage others to develop their practice.

S23: Be confident to identify, action and competently challenge issues and undertake difficult conversations where appropriate.

S24: Advocate for children through their child-centred approach, listening to the voice of the child; ensuring children's rights, views and wishes are heard, respected and acted upon at all times. Offer appropriate support and influence decisions in the best interests of the child.

S25: Competently action and carry out safeguarding procedures, using their professional curiosity, knowledge, insight and understanding.

S26: Explore and understand, challenge and question; knowing when to act to safeguard and protect children.

Behaviours

B1: Ethical, fair, consistent and impartial, valuing equality and diversity at all times within professional boundaries.

B2: Leaderful and motivating through consistent modelling of innovative and aspirational practice to other colleagues.

B3: Person-centred, friendly and approachable, demonstrating caring, empathetic and respectful qualities.

B4: Authentic and fun, demonstrating playful practice through animated and expressive play and quality interactions with children.

B5: Positive and proactive member of the team, being assertive and exercising diplomacy.

B6: Reflective practitioner.

B7: Creative and imaginative, demonstrating curiosity and inquisitiveness in order to be resourceful in all areas, including play and problem solving.

B8: Flexible and adaptable; responding to children's spontaneous activities.

B9: Receptive and open to challenge and constructive criticism.

Theme 1

The educator and developer of children

Chapters One and Two will support you in your duties as an educator and developer of children.

Duty	Knowledge / Skills / Behaviours
Duty 2 Provide playful, sensitive interaction opportunities that reflect children's needs, interests and motivations in order to facilitate and extend deep level learning.	**Knowledge:** 1 2 3 7 8 9 10 11 12 13 14 15 17 18 19
	Skills: 1 2 3 4 5 6 7 8 9 10 12 13 14 15 18 23
	Behaviours: 1 3 4 6 7 8
Duty 4 To be an effective key person and advocate for the child, supporting the child's developmental, emotional and daily needs within a secure and caring relationship. To ensure the effectiveness of the key person approach across the aspect or environment for which they are responsible.	**Knowledge:** 1 2 3 4 6 7 8 9 10 11 12 13 14 15 16 17 19 20 21
	Skills: 1 2 3 4 5 6 7 8 9 10 11 12 15 16 17 18 19 20 21 22 23 25
	Behaviours: 1 2 3 4 5 6 7 8 9
Duty 5 To take the lead and provide support in disseminating best practice in the use of observation, assessments and planning to meet children's needs and extend their holistic development within the aspect or environment for which they are responsible.	**Knowledge:** 1 2 3 6 7 8 9 10 11 12 13 15 18 19 21
	Skills: 1 2 3 4 5 6 7 8 9 12 13 14 15 16 18 20 23
	Behaviours: 1 2 3 4 5 6 7 8 9

DOI: 10.4324/9781041055358-2

1 The child at the centre of their development

Janet Harvell

This chapter focuses on the holistic development of the child and the early years practitioner's role in supporting this. Using a child-centred framework, you will explore key theories of child development, both classic and contemporary, which underpin practice and contribute to a growing knowledge and understanding of how children learn and develop. Developing skills in observing children will be identified as a key tenet of child-centred practice in this area. The importance of relationships between the child and primary carers is a key component which runs throughout this chapter.

Chapter objectives

In this chapter, you will:

- Explore the concept of childhood and what it means to be a child
- Examine your understanding of child development and factors that could impact on this
- Explore key theories linked to children's development and learning
- Examine the role of observation for professionals when supporting children's learning and development.

Introduction – defining childhood and what it means to be a child

For a book focused on the critical role of professionals and the ever-changing early years landscape, what better place to begin than by reflecting on what it means to be a child in today's society, and the impact of childhood experiences on development and future life chances?

DOI: 10.4324/9781041055358-3

When reflecting on 'What is a child?', it could be suggested that there is a simple answer to this question. The Convention on the Rights of the Child identifies a child as '*every human being below the age of eighteen years unless under the law applicable to the child, majority is attained earlier*' (UN, 1989, p2). This is referred to as childhood and covers the period of development between birth and adulthood, when children are learning how to become functioning adults. However, there is no typical childhood as children across the world have very diverse lived experiences, which means they will reach adulthood through differing stages of preparation. We know that development begins in the womb, continuing through to adulthood, although it is important to understand that development does not stop there. Although the brain reaches full size by mid-adolescence, it continues to develop and mature into the mid-to-late twenties (NIMH, 2024).

Consequently, it is essential to take into consideration that some 18-year-olds lack the life experiences needed to make appropriate adult choices. Therefore, it could be argued that a child should not be defined by an age, but rather their readiness to take an active and successful step into adulthood. Or should we instead consider adulthood from a cultural perspective, that equips children to be successful adults in their cultural environment? These challenges are reflected in the words of one young person stating that '*Now, I'm a full-grown man who still cannot stand out in the world – everyone and everything is ahead of me. People assume I have the same experience they gained during their childhood, while in reality, that is not the case*' (Najeeb, 2020). Therefore, as early years professionals it is important to reflect on the impact of children's culture and environment. You can explore this further in Chapter 8.

Critical reflection

What are your thoughts about childhood and when it ends?

Reflect on some 18-year-olds that you know/have known and whether they have had the life experiences needed to make appropriate adult choices.

Childhood development

The previous discussion highlights the challenges for those working with children and young people, and the significance of having a holistic understanding of the children we care for, by taking into account their environment, relationships and socio-economic situation.

Development is governed by genetic expression and biological patterning, and is directly influenced by our experience of the world. Earlier debates focused on whether it was nature (what you were born with) or nurture (how children were brought up) that had the most significant impact on children's potential. Now we recognise that nature **and** nurture are both equally instrumental in a child's development. The study of epigenetics adds to the debate.

Conkbayir (2017, p103) explains epigenetics as *'the study of gene expressions that do not involve changes to the genetic code but still get passed on to a least one subsequent generation'*. This suggests that both nature and nurture impact each other and have different influences on children's early learning. For example, as an early years practitioner this may mean that it is important to support parents with appropriate advice on nutritional food to address rising obesity rates, or to understand the impact of poverty on children's development, and the importance of families in developing strong and loving relationships with their children.

Generally, it is accepted that most children follow a similar sequence of development, although the timing of this is individual. In England, the Early Years Foundation Stage statutory framework (EYFS) (DfE, 2024) assesses children's development across seven areas of learning. These are divided into three prime areas: Communication and Language, Physical Development and Personal, Social and Emotional Development, and four specific areas of learning: Literacy, Mathematics, Understanding the World, and Expressive Arts and Design.

This is supported by 'Development Matters' (DfE, 2023) and 'Birth to five matters' (Early Years Coalition, 2021) which provide guidelines around developmental expectations between the ages of a) birth to three, b) three- and four-year-olds and c) reception age children (four-to-five-year-olds). Nevertheless, there are reservations that this might encourage practitioners to 'pigeonhole' children into what they can do within distinct age categories, rather than focusing on their individuality and unique needs. The National Association for the Education of Young Children (NAEYC) (2020) supports such Developmentally Appropriate Practice (DAP), defining this as,

> *methods that promote each child's optimal development and learning through a strengths-based, play-based approach to joyful, engaged learning. As a result, to be developmentally appropriate, practices must also be culturally, linguistically, and ability appropriate for each child.*
>
> *NAEYC, 2020, p5*

It is recognised that children can be affected detrimentally by their early experiences which can have a cumulative bearing on their development. Indeed, 'The 1001 Critical Days' document (Wave Trust, 2021, p5) underlines how *'the earliest experiences shape a baby's brain development and have a lifelong impact on that baby's mental health'*. Annie Murphy Paul's (2011) TED video 'What we learn before we're born' reinforces these points.

Having a knowledge of age-related human characteristics and sequential development enables professionals to make predictions within an age range about what activities, materials, interactions or experiences will be safe, healthy, interesting, challenging and achievable for each child. Planning for individual children's needs and stage of development (DAP), requires practitioners to make decisions based on what is known about a) a child's development and learning, b) their strengths, interests and needs and c) knowledge of the social and cultural contexts in which children live.

Factors that can affect children's development

It would be appropriate at this point to spend some time reflecting on the impact that some of these different factors could have on children's learning and development, both positively and negatively. Consider how different life experiences, family relationships, physical and mental health, nutrition, cultural beliefs, disability, housing conditions, political situation, genetic inheritance, environment, socio economics, and education and childcare services can impact on the development, aspirations and support available for each child. All these factors can have an influence on children's overall outcomes. By having an awareness of children's broader social contexts, professionals stand to have a clearer understanding of the extrinsic (external) and intrinsic (internal) factors which play a role in their development.

An extreme example of the impact of negative life experiences can be seen when reviewing the childhood of the American murderer Ronnie Lee Gardner (Cornwell, 2010). One of nine children, Ronnie suffered abuse by his father and brother, the family were economically deprived, the children were neglected and their tumultuous home life was characterised as violent and abusive – just a few of the adverse critical experiences that informed his childhood. Nevertheless, early years practitioners believe that the impact of most negative experiences can be overcome when an appropriate loving environment, and secure and supportive relationships are provided. The importance of the child–adult relationship is also recognised as having a significant impact on children's well-being and development, whether this is relationships within the home or at the early years setting.

As well as life experiences, a child may also have developmental delay in one or more areas including gross motor and fine motor skills, language delay, cognitive ability and social skills. Developmental disability can occur at any time during the developmental period, and usually lasts throughout a person's lifetime, although, at the time of writing there is research suggesting that some forms of autism can be reversed if caught early enough (Pinkstone, 2024). Most developmental disabilities begin before a baby is born, but some can happen after birth because of injury, infection or other factors (Maine Health, 2024).

Child poverty is recognised to have significant impacts upon development and was highlighted as a key issue during the recent 2024 UK Election, with all political parties promising to address the issue at a time when 4.3 million children (30% of children) in the UK are living in relative poverty (Save the Children, 2024). Such environmental stresses can have worrying impacts on all bodily systems including the brain and autonomic nervous system, neuroendocrine system, immune system, heart and cardiovascular system, and gut and metabolic systems (CDC, 2020).

Another environmental consideration that is gaining interest is the impact of gender on development and aspiration. Research in Sweden suggests that the use of gender-specific personal pronouns has an impact on what children believe they can achieve. The use of gender-neutral language, 'hen' rather than 'he' or 'she', was introduced in 2012 to address perceived male 'favouritism' and has become an effective tool *'for establishing gender-equality, challenging gender perceptions* [and] *perhaps even erasing traditional gender roles'* (Yeung, 2020, para 14).

🗣🔍 Critical reflection

Spend some time reflecting on your own life experiences, and those of another person that you know well. Consider how your environment, relationships and experiences have impacted on the person you are today.

The importance of theories of learning and development and observation

The previous discussions have reinforced the centrality of early years in laying secure foundations for children's cognitive attainment and future health and well-being; key to this is the role of the early years practitioner and their ability to understand children's development and how best to support them. A secure knowledge and understanding of the theory and the role of observation underpins this practice and the remainder of the chapter will focus on these two aspects.

Theories of learning and development

Theories help us to make sense of things that we have seen and experienced. Through research, experimentation and observation, theorists construct a rationale for why something happens, with the intention that this can be used to help us better understand what is happening, and how this information can be used to plan for children's learning and development. The early years practitioners will use a range of theories when reflecting on their work with children. These are summarised in Table 1.1. At this stage, it may be helpful to view these within their different fields of research, including:

- **Psychoanalytical theories** which focus on the formation of personality and behaviour as a result of childhood experiences and the impact of these on our psychological selves, our mental state and our emotions. Key proponents of this theory include Freud and Erikson (Gardner 2001). Psychoanalytical theories can support professionals in promoting children's emotional and psychological development, recognising the critical role of early childhood in shaping an individual's future.

- **Behavioural and social learning theories** reflect on the importance of the environment and nurturing experiences and how the child responds to differing stimuli. This includes the work of theorists: Watson, who built upon Pavlov's theory of 'classical conditioning', where children could be 'conditioned' (trained) to learn desired behaviours; Skinner, who believed that children learned language through appropriate stimulus and response (Coughlin, 2023); and Bandura whose experiments with the Bobo doll explored how children learned behaviour from social modelling (Willan, 2024). Behavioural and social learning theories show us that it is important to reflect upon the impact of those who are in close proximity to children.

- **Biological theories,** including Attachment Theory and Epigenetics, argue that it is heredity and innate biological processes that govern growth and development. Theorists include: Gessell, who promoted the Maturation Theory, where children's physical skills would develop as a result of internal processes, and did not need specific support to develop (Goodsir, 2023); Lorenz, who promoted the concept of sensitive/critical periods for learning, and that if these were missed these critical behaviours might fail to develop – more current/recent research, as discussed earlier, identifies that development continues through childhood and brain plasticity means that humans continue to learn and develop throughout their lives (Willan, 2024); and Bowlby, who is known for his work into Attachment Theory which has informed early years practice and the importance of primary attachment figures (Willan, 2024). The maturationist view helps professionals to recognise that children generally develop sequentially along common patterns of development, recognising the 'nature' component.

- **Constructivist theories** of cognitive development identify that children are active in their own learning as they progress through stages of constructing their own knowledge by making sense of their world through repetitive forms of behaviour. Piaget called these repetitive behaviours 'schemas' and suggested that children used these schemas to help make sense of the world. This supports children in assimilating new information until equilibrium is achieved. MacDougall and Brown (2016, p106) explain equilibrium as *'the continuous adjustment to existing schema when we learn new concepts and acquire new information'*. Constructivist theories show how we can support children's development, by encouraging problem solving and providing appropriate resources, with plenty of time and opportunities to engage in, and strengthen, their growing knowledge and understanding through their experiences.

- **Social constructivist theory** emphasises the impact of the socio-cultural environment and the social aspect of learning, particularly the importance of learning with others and how the more able adult or child can help children to take the next step in the learning process. Both Dewey and Vygotsky held similar beliefs to Piaget, but believed strongly that society informs children's development, and the roles of cultural values and customs dictate what is important to learning and the significance of support from more expert others. Vygotsky identified this as the Zone of Proximal Development (ZPD) (Willan, 2024), which is the space between what a child is currently able to do without support, and what they can achieve with adult assistance, or support from more able peers. For example, a young child developing language and speech may mispronounce new words, and the adult can support them by responding with the correct pronunciation. Social constructivist theories support professionals in using their interactions with children to stretch and challenge them.

- **Motivational theory** The psychologist Maslow (1943) originally developed the Hierarchy of Needs as a motivational theory which states that individuals can only reach their full potential once basic needs have been met. There are five key needs that need to be met in order for individuals to be able to reach their full potential (Willan, 2024). As shown in Figure 1.1, Maslow's hierarchy of needs is often represented within a triangle where each level needs to be met before moving up to the next level, Level one represents **Physiological Needs**, the need for food, warmth and shelter; Level 2 identifies the need for **Safety**; Level 3 the need for **Love and Belonging**; Level 4 **Esteem**; and Level 5 **Self-Actualisation** (being the best that an individual can achieve).

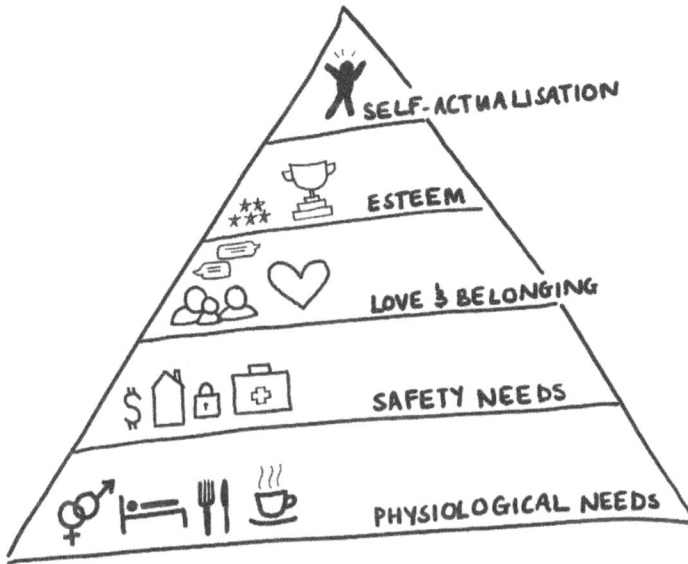

Figure 1.1 *Maslow's (1943) Hierarchy of Needs*

This theory suggests that each of the lower needs must be met before individuals can achieve self-actualisation. Consider this when reflecting on the lives of refugee children who have had to flee their homes, facing danger when seeking refuge, whilst losing their sense of belonging as they must leave behind all that has meant anything to them, including loved ones. With their basic needs being unable to be met, self-esteem is challenged, and children's focus is on self-preservation, with limited capacity for learning and ultimately self-actualisation. The experiences of refugee children will be explored further in Chapter 8. In practice, some of the children that you work with may not have secure, warm homes, quiet places to sleep or sufficient food. Without these most basic needs being met, children may have difficulty being ready to learn or reaching their full potential.

• **Bronfenbrenner's ecological systems theory** identifies that a range of environmental systems shape a child's development. This theory acknowledges that children do not grow up in isolation but over time are influenced by the biological, social and cultural environments they live in (Children, Families, Schools and Communities, 2023). Within this theory, our key systems are identified. This is generally represented by a diagram with the child at the centre surrounded by four concentric circles representing the Microsystem, Mesosystem, Exosystem and Macrosystem (see Chapter 2 for an example). Bronfenbrenner continued to revise his theory with the Bioecological Systems model and the addition of the Chronosystem. This acknowledges the influence of the biological context, that is children's individual characteristics, their own context and history and how these impact on their interactions.

○   The **Microsystem** includes the direct context which the child inhabits and those direct relationships, interactions, activities and experiences within their immediate surroundings. This includes their parents, family, home setting, school, nursery and friends. These have the most impact on the child as they make sense of their environment and social conventions.

○   The **Mesosystem** relates to the relationships between people involved in the child's life. For example, the impact of interactions between parents with daycare providers and teachers which can have an impact on the child.

○   The **Exosystem** focuses on the localised context that has an indirect influence on the microsystem and mesosystem. This includes those people or institutions that although not directly part of the child's life, have an indirect influence on them. For example, the parent's work setting could impact on the time a parent is able to spend with their child; similarly, the range of community resources available could have a positive and/or negative impact on the child's experiences.

○   The **Macrosystem** represents the laws, customs, culture, social class, values and belief systems that can have a broader impact on the child. For example, the UK is currently debating the limitations of the two-child benefit system (BBC News, 2024). If the current policy was changed to include all children, this could mean that 250,000 children were lifted out of poverty.

○   Finally, the **Chronosystem** reflects the longer-term context and changes in the environment over the lifetime of a child and the impact that this can have. For example, the birth of sibling, the outbreak of war or famine.

Bronfenbrenner's ecological systems theory supports professionals in understanding the impact that children's broader social contexts have upon their development. This encourages a more holistic approach to supporting children and families.

Critical reflection

Consider which of these theories you see evidence of in practice and which of them align most with your own values for practice.

By having a secure understanding of a range of theories, professionals can better understand and support children's learning environments that nurture children's holistic development needs. Similarly, these theories have had a significant influence on the development, and adoption, of educational practices and policies. When reflecting on different pedagogical and curriculum approaches, different theories have been critical in informing these. For example, the UKs SureStart policy was modelled on the American Head Start programme which was co-founded by Bronfenbrenner (Welshman, 2009). Many curricula favour one or a mix of theories when developing a curriculum that is most effective for children's learning. For example, Reggio, EYFS, Steiner and Montessori.

Table 1.1 *'Theories in a Nutshell', provides examples of what these theories could look like in practice*

Theory	Theorist	What this means for the early years setting and professionals
Constructivists Children learn through being active, through exploring and investigating – constructing their own knowledge	**Piaget** Children's development occurs in stages and is influenced by their environment – sensori-motor (birth to 2 years), pre-operational (2–6 years), concrete-operational, (6–12 years), formal-operational (12 years onward) – UK curricula reflects these stages. Schemas – repeated behaviours/ actions which help children to organise, interpret, make sense of things/information – learning through experience.	- Children using symbols in their play (e.g. a cardboard box is a computer, or plastic blocks as cakes (pre-operational) - Children talking to dolls and soft toys - Babies exploring toys, putting in their mouths (sensori-motor) - Children repeating the same things over and over again – develop logic (concrete-operational) - Engaging in schematic behaviour, e.g. continually lining up play toys, deconstructing and reconstructing toys - Using milestones to assess children's development
	Vygotsky Social constructivist – children learn from those around them (adults and peers); importance of 'cultural tools' such as communication and language; development of inner speech and self-talk. ZPD (Zone of Potential Development), ZAD (Zone of Actual Development) – 'less able' learning new skills from 'more able' adults/peers.	- Practitioners talking to children engaged on a task, questioning and making suggestions about what they might do - Children discussing a topic of mutual interest with each other and/ or an adult - Children engaged in emergent writing - Children talking to themselves as they play - Children explaining to each other

(continued)

Table 1.1 (Cont.)

Theory	Theorist	What this means for the early years setting and professionals
	Bruner Notion of scaffolding builds upon Vygotsky's ideas on how to support children as they learn new concepts. Professionals provide a 'framework' for supporting children's learning and development. Three modes of representation which children go through when learning new things. Enactive (action), iconic (image) – visually summarises and symbolic (language) where the child uses words and symbols.	- Professional/adult providing resources at critical moments to encourage children to develop existing knowledge and understanding - Babies experimenting with movement - The use of symbols, e.g. mark making - Observing what child is able to do and planning activities to extend this
Behavioural and social learning	**Skinner** Where learning a new response which is defined as any relatively permanent change in behaviour – 'conditioning'. Children learn through seeking approval. Positive reinforcement – where behaviour is repeated as a result of rewards (stimulus and response). Ignoring unwanted behaviour, praising positive behaviour.	- Behaviour management strategies, e.g. reward wanted behaviour and ignore unwanted behaviour; where behaviour is reinforced every time it occurs, it tends to occur more often, e.g. - Children using new skills as a result of praise - Social development and social and cultural mores
	Bandura Children learn through observing others (social modelling) (Bobo doll).	- Children imitating speech and actions in role play - Social development and behaviour management
	Watson Classical conditioning – children can be conditioned to learn desired behaviours – unconscious automatic learning	- The blowing of bubbles to instigate 'tidy up time' - Staff ensure children associate positive emotional experiences with learning

Table 1.1 (Cont.)

Theory	Theorist	What this means for the early years setting and professionals
Psychoanalytical	**Freud** The importance of early experiences and the role of the unconscious mind (the Id – ego – super ego). Different ages result in different stages of development/ libido – and how adults respond to these – oral, anal, phallic, latency – and potential impact on adulthood.	- In a baby the mouth is the primary source of interaction – babies exploring everything with their mouths - Children learning to control bowel movements and how they are supported in this - Baby crying when hungry - Supporting children's understanding of social/cultural mores, e.g. learning rules and values of society
	Erikson Identified eight stages in the development of personality linked to social and cognitive development – from infancy to adulthood (builds on Freud). The importance of relationships. Children will only progress as a result of praise.	- Professionals providing nurturing environments that promote trust and encourage independence – children being encouraged to have a go - Children talk about achievements at circle time - Supporting emotional development
Attachment	**Bowlby, Ainsworth, Elfer** Forming of strong attachments to main carer. Potential concern if no attachments formed in the first year.	- How children separate from main carer; transitions; attachment - Emotional and social development - The role of the key person
	Konrad Lorenz Focus on attachment/imprinting. Sensitive/critical periods of learning.	- Bond formed between newborn and caregiver prompted by visual and auditory stimuli

(continued)

Table 1.1 (Cont.)

Theory	Theorist	What this means for the early years setting and professionals
Biological	**Arnold Gessell** Maturation theory – whereby children's physical skills will develop as a result of internal processes and do not need any specific support. Does not take into effect the impact of the social environment.	- As children get older their bodies grow and mature, their abilities also develop (physically and mentally), practitioners use this when assessing children's progress along expected developmental milestones - Child development proceeds along a largely determined 'natural' path
Motivational	**Maslow** Hierarchy of Needs and the need to meet basic needs to be able to achieve potential.	- Ensuring basic needs being met, i.e. sufficient sleep, food, feeling safe, loving environment and need for being appreciated and valued - Awareness of the impact that negative experiences could have on children's learning and development
Ecological systems	**Bronfenbrenner** The impact of different environmental systems which shape development.	- Understanding the impact of quality relationships on children's learning and development, e.g. family, neighbours, school, doctor, etc. The importance of the setting in developing supportive and nurturing connections between the setting and the home

Theories provide insight and should act as a filter to help us determine what behaviours and observations are relevant when seeking to answer specific questions or provide us with guidance on how we might better support children when dealing with a particular circumstance/event/approach.

The role of observation in our practice

The significance of observations, and how these are used to support children's learning and development, has long been recognised and was key to the development of many theories discussed previously. Observation is central to our understanding of the children we care for and is crucial when determining appropriate activities to support progression in learning and development. By observing children's actions, behaviours, social engagement and language we are better able to understand why things may be happening and possible next steps to be taken.

The type of observation to be completed will be determined by what aspect of the child's development you are wanting to explore. Apart from accuracy, one of the most important things to remember when observing is to retain an objective form of writing; that is recording just what you have seen and heard, and not interpreting the observation as you go along. For example, the statement 'Jane was upset when she spilt the sand on the floor', is subjective; instead the observation should identify that 'Jane spilt sand on the floor and started to cry', which is a more objective statement. Analysis occurs afterwards when you review the observation in full to see what it is telling you; at this stage it may then be appropriate to reflect on Jane's emotional state. The reason for this is that whilst recording an observation, we do not have all of the facts to hand that would enable us to make an informed analysis at this stage.

The most common method of observation is the **narrative** which, as its name suggests, is a written description of what is seen and heard. But other observation methods include a **time sample** where you record the child's activity at set intervals over a period of time. For example, every ten minutes during a session. This can provide you with a holistic understanding of the child's experiences during their session, identifying what activities a child engages with, and with whom, providing an informed understanding of the child's interests over the course of the session. Do they flit between activities, or focus on one area of play? A **sociogram** supports your understanding of who children interact with and any specific friends they might have, whilst the **tracking** observation enables the professional to track a child's movements in the setting during a period of time. This can be used to analyse the effectiveness of the available resources and the time spent engaging with these (Harvell and McMahon, 2023). More recently, digital technologies have been used within the observation and assessment process with practitioners using bespoke apps to record and analyse videos and photographs of children in the setting which can then be shared with parents on secured websites (Harvell and McMahon, 2023). At the same time, it is important not to forget basic information when observing children, i.e. the time and date, location and what was going on at the time. For example, consider how the observation might be different if: it takes place first thing in the morning, or in the afternoon, or if you were observing a child playing by themselves or as part of a group, or playing inside or outside.

Analysing your observation

Once you have completed an observation, it is now important to analyse what your observation has told you about individual children. This should include,

*   Whether there were any factors that could have impacted on the observation. For example, has the child been involved in an argument with friends that could impact upon their mood or engagement with an activity. Did parents/carers say that their child was feeling very tired, or very excited about an upcoming event? If so, you will need to consider if this could have impacted on what you were observing.

*   What observation method did you use and why? For example, you wanted to focus on social groupings and whether the child has any specific friends they enjoy spending focused time with.

- What learning was observed? Is the child within the expected developmental range? What makes you say this, what evidence is there from the observation to support this? Is there any evidence from your understanding of different theories that supports this?

🗪 Critical reflection

The next time you complete an observation in practice, use the above questions to scaffold your thinking. How has this impacted your practice with regards to making observations meaningful for capturing and supporting children's development?

Chapter summary

This chapter has focused on several key issues including what it means to be a child in today's society, the construct of child development and factors that could impact upon this. A range of theories were introduced, providing an insight into how these could be used to better inform our understanding of children and their holistic development. Finally, the role of observation has been examined and the use of this in supporting learning and development was considered. This has reinforced the impact that social and cultural circumstances have on children's holistic learning and development. This forms a strong foundation as you continue to consider the role of the early years practitioners in the dynamic area of early years.

Further reading

Excellent Site for Understanding Bronfenbrenner. Available at: www.earlyyears.tv/urie-bronfenbrenner-ecological-systems-theory-bioecological-model

Murphy-Paul, Annie TED Talk (2011) *What we learn before we're born*. Available at: www.ted.com/talks/annie_murphy_paul_what_we_learn_before_we_re_born?subtitle=en

References

BBC News (2024) *Why is There Fresh Controversy Over the Two-Children Benefit Cap*. Available at: www.bbc.co.uk/news/articles/c87rp0xr3ydo#:~:text=Campaigners%20brought%20a%20legal%20challenge,dismissed%20their%20case%20in%202021 (Accessed 25 July 2024).

Centre on the Developing Child (CDC) (2020) *Connecting the Brain to the Rest of the Body. Early Childhood Development and Lifelong Health are Deeply Intertwined*. Available at: https://developingchild.harvard.edu/resources/connecting-the-brain-to-the-rest-of-the-body-early-childhood-development-and-lifelong-health-are-deeply-intertwined/ (Accessed 20 July 2024).

Children, Families, Schools and Communities (2023) *Bioecological Systems Theory*. Available at: https://rotel.pressbooks.pub/children-families-schools-communities/chapter/bioecological-systems-theory/#:~:text=Bronfenbrenner's%20bioecological%20systems%20theory%20looked,children%2C%20families%2C%20and%20parenting (Accessed 20 July 2024).

Conkbayir, M (2017) *Early Childhood and Neuroscience: Theory, Research and Implications for Practice*. London, Sage.

Cornwell, R (2010) *The Doomed Life of a Troubled Killer Who Never had a Chance*. Available at: www.independent.co.uk/voices/commentators/rupert-cornwell/the-doomed-life-of-a-troubled-killer-who-never-had-a-chance-2004759.html (Accessed 10 July 2024).

Coughlin, A (2023) Promoting communication, language and literacy. In: Hayes, C. (ed.), *The Early Years Handbook for Students and Practitioners: An Essential Guide for the Foundation Degree and Levels 4 and 5*. Oxon, Routledge.

DfE (2023) *Development Matters. Non-Statutory Curriculum Guidance for the Early Years Foundation Stage*. Available at: https://assets.publishing.service.gov.uk/media/64e6002a20ae89001 4f26cbc/DfE_Development_Matters_Report_Sep2023.pdf (Accessed 20 July 2024).

DfE (2024) *Early Years Foundation Stage Statutory Framework. For Group and School-Based Providers*. Available at: https://assets.publishing.service.gov.uk/media/65aa5e42ed27ca001327b2c7/ EYFS_statutory_framework_for_group_and_school_based_providers.pdf (Accessed 20 July 2024).

Early Years Coalition (2021) *Birth to 5 Matters: Non-statutory Guidance for the Early Years Foundation Stage*. St Albans, Early Education. Available at https://birthto5matters.org.uk/wp-content/ uploads/2021/04/Birthto5Matters-download.pdf

Gardner, S (2001) Psychoanalysis: Overview. *International Encyclopedia of the Social & Behavioral Sciences*. Available at: www.sciencedirect.com/topics/neuroscience/psychoanalytic-theory (Accessed 23 July 2024).

Goodsir, K (2023) The physical development of children. In: Hayes, C. (ed.), *The Early Years Handbook for Students and Practitioners: An Essential Guide for the Foundation Degree and Levels 4 and 5*. Oxon, Routledge.

Harvell, J and McMahon, S (2023) Observation. In: Hayes, C. *The Early Years Handbook for Students and Practitioners: An Essential Guide for the Foundation Degree and Levels 4 and 5*. Oxon, Routledge.

MacDougall, I and Brown, J (2016) The Foundation Years: Babies. In: Trodd, L. (ed.), *The Early Years Handbook for Students and Practitioners: An Essential Guide for the Foundation Degree and Levels 4 and 5*. Oxon, Routledge.

Maine Health (2024) *Development Disorders Diagnosis, Causes, Types and Treatment*. Available at: www.mainehealth.org/care-services/pediatric-care-child-health/developmental-disorders (Accessed 10 October 2024).

Maslow, A H (1943) A theory of human motivation. *Psychological Review*, 50(4), 370–396. https://doi.org/10.1037/h0054346

NAEYC (2020) *Principles of Child Development and Learning and Implications That Inform Practice*. Available at: www.naeyc.org/resources/position-statements/dap/principles (Accessed 8 July 2024).

NAEYC (2020) *Developmentally Appropriate Practice National Association for the Education of Young Children.* Available at: www.naeyc.org/sites/default/files/globally-shared/downloads/PDFs/resources/position-statements/dap-statement_0.pdf (Accessed 5 November 2024)

Najeeb, R (2020) *A Universal Definition of What It Means to be a 'Child'.* Available at: www.unicef.org/sudan/stories/universal-definition-what-it-means-be-child (Accessed 18 November 2024).

NIMH (2024) *The Teen Brain: 7 Things to Know.* Available at: www.nimh.nih.gov/health/publications/the-teen-brain-7-things-to-know#:~:text=Although%20the%20brain%20stops%20growing,the%20last%20parts%20to%20mature (Accessed 7 July 2024).

Paul, A (2011) *What We Learn Before We're Born.* Available at: www.ted.com/talks/annie_murphy_paul_what_we_learn_before_we_re_born?subtitle=en (Accessed 10 July 2024).

Save the Children (2024) *4.3 Million Children in Poverty are Being Failed – The UK Government Needs to Wake Up.* Available at: www.savethechildren.org.uk/news/media-centre/press-releases/children-in-poverty-are-being-failed-the-uk-government-needs-to-#:~:text=2023%2F24%20stats%3A,100%2C000%20more%20than%20last%20year (Accessed 20 July 2024).

UN (1989) *Convention of the Rights of the Child.* Available at: www.unicef.org/media/52626/file (Accessed 7 July 2024).

Wave Trust (2021) *The 1001 Critical Days. The Importance of the Conception to Age Two Period.* Available at: www.wavetrust.org/1001-critical-days-the-importance-of-the-conception-to-age-two-period (Accessed 10 July 2024).

Welshman, J (2009) From head start to sure start: Reflections on policy transfer. *Children and Society,* 24(2), 89–99.

Willan, J (2024) *Early Childhood Studies. A Multidisciplinary Approach.* London, Bloomsbury.

Yeung, P (2020) *Why Sweden's Gender-Neutral Pronoun is a Model to follow. Rather than him and her, We Should be using Hen.* Available at: https://apolitical.co/solution-articles/en/why-swedens-gender-neutral-pronoun-is-a-model-to-follow (Accessed 10 July 2024).

2 Supporting children to be healthy and well

Olivia Storey and Angela Hodgkins

This chapter will consider a holistic and context-sensitive approach to well-being which identifies the role of children's social worlds in supporting health and well-being. It will critically explore contemporary issues facing children and families in terms of being well, such as the impact of social policy and rising concerns about children's mental health. This chapter examines health and well-being across the life course but with specific emphasis on prenatal and postnatal phases and early and mid-childhood. It will consider a range of definitions and understandings of health and well-being, exploring how these are impacted by cultural and social determinants. It will explore how practitioners and families can best support children's health and well-being.

◎ Chapter objectives

In this chapter, you will:

- Explore definitions and interpretations of health and well-being
- Examine factors affecting health and well-being
- Analyse ways of supporting children's health and well-being
- Explore the importance of self-regulation and resilience
- Consider ways of developing attachment relationships with children.

Introduction

Perhaps one of the most fundamental roles of the EY professional is to promote the health and well-being of the people we work with. This chapter pushes the boundaries

DOI: 10.4324/9781041055358-4

of our understanding of health as merely being the absence of illness towards more holistic perspectives of being well. Within this new lens, you will be supported in developing your practice in a way which promotes best outcomes for the children and families you work with.

Definitions and interpretations of health and well-being

In order to support children to be healthy and well, it is useful to first define the concept of health and well-being. A positive definition of health and well-being is concerned with what an individual possesses in terms of their health. Whereas a deficit approach, focuses on any health problems and needs requiring intervention. Using a positive definition of health and well-being, the goal is to live in a way that enables individuals to achieve the best health possible and to maximise an individual's well-being and quality of life. Individuals are viewed as capable of managing their own health choices to prevent the need for medical cure, care and therapy. In this sense, principles from a strength-based viewpoint such as respect, shared power and social justice are valued. Conversely, a negative definition of health refers to an absence of disease; it is where an individual believes they have a good state of health because they do not have an illness or disability (Schick, 2022).

The World Health Organisation (WHO, 2024, np) describes health as a state of 'complete physical, mental and social well-being and not merely the absence of disease or infirmity', including both a negative and positive characterisation of health. The criticisms of one approach may be overcome with the strengths of the other by combining both the positive and negative definitions together. However, what may be more helpful is to apply the definitions based on the individual's personal needs and context. In addition to the negative and positive approaches to health, a holistic understanding is also included in the WHO definition, whereby all aspects of a person's lifestyle are considered: physical, intellectual, emotional, spiritual and social. By including this outlook, it is acknowledged that health can be affected by cultural and educational factors.

Nationally, a contemporary issue influencing children's health and well-being is the sustainability of public healthcare. Common rhetoric in the 2024 UK general election involved the need to save the National Health Service from crisis, referring to challenges regarding the availability of health services and waiting times for GP and hospital appointments (Labour Party UK, 2024). Correspondingly, research highlights the concerns of community health service leaders in relation to post-pandemic waiting times for initial assessments and treatments for health services (NHS England, 2023). A positive definition of health supports an active approach which enables individuals to use their own knowledge and skills to avoid and manage ill health and ailments, rather than waiting to be seen by a professional. By adopting this outlook, the demands on the NHS and private health services could be alleviated; inappropriate appointments might be avoided by suitable self-care and signposting, reducing waiting times for those with greater needs (NHS England, nd).

Despite the potential benefits, there is however a danger with this perspective. Using a positive definition of health can place a disproportionate level of blame onto certain individuals, for instance a family with poor health may view themselves in a distorted way and conclude incorrectly that their health is exclusively a direct result of poor life choices. They may also experience unfair prejudice.

Alternatively, to work out if an individual is healthy using the negative definition, the starting focus is whether an individual fits into the 'not healthy' category: do they have an illness or injury, do they have a disease? If the answer to these questions is 'no', then the individual is healthy. This viewpoint towards health can therefore be argued as pessimistic and leading to reactive as opposed to proactive steps towards health and well-being as it tends to rely on visible difficulties and biomedical models. It is only when there is a problem that a medical professional will step in with treatment. A further criticism can therefore be made that this perspective is disempowering to individuals, rendering them powerless and dependent on the intervention of health experts. Many families in the UK today are facing significant wait times for an appointment with a GP – in February 2023 over 4,000,000 patients waited over two weeks after the time of booking before attending their appointment (NHS England, 2023) – and so such an approach to help may lead individuals to worry and suffer until appropriate healthcare is available. Nevertheless, for some children and families this stance is helpful. This is because having a diagnosis can relieve guilt and share responsibility, leading to access of welcomed resources.

🗣 Critical reflection

Given the acknowledged value above of a strength-based approach to health and well-being, produce a mind map that highlights factors that affect children's health and well-being.

Factors affecting health and well-being

Health is influenced by a multitude of circumstances. One of the most recognised models to describe the factors affecting a child is the bio-ecological framework (Bronfenbrenner, 1979). This theory views child development as a complex system of relationships. It describes how a child's life and development is affected by multiple levels of the surrounding environment, from immediate family and childcare settings to broader cultural values, laws and customs. These levels are called the microsystem, mesosystem, exosystem, macrosystem and chronosystem (see Figure 2.1). Factors at each of these levels/layers can affect a child's physical and mental health.

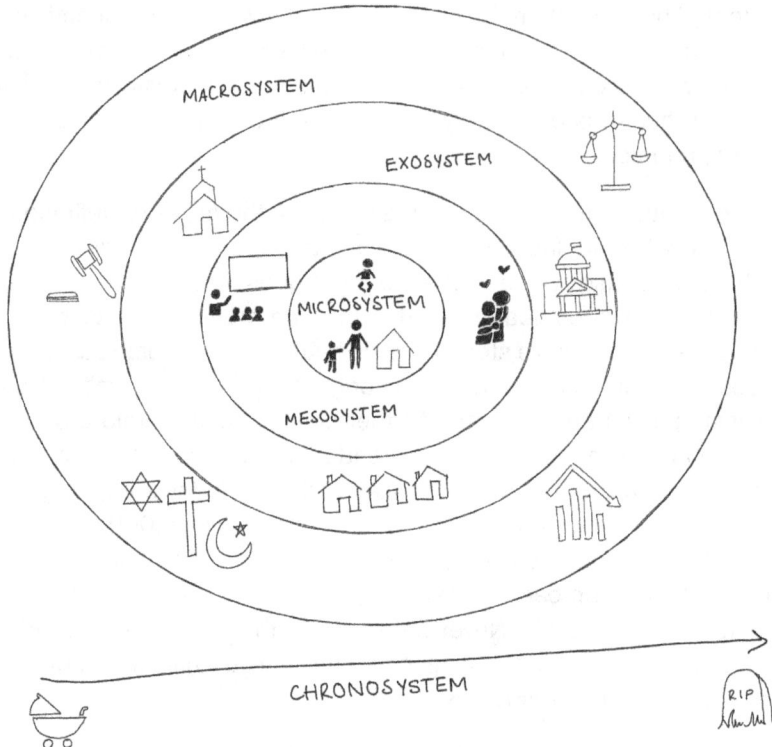

Figure 2.1 *Bronfenbrenner's (1979) bio-ecological systems model*

- **The microsystem** – this includes the things that are closest to the child and therefore have the most influence: the child's immediate family, home and any early years settings that the child attends regularly.

- **The mesosystem** – this system consists of relationships between those in the microsystem: e.g. relationships between members of the family, the relationship between parents and the setting.

- **The exosystem** – things that do not directly affect the child but still influence them: parents' work, community/neighbourhood, local government policy and funding.

- **The macrosystem** – the society the child is living in: culture, laws, attitudes and values and socio-economic status.

- **The chronosystem** – this relates to changes over time in the child's life: e.g. transitions, puberty, effects of the pandemic.

❝❝ Case study – Madelina

Madelina is seven years old, she lives on the outskirts of a large city in an apartment with her mother and four siblings (aged nine, five and two-year-old twins). The apartment is on the second floor of a block in an area of deprivation; the building is damp and has no out-side play area. The community is made up of mostly refugees and immigrants, and there is an active and supportive community centre in the next apartment block. The community centre provides free English lessons, a cookery class and a stay and play toddler group.

The family are originally from Romania but are legal immigrants who have been settled in the UK since Madelina was two years old. The children's father no longer lives with them, and they have little contact with him, due to a volatile relationship and a history of domestic abuse between the parents. Madelina's mother is not able to work, as she has no childcare for the younger children. Madelina attends the local school, where she has lots of friends; she is happy at school and her achievements are comparable with her peers.

Madelina's family have experienced racial abuse on the streets where they live; they have been sworn at and told to 'go back to where you came from'. Madelina's mother always retaliates angrily. Once, a bottle was thrown at the family; none of them were hurt, but Madelina's mother reacted by yelling and chasing them, which frightened the children. The school has a wide mix of children from different nationalities and cultures and there have been no incidents of racism in school. Madelina's mother is worried, as she has heard about racism at the secondary school.

Madelina's family are Orthodox Christians and their values reflect this. Within her culture, respect for elders is paramount, and mothers generally have a lot of authority in the family. Madelina and her siblings know that they are loved and that they must respect their mother's rules.

⊙⊙ Critical reflection – Madelina's bio-ecological systems

Can you identify factors affecting Madelina's life in each of the bio-ecological systems (Table 2.1)? As you will see, some effects will be positive (e.g. a loving parent) and others will be negative (racism).

Table 2.1 Bio-ecological system activity

	Factors affecting Madelina	Potential risks	Potential strengths
Microsystem	Family – Home – School –		
Mesosystem	Family relationships – Parent and school –		

(continued)

Table 2.1 (Cont.)

	Factors affecting Madelina	Potential risks	Potential strengths
Exosystem	Neighbourhood – Romanian community –		
Macrosystem	Government funding – Culture – Attitudes toward refugees & immigrants –		
Chronosystem	Moving from Romania – Schools –		

Even before Madelina was born, circumstances in her environment will have affected her growth and life chances. These factors are discussed next.

Nature, nurture and epigenetics

Both nature and nurture, as we have explored in the previous chapter, influence people's lives. This is also relevant to health and well-being. The nature/nurture debate is a psychological debate about which has the most influence. Nature is what we think of as pre-wiring and is influenced by genetic inheritance and other biological factors. Nurture is generally taken as the influence of external factors after conception, e.g., the product of exposure, life experiences, and learning, the factors included in Bronfenbrenner's model above.

🗣️ Critical reflection – nature vs nurture

Think about your own experiences/life

- What do you think you may have inherited from your biological parents? (think about physical attributes, health and behavioural tendencies).

- Which parts of your personality do you think are 'in your nature'?

- Which parts of your personality do you think have been shaped by your upbringing? (think about your parents/carers' parenting style, your role models and life events).

- What events and experiences have influenced your life?

The activity above is to help you to consider whether you think nature or nurture has had the most influence on you. However, the nature/nurture debate is much more complex than it seems at first. For example, if you are a quiet, shy person, is it because shyness has been inherited from your parents through your genes? Or is it because you have spent your life living with shy, quiet parents? If you are overweight, is that because of your genes? Or the way you were brought up around food? The debate around nature and nurture has been furthered by a new scientific theory.

This relatively new area of research, epigenetics, has revealed that environmental circumstances can affect how a person's genes work. Experiences in childhood can change whether, and how, a child's genes release the information they carry (Harvard, 2023). When a child has positive experiences (e.g. supportive relationships), negative genes can be 'turned off', but when a child has negative influences (e.g. a stressful life), negative genes can be 'turned on'. An example is a child born to two tall parents. If the child has plenty of healthy food and exercise, he/she is likely to grow to be a tall adult. However, if the child lives in poverty and does not have enough (or the right kind of) food, and/or the child's mother smokes throughout pregnancy, growth is then stunted through malnutrition, causing the child to grow to below average height.

A study by Alegria-Torres, Baccarelli and Bollati (2011) showed that 'higher maternal care ... reduces responses to stress' (p270). In animal studies, it was observed that when mother animals (such as rats) frequently lick and groom their pups, it leads to a biological change in the pups' brains (hypomethylation of the glucocorticoid receptor gene). Hypomethylation is a process that typically makes genes more active. Therefore, increased licking and grooming by the mother can result in higher activity of the glucocorticoid receptor gene in the pups' brains. This gene plays a critical role in regulating the stress response, so this increased activity can influence how the pups respond to stress throughout their lives. Changes in genetics can be caused by a multitude of factors (Figure 2.2).

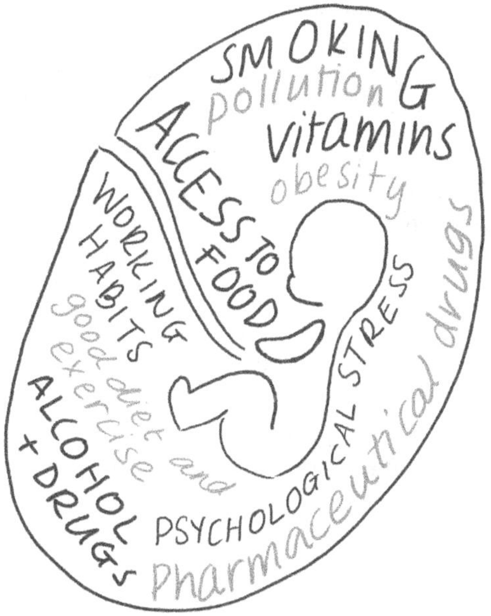

Figure 2.2 *Epigenetic factors*

As we can see, there are things that we can do to provide the best possible conditions for children to grow and thrive, such as providing a healthy lifestyle with a good diet and exercise. When a child experiences a poor lifestyle or adverse life experiences, resilience and self-regulation can benefit the child.

Supporting a healthy approach

> ## ❝ Case study – Mr Garcia – should Kam go home?
>
> In line with the organisation's policy in which he works at, the teacher, Mr Garcia, sent a class text to the parents and guardians regarding the presence of flu-like symptoms and illness in the school. The text highlights the sickness policy regarding absence from school, and some guidance regarding infection control, such as the importance of handwashing to prevent the spread of illness. Mr Garcia made sure that the classroom was well ventilated and reminded the children about how to prevent bugs and infection from spreading, e.g. by covering their mouth and nose when coughing or sneezing with a tissue.
>
> Kam, a child in Mr Garcia's class, is withdrawn and quiet during the maths quiz. Usually, she appears to enjoy such classroom activities and participates fully. She is also presenting with a runny nose and has flushed cheeks. Mr Garcia, noticing this, asks Kam if she is feeling okay. She becomes visibly upset, stating that she is feeling warm and unwell and asking to go home. Mr Garcia suggests to Kam that she has a drink from her water bottle. He then passes his concerns to Mr Anslow in the school office via the class phone, asking him to call Kam's father.
>
> Mr Anslow phones Kam's father to discuss the observations of Kam. He also checks if he had received the text about the various illness at the school currently. Kam's father explained that the family pet had died unexpectedly the previous evening, and this had been extremely sad. Mr Anslow, considering how difficult this is likely to be to all the family, offers his condolences. After listening to Kam's father, Mr Anslow acknowledges that this information may explain some of the observations of Kam but also reiterates his concerns regarding Kam's symptoms. He puts forward the benefits of Kam going home. He states that at home she can rest, whilst rehydrating and having regular paracetamol to bring her temperature down. Kam's father states that he will pick up Kam on the next break. Mr Anslow explains that he will update Mr Garcia about what has been discussed and will contact Kam's father if anything changes.

To assess what conditions would support a child and their family's health and well-being as much information as possible about the individual and their circumstances needs to be collected, therefore, when promoting health and well-being it is crucial that a non-judgemental approach is adopted. Mr Garcia and Mr Anslow adopt a child/family-centred approach (in line with *Working Together to Safeguard Children*, HM Government, 2023), observing Kam's behaviour, asking Kam and her father questions and listening to gain a greater understanding of Kam's health and well-being.

Mr Garcia and Mr Anslow may draw on all three definitions and approaches to health and well-being when supporting Kam and her family. Table 2.2 highlights some of the potential implications of applying the different perspectives relating to definitions of health in the above case study.

Table 2.2 *Helpful and challenging implications of applying the different perspectives relating to definitions of health in Kam's case study*

Perspective and definition	Helpful	Challenging
Negative	Public health campaigns and NHS resources inform the public about symptoms to be aware of regarding infectious illness caused by viruses.	Illnesses like the flu are experienced subjectively and so can be difficult to diagnose. Individual and/or contextual factors may provide a better explanation of health in some situations. For instance, a life event (the death of a pet) may explain changes in behaviour, social withdrawal and emotional well-being. Another possibility is that Kam has a history of various allergies and is presenting with a runny nose on a day when there is a high pollen count.
Positive	Infection control via lifestyle choices (wearing PPE, effective personal hygiene practices, avoiding contact with others if symptoms of a contagious illness are present) reduces the spread of infectious illness.	The amount of responsibility for a parent to manage their child's health or their own health can be overwhelming: when is it okay for a child to be exposed to an illness to build up immunity, and when is it too risky?
Holistic	Individual needs, difference and diversity are acknowledged as well as the needs of society overall. For example, some children may be immunocompromised due to health conditions or medical treatments. By considering various aspects of health, equity is promoted, and vulnerable individuals can be protected.	Actions which can benefit one aspect of health can be detrimental to another. Self-isolating may reassure worries of contagion but have a negative impact on social well-being and immunity.

Supporting individual needs and early intervention

Health literacy, an individual's capacity, ability and confidence to access, comprehend and use health information and services, has been linked to individual's health-related quality of life (Naimi et al, 2017). One way for early years practitioner to support the development of their own and others' health literacy is by signposting, accessing and working in partnership with the appropriate health services available in a timely manner. Being aware of the numerous services, practitioners and wealth of information available when supporting children and their families can be overwhelming but is incredibly important. The UK's public health framework, the Healthy Child Programme (OHID, 2023), supports the opportunities and value of early intervention to promote well-being and to identify and address individual needs and interventions. The Healthy Child Programme Schedule of Interventions Guide (NHS England, 2022) splits resources into four sections: community, universal, targeted and specialist. These are available across the life course, from preconception to 19 years of age, or 25 depending on statutory entitlement. In accordance with the NHS England's (2019) Comprehensive Model for Personalised Care these services and resources should be applied based on the complexity of the individual's needs and the changes in health and well-being throughout their life. Community and universal services are available to all, with community referring to support delivered by frontline workers in the community and universal support being offered to all including screening, immunisations, advice and referral to specialists. Targeted support involves expert advice and support for specific issues, and specialist support concerning specialist practitioner treatment.

Research supports the rationale of adopting a more community-centred approach to enable positive health outcomes for disadvantaged groups (O'Mara-Eves et al., 2015). The Healthy Child Programme (OHID, 2023) encourages and promotes the use of community health services, enabling children and families the opportunity to gain knowledge to make their own health and well-being decisions, as well increasing the chance to form supportive social networks. In addition to this, the Healthy Child Programme (OHID, 2023) aims to stop diseases through the promotion of universal childhood immunisations and ensures that risk factors are identified and monitored via developmental reviews, such as the two-and-a-half-year review. Interventions can therefore be put into place which can assist children's development. By being aware of, and working alongside various universal services, health conditions can be managed and negative impacts on day-to-day activities are reduced. The aims of targeted and specialist services include supporting the development of skills to enable individuals to '*live well with their health conditions*' (NHS England, 2019, p17).

Critical reflection

- Look at the examples of how different health services can be accessed and used by early years practitioners in Table 2.3. Think about the health needs of the children you work with; research and make a list of the community, universal, targeted and specialist health resources and services available to them.

- Trusting relationships and collaboration are key to community-centred public health according to research by Public Health England (PHE, 2020). Consider strategies to maintain effective relationships whilst promoting and supporting health and well-being. How can you share information in a way that is not patronising, judgmental, discriminatory or insensitive?

Table 2.3 *Examples of how early years professionals can promote and utilise health services and resources*

community	universal	targeted	specialist
A notice about weekly baby weigh-in sessions, at the local community hub, is included in the newsletter for families whose children attend a preschool.	The national child measurement programme – parents are given the opportunity for their children to be measured and weighed at school or to opt out of this.	After an early years practitioner signposted a mother to the GP, due to her difficulties following birth, she is now receiving support from perinatal mental health services.	A child is receiving speech and language therapy after a referral was made by a nursery practitioner.
A parent talks to a nursery practitioner about concerns she has regarding her child's nutrition and health, the practitioner mentions vitamin collections for babies and children at maternity outreach hubs.	Links to the NHS webpage about the eligibility for immunisations for infants at 4 months old and statistics about the rising cases of whooping cough locally are included in the weekly nursery newsletter.	The manager of a nursery includes the details and web links for a virtual support group for parents and carers of children with additional needs, run by a charity organisation, as a post on the 'Tapestry' app he uses to share information with families.	A father informs a child's key worker that their child is attending sessions with a psychologist through CAHMS following a bereavement, to help with managing feelings. The key worker accesses and uses the open resources on the CAHMS website to support his practice.
A flyer is placed in the entrance hallway at a nursery for an antenatal class run by midwives at a local village hall, focusing on nutrition and exercise in pregnancy.	A parent shares the findings from their son's 9 month check with the health visitor as part of the induction process at the nursery her son is to attend.	A parent is completing a parenting course at a Children and Family Centre. This centre offers targeted support for children with complex medical and physical needs, autism and behavioural difficulties. The parent shares the strategies and knowledge she has gained from the course with her daughter's teacher at school. The teacher records this information to support her own interactions with this child.	Following his 2–2 ½-year review, a child in the preschool has received specialist equipment and is on a treatment plan from a physiotherapist. The preschool has received suggestions about group activities that would provide targeted support for this child from the physiotherapist.

Self-regulation and resilience

Self-regulation is the ability to understand and manage your behaviour and your reactions to feelings and things happening around you. For children, it takes time to develop the ability to regulate their reactions to strong emotions (anger, excitement, etc.) and to calm themselves down when necessary. '*When a child can self-regulate, they are able to think before they act, self-calm or re-organize when they are met with overwhelming or stressful input*' (Conkbayir, 2022, p 2).

Shanker (2020) identified five domains of self-regulation, and each one has its own stressors which impact on the development of the child's regulation skills (see Table 2.4).

Table 2.4 *Domains and stressors of self-regulation (based on Shanker, 2020)*

Domain	*Stressors*	*How we can help*
Biological domain (physical health and well-being)	Poor diet, lack of exercise, lack of fresh air, insufficient sleep, illness, pain, over-stimulation, physical abuse.	Make sure that young children's physical needs are met. Get to know the child individually, learn what triggers their stress response. Comfort babies when they are upset; leaving them to cry does not help the child to learn self-regulation.*
Emotional domain (recognising emotions and changing your own behaviour)	Abuse, trauma, bereavement, transitions, anxiety, depression, changes in routine.	Adults should guide young children through strong emotions that are frightening for them. Build a connection with the child. The ability to regulate their own emotions is important for every area of a developing child's life.
Cognitive domain (mental processes: attention, memory, problem-solving)	Lack of stimulation, abuse and neglect, frustration.	Avoid making children sit still for long periods until they are ready to do so. Help children develop executive functioning skills (memory, decision-making, concentration, flexibility and planning ahead). Resist pressure on 'school readiness'. Provide opportunities for free-flow play.

Table 2.4 (Cont.)

Domain	Stressors	How we can help
Social domain (communication, empathy, friendships, managing conflict)	Abuse, lack of friends, bullying, loneliness, awkwardness in social situations.	Support children in making and maintaining friendships. Help children to manage conflicts and arguments themselves. Provide a good variety of play activities for children. Talk with children about feelings.
Prosocial domain (emotional intelligence, care for others)	Difficulty reading non-verbal cues, difficulty knowing right and wrong, injustice and exploitation.	Role model positive social behaviour. When a child displays unwanted behaviour, help them to understand why the behaviour is unwanted. Try to understand and deal with the root causes of unwanted behaviour.

*A note on leaving babies to cry – Conkbayir (2022) points out that in the first stage of life, babies have no control over their nervous system; therefore, they need compassionate adults to help them regulate.

> *We would not turn away a friend or relative who is crying or expressing the need for comfort. So how can we deem this ethical when it comes to our youngest and most vulnerable, whose nervous systems and consequent ability to regulate themselves are still nascent and thus wholly dependent on us for regulation?*
>
> Conkbayir, 2022, p8

Emotion coaching vs behaviour management

In our society, behaviour management has often been based on traditional theories, for example, operant conditioning theory (Skinner, 1963), where positive behaviour is rewarded, and negative behaviour is given consequences. Rewards given for following the behaviour rules, particularly in schools, include stickers, star charts, house points and verbal praise. Sanctions can include warnings, isolation and, for older children, detention. However, this approach does not tackle '*the complexities of social and emotional needs of pupils, particularly those who are vulnerable, in need and/or high-risk of under achievement*' (Rose, 2023, np).

In early years settings, stars, stickers, and behaviour charts are commonly used to 'manage' children's behaviour. These charts aim to encourage specific behaviours by offering rewards. Children often mimic their peers, hoping to earn similar rewards. However, according to Davis (2022), there is a major issue with this approach: these charts publicly display children's rewards and punishments. This can potentially harm their self-esteem. Also, Davis (2022) notes the assumption that all children can control their behaviour, which is not true for very young children. At ages two to three, children are still developing self-control, a process that requires warm interactions with caregivers and a secure environment – something not all children experience.

'Time out' is another strategy commonly used in the UK. Putting children on 'the naughty step' or 'the thinking chair' has been used for the management of behaviour in early years settings. The word 'naughty' is frowned upon in the early years profession these days, due to our understanding of the dangers of labelling children with negative words, but the 'time out' strategy can still be seen in some settings. New thinking leads us to see the practice as damaging to children, particularly very young children. What children need, within a nurturing and compassionate relationship, is help from adults to manage their own emotions and behaviour. This is why 'emotion coaching' is gaining popularity in the UK (Rose and Gilbert, 2018).

Emotion coaching requires early childhood practitioners to help young children understand and regulate their emotions. In the approach, adults working with the child are encouraged to provide support, to help the child recognise and label the emotion they are feeling (Krawczyk, 2017). It is important to validate the child's emotion (Gus, Rose and Gilbert, 2015), so the child feels listened to and understands that their emotions are accepted, as can be seen in Figure 2.3.

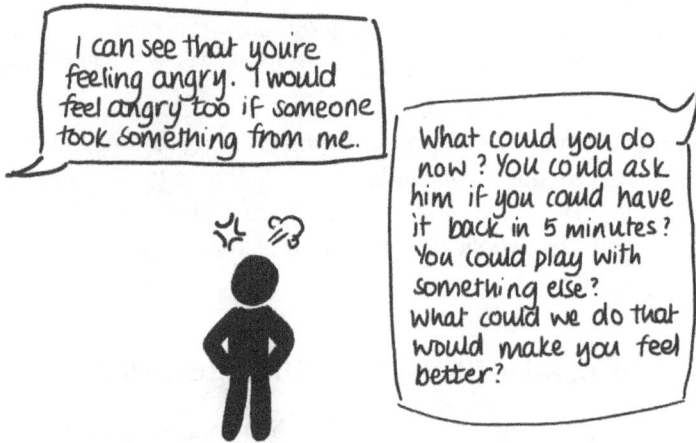

Figure 2.3 *Emotion coaching*

Attachment and relationship building

Theories of attachment

One of the most important responsibilities of an early years practitioner is to build secure attachments with young children. Children need secure attachments to enable them to feel able to explore their world whilst feeling safe. Initially, Bowlby (1969) developed a theory of attachment, stating that babies are biologically wired to form attachments with key figures and that these attachments form the basis of their future relationships. Bowlby outlined stages in young children's development of attachments (see Table 2.5)

Table 2.5 *Stages of attachment (adapted from Bowlby, 1969)*

Birth–3 months	Pre-attachment stage	The baby starts to form bonds with people and objects
6 weeks–7 months	Indiscriminate attachment	The baby begins to prefer some familiar people
7–11 months	Specific attachment	Babies begin to show stranger anxiety and separation anxiety when away from their attachment figure
2 years +	Multiple attachments	Children form more than one bond with the people they spend most time with

Following Bowlby's work, Ainsworth (1978) carried out investigations which identified specific types of attachment. Her research identified three types: avoidant, resistant and securely attached. A fourth type, disorganised attachment, was later added (Main and Soloman, 1986). Ainsworth's study illustrates the way that children who are securely attached to a caregiver can explore their environment confidently, knowing that their secure base will be there if they need to return to it for comfort and security. However, if the attachment is insecure, there are likely to be consequences for the child when they start attending a childcare setting. Figure 2.4 below outlines the four attachment types, the causes of these and likely consequences for the child.

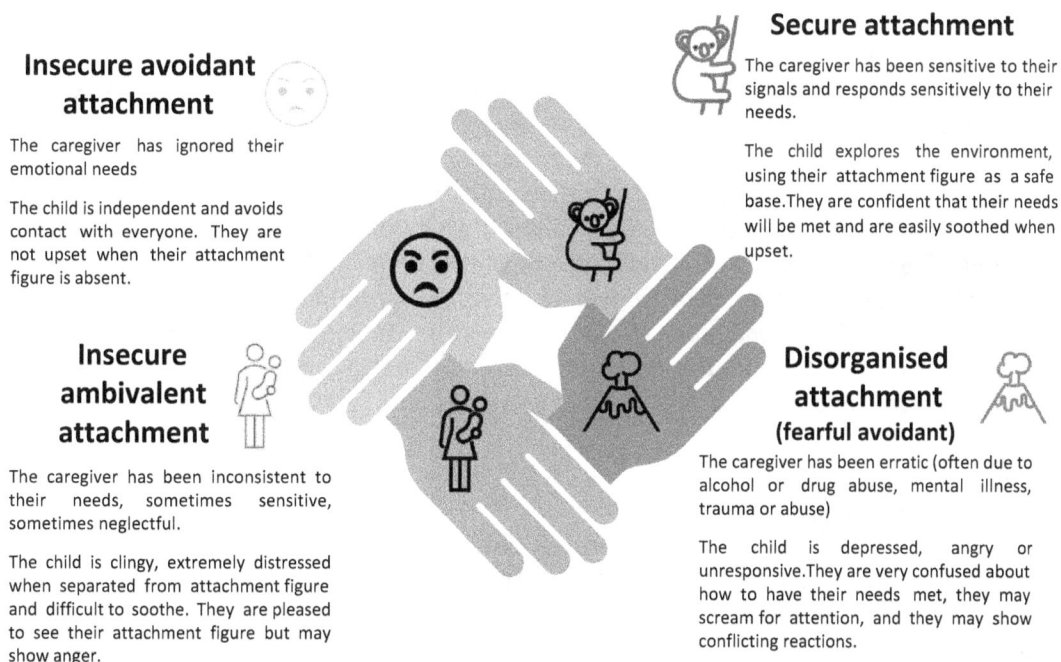

Secure attachment

The caregiver has been sensitive to their signals and responds sensitively to their needs.

The child explores the environment, using their attachment figure as a safe base. They are confident that their needs will be met and are easily soothed when upset.

Insecure avoidant attachment

The caregiver has ignored their emotional needs

The child is independent and avoids contact with everyone. They are not upset when their attachment figure is absent.

Insecure ambivalent attachment

The caregiver has been inconsistent to their needs, sometimes sensitive, sometimes neglectful.

The child is clingy, extremely distressed when separated from attachment figure and difficult to soothe. They are pleased to see their attachment figure but may show anger.

Disorganised attachment (fearful avoidant)

The caregiver has been erratic (often due to alcohol or drug abuse, mental illness, trauma or abuse)

The child is depressed, angry or unresponsive. They are very confused about how to have their needs met, they may scream for attention, and they may show conflicting reactions.

Figure 2.4 *Attachment types*

Critical reflection

Looking at the descriptions above, what sort of support do you think a child with each type of attachment would need when they start attending an early years setting?

Key person approach

Given the evidence from the aforementioned attachment research, a key person approach, where a named person builds a relationship with a particular child is ideal, and this is what the EYFS guidance (DfE, 2023) advocates. The key person is responsible for meeting the child's needs and is a crucial link between home and the care setting *'providing reassurance and creating close, supportive, ongoing relationships with families'* (Early Education, 2021, p17). The 'unique child' (DfE, 2023) is a principle of early years practice, and it requires practitioners to demonstrate empathy and compassion. This close relationship between child and key worker is also important because every child needs to feel 'known'. The birth to five guidance (Early Education, 2021) stresses the importance of this fact. Feeling known, having confidence in the fact that the people around you know about who you are, your characteristics and your needs, is a basic human need (Purvanova, 2013), therefore, information sharing and partnership with families is crucial, particularly during times of transition.

Transitions

A transition for a young child is a process, a change, which can be environmental or emotional, such as the transition from home to an early years setting, or from nursery to school (Seaman and Giles, 2021). Transitions from one room to another within a setting can be just as significant for a young child, as can transitions from one carer to another or even from one part of the day to another (Klette and Killen, 2019). Children are particularly vulnerable at times of transition; feelings can be mixed but most children feel a degree of anxiety and insecurity (Early Education, 2021). Research by Datler, Datler and Funder (2010, p82) identified *'the primitive and often catastrophic emotions of very young children during their process of transition from home care to out-of-home care'*. Therefore, transitions within early years settings should be managed sensitively, with partnership between the child, the child's family and practitioners, all working together to provide as smooth a changeover as possible.

Independence

As children adjust to a new environment, fostering independence is crucial. In early years settings, practitioners must strike a balance between protection, risk and challenge. While it is essential to safeguard the children, it is equally important not to overprotect them and instead to encourage them to take risks to challenge their physical abilities (Johnston et al, 2018). For instance, allowing a toddler to use a hand trowel for gardening can make them feel competent and useful. If we then supervise the activity and hand washing after the activity, we will also ensure the children's safety (Hodgkins and Prowle, 2023, p41).

Communication

Communication with children encompasses a variety of skills, including verbal communication, non-verbal communication and touch. As early years practitioners, communicating with children is of the utmost importance. Research by Fuertes et al (2024) indicated that the more time adults spent playing with children, the more positive their communication became, and the more positive the communication, the more learning was evident. Good practice in communication with young children includes:

- **Active listening** – showing the child that you are listening by asking questions, repeating what they say back to them and using gestures (smiling, nodding). This helps the child feel that they are heard and understood.

- **Speaking clearly** – making sure that communication is appropriate to the child's age and stage of development.

- **Positive language** – using kind, positive language sets a good example to children. Insulting words such as 'naughty', 'stupid', etc. should never be used.

- **Explain feelings** – help children to understand their emotions by naming them, e.g. 'I can see that you are feeling sad now that it's time to pack away the bikes. I understand that you are disappointed, but it's time for them to go away now and you can play with them again tomorrow'.

- **Specific praise** – help children to understand what behaviour you like to see by being specific. For example, instead of saying 'good girl!' say 'I see you have put all of your toys away, that's really helpful.'

- **Focus on behaviour, rather than labelling the child** – instead of saying 'you are too noisy', say 'I don't like it when you shout loudly while I am talking.'

- **Be a good role model** – treat children with kindness and empathy and they will do the same.

- **Listen to the child's voice** – value what children have to say and pay attention to what they are communicating.

Touch

Touch conveys safety and acceptance for babies and young children unable to communicate verbally. Being touched is a human right, but touching the children in our care can be a source of worry in some settings, due to the anxiety surrounding abuse. Professor McGlone from the Fit and Healthy Childhood All-Party Parliamentary Group says,

> *My view is that **not** touching children is a form of abuse ... touch is a necessity as much as food. What we are doing is removing an essential experience for young children.*
>
> cited in Goddard, 2020, np

The answer to this anxiety is to follow the policies and procedures of your setting and to get advice from your supervisor if you are unsure of the rules.

Chapter summary

This chapter has provided a thorough exploration of health and well-being, emphasising a positive and holistic approach. It examined various factors affecting health, including environmental influences and the nature versus nurture debate, and highlighted the importance of self-regulation, resilience and strong attachment relationships.

Practical strategies for supporting children's health and well-being were discussed, alongside contemporary issues like public healthcare sustainability. The chapter also underscored the significance of health literacy and the role of early years practitioners in enhancing it through partnerships with health services.

The key person approach was highlighted as essential for building close, supportive relationships with children, particularly during transitions. Effective communication and the appropriate use of touch were also emphasized as crucial elements in fostering a nurturing environment for young children.

Further reading

Conkbayir, M (2022) *The neuroscience of the developing child: Self-regulation for wellbeing and a sustainable future*, London: Routledge.

Rose, J (2023) Improving Behaviour – why rewards and sanctions are just not enough, *Teaching Times*, available at: www.teachingtimes.com/improving-behaviour-why-rewards-and-sanctions-are-not-enough/

References

Ainsworth, M, Blehar, M, Waters, E and Wall, S (1978) *Patterns of attachment: A psychological study of the strange situation*, Hillsdale, NJ: Erlbaum.

Alegria-Torres, J, Baccarelli, A and Bollati, V (2011) Epigenetics and lifestyle, *Epigenomics*, 3(3), pp. 267–277.

Bowlby, J (1969) *Attachment and loss, Vol. 1: Attachment. Attachment and loss*, New York: Basic Books.

Bronfenbrenner, U (1979) *The ecology of human development: Experiments by nature and design*, Cambridge, MA: Harvard University Press.

Conkbayir, M (2022) *The neuroscience of the developing child: Self-regulation for wellbeing and a sustainable future*, London: Routledge.

Datler, W, Datler, M and Funder, A (2010) Struggling against a feeling of becoming lost: A young boy's painful transition to day care, *Infant Observation*, 13(1), pp. 65–87.

Davis, E (2022) Behaviour charts: Good or bad? *Nursery World,* 1st March 2022.

Department for Education (2023) *Statutory framework for the early years foundation stage.* Available at: www.gov.uk/government/publications/early-years-foundation-stage-framework--2 (Accessed 3rd July 2024).

Early Education (2021) *Birth to 5 Matters: Non-statutory guidance for the Early Years Foundation Stage.* Available at: www.birthto5matters.org.uk (Accessed 20th July 2024).

Fuertes, M, Fernandes, I, Azevedo, A, Morais, I, Tadeu, B and Tempera, T (2024) What do adults learn through play regarding interactions and communication with children? *European Early Childhood Education Research Journal*, published online ahead of print. DOI: 10.1080/1350293X.2024.2332456

Goddard, C (2020) EYFS best practice in schools – Be in touch, *Nursery World*, 16th March 2020. Available at: www.nurseryworld.co.uk/features/article/eyfs-best-practice-in-schools-be-in-touch (Accessed 3rd March 2024).

Gus, L, Rose, J and Gilbert, L (2015) Emotion coaching: A universal strategy for supporting and promoting sustainable emotional and behavioural well-being, *Educational and Child Psychology*, 32(1), pp. 31–41.

Harvard University (2023) *What is epigenetics?* Available at: https://developingchild.harvard.edu/resources/what-is-epigenetics-and-how-does-it-relate-to-child-development/ (Accessed 22nd July 2024).

HM Government (2023) *Working together to safeguard children 2023: A guide to multi-agency working to help, protect and promote the welfare of children.* Available at: https://assets.publishing.service.gov.uk/media/669e7501ab418ab055592a7b/Working_together_to_safeguard_children_2023.pdf (Accessed 16th October 2024).

Hodgkins, A and Prowle, A (2023) *Strength-based approaches with children and families*, St Albans: Critical Publishing.

Johnston, J, Nahmad- Williams, L, Oates, R and Wood, V (2018) *Early childhood studies: Principles and practice*, 2nd ed, London: Routledge.

Klette, T and Killén, K (2019) Painful transitions: A study of 1-year-old toddlers' reactions to separation and reunion with their mothers after 1 month in childcare, *Early Child Development and Care*, 189(12), pp. 1970–1977.

Krawczyk, K (2017) *A whole school single case study of Emotion Coaching (EC) training and the impact on school staff.* Unpublished PhD thesis. University of Birmingham.

Labour Party UK (2024) *Change: Labour party manifesto 2024.* Available at: https://labour.org.uk/wp-content/uploads/2024/06/Change-Labour-Party-Manifesto-2024-large-print.pdf (Accessed 18th July 2024).

Main, M, and Solomon, J (1986) Discovery of an insecure-disorganized/disoriented attachment pattern. In T. B. Brazelton & M. W. Yogman (Eds.), *Affective development in infancy* (pp. 95–124). New York: Ablex Publishing.

Naimi, A, Naderiravesh, N, Bayat, Z, Shakeri, N and Matbou, M (2017) Correlation between health literacy and health-related quality of life in patients with hypertension, in Tehran, Iran, 2015–2016, *Electronic Physician*, 9(11), pp. 5712–5720.

NHS England (2019) *Universal Personalised Care: Implementing the Comprehensive Model*. Available at: NHS England report template – NHS logo (Accessed 14th October 2024).

NHS England (2022) *Healthy Child Programme Schedule of Interventions Guide*. Available at: www.e-lfh.org.uk/pathways-healthy-child/ (Accessed 9th July 2024).

NHS England (2023) *Enhanced access to GP services*. Available at: www.england.nhs.uk/gp/investment/gp-contract/network-contract-directed-enhanced-service-des/enhanced-access-faqs/ (Accessed 27th November 2024).

NHS England (nd) *600 GP hours released a year after reducing inappropriate appointments – Chiswick Health Practice* [Online] Available at: www.england.nhs.uk/gp/case-studies/600-gp-hours-released-a-year-after-reducing-inappropriate-appointments-chiswick-health-practice-london/ (Accessed 8th July 2024).

O'Mara-Eves, A, Brunton, G, Oliver, S, Kavanagh, J, Jamal, F and Thomas, J (2015) The effectiveness of community engagement in public health interventions for disadvantaged groups: A meta-analysis, *BMC Public Health*, 15(1), pp. 129–152.

Public Health England (2020) *Community-centred public health: Taking a whole system approach briefing of research findings*. Available at https://assets.publishing.service.gov.uk/media/5e184c78e5274a06b1c3c5f9/WSA_Briefing.pdf (Accessed 28th September 2024).

Purvanova, R (2013) The role of feeling known for team member outcomes in project teams, *Small Group Research*, 44(3), pp. 298–331.

Rose, J (2023) Improving Behaviour – why rewards and sanctions are just not enough, *Teaching Times*. Available at: www.teachingtimes.com/improving-behaviour-why-rewards-and-sanctions-are-not-enough/

Rose, J., Gilbert, L. And Richards, V. (2018) *Health and well-being in early childhood*, London: Sage.

Schick, A. (2022) Health as temporally extended: Theoretical foundations and implications, *History and Philosophy of the Life Sciences*, 44(3), pp. 32–32.

Seaman, H and Giles, P (2021) Supporting children's social and emotional well-being in the early years: An exploration of practitioners' perceptions, *Early Child Development and Care*, 191(6), pp. 861–875.

Shanker, S (2020) *Reframed*, Toronto, Buffalo and London: University of Toronto Press.

Skinner, B (1963) Operant behaviour, *American Psychologist*, 18(8), pp. 503–515.

World Health Organization (2024) *Constitution*. Available at: www.who.int/about/governance/constitution (Accessed 22nd July 2024).

Theme 2
The custodian

Chapters Three and Four will help you in your duties as a custodian for children.

Duty 1 Promote the health and well-being of all children, self-regulation and resilience through learning rich environments, opportunities for challenging play and a healthy attitude towards risk taking.	**Knowledge:** 1 2 3 4 6 7 8 9 11 14 15 16 17 18 19 20 21
	Skills: 1 2 4 6 10 15 16 17 18 19 21 22 23
	Behaviours: 1 2 3 4 5 6 8
Duty 7 Ensure full compliance with all safeguarding legislation, policies and strategies at a national, local and setting-based level are promoted, implemented and embedded respectfully within practice, providing appropriate support to colleagues as, or supporting, the Designated Safeguarding Lead.	**Knowledge:** 1 3 4 5 6 7 8 16 17 18 19 20 21 22
	Skills: 2 10 11 16 18 20 21 22 23 24 25
	Behaviours: 1 2 3 5 6 9
Duty 13 Ensure compliance with all Health and Safety legislation, policies and strategies at a national, local and setting based level.	**Knowledge:** 10 15 16 19 20 22
	Skills: 2 5 10 17 19
	Behaviours: 1 5

DOI: 10.4324/9781041055358-5

Duty 14 Maintain effective administrative systems including development records, assessment, report writing and record keeping, such as risk assessments and safeguarding concerns.	**Knowledge:** 1 2 3 5 8 11 12 13 14 16 19 20 21
	Skills: 1 3 4 11 12 13 16 18 19 20 23 24
	Behaviours: 1 5 6

3 Understanding, applying and managing legislation and regulatory frameworks

Michelle Malomo, Emma Laurence, and Amanda McCully

Social policy impacts children and families in all areas of their lives. It can empower or disempower young children and their families through its impact on the level of provision, access and suitability of services for children with differing needs. This chapter considers current legislation, professional guidance and national and local policy initiatives, supporting you to analyse critically so that you may lead practice in relating these to the needs of children and families. Within the chapter, there is a focus on the rights of children, inequality and social justice in order to evaluate policy, practice and provision through examination of a rights-based perspective. This will provide you with an informed awareness of how policy impacts on your leadership of practice and the quality of provision.

Chapter objectives

The aim of this chapter is:

- To understand how legislation, policy and regulations for early childhood education and care arises from socio-political debates: locally, nationally, internationally

- To explore the impact of key government policies which aim to reduce educational inequalities.

- To support you in reflecting on your own leadership in applying relevant social policy to practice and how effectively this contributes to quality provision at the setting.

Introduction

Beige (2021, p4) suggests that it is professionals who 'work on the ground that determine the experiences children receive, regardless of the policies that circulate above them'. This opening statement is at the heart of this chapter. The chapter will consider the importance of you understanding legislation, policy and regulation but more importantly it will challenge

DOI: 10.4324/9781041055358-6

you to consider your position within these and how important this is when leading practice within this area. On reflection, writing about this area of practice is often challenging because the narrative for practice seems to be set and to some degree prescriptive in nature. However, this is not the reality nor is it the aspiration that we have for legislation, policy and regulation within early childhood. As the chapter progresses, we will hopefully inspire practice that blossoms beyond the compliance model of practice. Throughout this book you will have seen that different authors have referred to Bronfenbrenner's ecological systems model (1979). This chapter will consider the impact of legislation, policy and regulations in the macrosystem of this model and how this can have an influence on holistic developments and outcomes for children.

When thinking about legislation and regulations that underpin the sector, we think that EY professionals potentially sit in one of two camps. Before this thinking is explored though, there is a disclaimer. Legislation, policy and regulations are essential, crucial and necessary and compliance with these is the day-to-day bedrock of practice. However, how do you see legislation, policy and regulations within your day-to-day practice? Observations of approaches range from the those that hold on tightly to these 'documents' and they often become the only accepted discourse of how we do our work, with the fear that any free thinking about meaning, and interpretation of these documents could lead to regulatory bodies judging practice to be 'less than'. The reality is that often what has been interpreted is just one way of being compliant and without creative and innovative thinking, practice becomes limited rather than being inspired for good.

However, it is also encouraging to see EY practitioners that use these as the very baseline of practice but then they have the courage to think beyond the compliance of practice to a deeper more reflective interpretation that centres legislation and regulation as the springboard for best practice. It takes bravery and courage to lead practice in this manner. Within this chapter we will explore how you might develop practice like this.

What is a custodian?

When reflecting on how to describe the responsibilities of early years practitioners in this area of practice the idea of them being a custodian seemed appropriate. The Cambridge dictionary defines the custodian as;

> *A person with responsibility for protecting or taking care of something or someone who tries to protect ideas or principles*
>
> *Cambridge dictionary, 2025*

This definition seems to sum up the responsibilities that need to be acknowledged but also offers hope to the notion of protecting the ideas and principles whilst enabling the practitioner to lead practice that moves beyond a compliance interpretation. It is the intention within this chapter that we will encourage you to delve deep so that you have the knowledge to then develop the skills and behaviours to do this.

When looking at this topic it can be overwhelming as there is a need to be compliant and (as discussed in Chapters Seven and Ten) more importantly to 'do the right thing'. This is also the underlying foundation of this chapter. To be able to move beyond the compliance model we need to consider where we stand within legislation, policy and regulations. Once an understanding is gained, we can move through this chapter in a reflective and developmental manner.

Critical reflection – my relationship with legislation policy and regulations

Malomo and Laurence (2022, p92) suggest that fear often creates a shadow impeding meaningful reflection when working with children and their families as we avoid considering the things we are afraid of. However, it is important to understand that avoiding reflecting on certain aspects of practice due to this discomfort hinders progress. However, as Malomo and Laurence (2022, p92) make clear, *'courage and empowerment can be cultivated by leaning into this discomfort'*.

- Having considered this citation reflect upon your own professional fears that you have when considering legislation, policy and regulations. Note these down and use these as you delve into the chapter.

- Is there a piece of legislation that you need to gain further knowledge and understanding of? How might this be helpful in developing and leading practice within your setting?

Contemporary context for legislation, policy and regulations

Before we delve into relevant legislation, policy and regulations it is important to rise above our own practice and look down and consider the social policy/cultural landscape in which current practice sits. This type of *'reflection may involve taking a "balcony perspective", where you step back and consider the bigger picture, complicated by several factors, including other people's hidden agendas'* (Paige-Smith and Craft, 2018, p161). Often, we can be so consumed with the pressure of day-to-day practice we fail to have a mindful and reflective moment to consider what might have had an influence.

Currently within the United Kingdom *'4.3 million children are in poverty across the UK. That's 30% of all children. In the ten years between 2012/13 and 2022/23, the number of children in poverty rose by 700,000 (from 27% to 30%)'* (Action for Children, 2024). This data provides a sobering read despite the intention to eradicate childhood poverty by 2020 (HMG, 2010).

This is in part because of the extended cost of living crisis that has been experienced within the UK. The Joseph Rowntree Foundation (2024) states that '*seven million low-income households (60%) were going without the essentials in the previous 6 months, including 5.4 million experiencing food insecurity in the previous 30 days and 4.3 million low-income households (37%) were in arrears on at least one household bill or credit commitment*'. This has had an impact on those that work within the sector. Hodgkins, Malomo and Solvason (2024) uncovered in research with teaching assistants that '*one in seven said they had used a foodbank, community larders, or apps to enable them to obtain reduced-cost food, and over a quarter (26%) said they had to take on a second or third job to make ends meet*'. The cost of living crisis is part of many of those who work within sectors, lived reality. This shared story with the children and families that we work with places the sector right in the heart of this context. Solvason, Sutton-Tsang and Stobbs (2025, p10) state that '*low wages have always been an issue for professionals working in ECEC and those who stay in the sector clearly do not do it for financial recompense. It is morally wrong, however, that the passion and compassion of ECEC practitioners continues to be taken advantage of by a government that consistently raises demands without providing the resources to enable this*'. There is therefore an urgency for social policy to address this crisis.

What is policy?

The National Audit Office (2001, np) defines policy as '*the translation of government's political priorities and principles into programmes and courses of action to deliver desired changes*'. The implementation of government policy may require new legislation (Acts of Parliament) or amendments to previous legislation. However, not all policy requires changes to legislation, and may be implemented through government guidelines, codes of practice and standards; these guidelines and codes, etc. are also called government policy. Therefore, policy is not the same as law but there is sometimes overlap between the two. Most government policy requires implementation at local authority and/or private and voluntary organisational level. This usually results in these organisations creating local applications of government policy; thus we have local authority policies, agency policies and settings' policies. As you can see the word policy applies to all levels of implementation and application at the local level.

International influences on policy and how this influences national and local policy

This section of the chapter will explore how international and national social policy and legislation and will inevitably have an impact on the local policies that we work with.

Westwood (2017) states that when we consider international perspectives, we are able to compare and critically analyse systems, policy and practice and how this has an impact for children. Taking this approach also helps us see how international conventions have an impact on national interpretations and in turn affect our practice.

International declarations, conventions and goals

Universal Declaration of Human Rights (1948)

In December 1948, a declaration was made by the United Nations General Assembly. There was a desire at the end of World War Two for a new declaration that would prevent the abuse of human rights that had been seen through the war. This was seen as a milestone document in the history of human rights as it made a universal declaration of a common standard for all peoples and all nations. It was drafted by representatives from all regions of the world and from diverse cultural backgrounds and is the foundation for all international human rights legislation.

The United Nations (2025a, np) states that,

> Human rights are rights we have simply because we exist as human beings – they are not granted by any state. These universal rights are inherent to us all, regardless of nationality, sex, national or ethnic origin, colour, religion, language, or any other status. They range from the most fundamental – the right to life – to those that make life worth living, such as the rights to food, education, work, health, and liberty.

There are many Acts of Parliament that have been developed since this to reflect and ensure that these rights are upheld within law. However, it is the development of the United Nations Convention on the Rights of the Child (UNCRC) as an interpretation of these rights for children that has had a profound influence on both national and local policy.

UNCRC (1998)

UNICEF (2025) describe the UNCRC as 'the most complete statement of children's rights ever produced and is the most widely ratified international human rights treaty in history'. They explain that each of the rights is interconnected and ensures that each child has the right to: relax and play (Article 31), freely express themselves (Article 13), be safe from violence (Article 19), receive an education (Article 28), have their identity protected (Article 8), enjoy a sufficient standard of living (Article 27), know their rights (Article 42) and have good health and access to health services (Article 24). When considering this list there is a visible link to national legislation. National and local policy highlights the UK's intention to not only ratify the convention but also to ensure that as a country we make sense of these rights in the context of culture and childhood.

The UNCRC (United Nations Convention on the Rights of the Child) (UNICEF, 2025) is a legally binding agreement signed by 196 countries. All UN member states except for the United States have ratified the Convention. With the recent changes in leadership within the USA, the reneging on climate pledges and decisions that intend to maintain internal control of policy, it is unlikely that this position will change soon.

Sustainable development goals (SDGs)

In 2015, world leaders came together to make *'a historic promise to secure the rights and well-being of everyone on a healthy, thriving planet when they adopted the 2030 Agenda for Sustainable Development and its 17 Sustainable Development Goals (SDGs)'* (United Nations, 2025b, np). The Agenda for Sustainable Development has become the road map for countries to end poverty, tackle inequalities and protect the planet. The SDGs set goals for countries to tackle these by offering *'the most practical and effective pathway to tackle the causes of violent conflict, human rights abuses, climate change and environmental degradation and aim to ensure that no one will be left behind'* (United Nations, 2025b, np). The 17 SDGs include items such as, No poverty, Zero hunger, Good health and well-being, Quality education, Gender equality, Climate action and Peace. These goals support leaders in the early years sector to take a sustainable approach to their practice and curriculum, and ensure that they cultivate sustainability within the lives of the children and families that are part of their settings. Chapter 8 explores this in more detail.

Salamanca statement

In 1994 the United Nations Educational, Scientific and Cultural Organization (UNESCO) brought together 92 governments and 25 international organisations. The statement required that *'all children should learn together, wherever possible, regardless of any difficulties or differences they may have. Inclusive schools must recognize and respond to the diverse needs of their students'* (UNESCO, 1994). This was a shift in approach. Within national policy this is reflected in the SEND code of practice: 0-25 (2014).

National policy and legislation

In the 21st century national policy has been informed by international studies as to the effectiveness of ECEC, alongside understandings of the benefits of good provision for children, families, society and the economy (Children's Commissioner for England, 2020). Wood, Kay and Travers (2023) suggest that policy and leadership are key to raising quality within the sector. For *'raising quality is associated with social justice – equality of opportunity, anti-discriminatory practice and inclusion with a particular focus on children considered to be disadvantaged, vulnerable or at risk'* (Wood, Kay and Travers, 2023, p146). Therefore, successive governments have introduced both policy and legislation to address this. A deeper delve into safeguarding policy/legislation is covered in Chapters Seven and Ten, but it is important that there is an understanding as to how this national policy and legislation was developed.

The Children Act 1989 and 2004

The Children Act was introduced as an *'act to reform the law relating to children; to provide for local authority services for children in need and others; to amend the law with respect to children's homes, community homes, voluntary homes and voluntary organisations; to make provision with respect to fostering, child minding and day care for young children and adoption; and for connected purposes'* (HMG, 1989, p1). This Act was further developed in 2004 and alongside the statutory guidance of Working Together to Safeguard Children (DfE, 2023) provides the core legal requirements for safeguarding practice. The Children Act had three key principles; the concept of parental responsibility, the importance of a child's welfare when a court is considering their care and the understanding that children are best looked after by their family unless an intervention is essential. Section 31 of the Act sets out the circumstances whereby a court may place a child in a local authority's care. The amendments in 2004 require that agencies including local authorities, the police and health services, are under a duty to ensure they consider the need to safeguard and promote the welfare of children when carrying out their functions (section 11). At the time of writing, the Children's Wellbeing and Schools Bill is being considered in parliament, which seeks to further reform aspects of the Children Act to further support our most vulnerable children.

Every Child Matters agenda (ECM)

Following the Laming report (2003) into the death of Victoria Climbie, recommendations were made and as a response the then Labour government implemented the ECM agenda (HM Treasury, 2003). This agenda aimed to reform services for children. The agenda set out the following five aspirations for every child:

- have the support needed to be healthy

- stay safe

- enjoy and achieve

- make a positive contribution and

- achieve economic well-being.

These aspirations became the focus for all professionals working with children. However, the ECM agenda was dropped by the coalition government in 2010. Having the ECM agenda to support collaborative working was inspirational and many practitioners use this still as a focus for good practice.

Early Years Foundation Stage (EYFS)

The EYFS (DfE 2024) was introduced in 2008 to provide a framework that would provide universal high-quality environments for children in their preschool years. The EYFS was established in response to the requirements laid down within The Childcare Act (2006). The EYFS sets out the standards for learning, development and care of children from birth to five years. This is a statutory (non-optional) requirement for those working within the sector.

Local policy

Having explored the international and national influences, this section of the chapter will support you to think about how these have influenced day-to-day practice. The policies and procedures that you have within your setting are your local policies. At times, local policy can become an exercise in being compliant. In our experience it is when policies and procedures are brought to life that they can be meaningful and enhance practice beyond compliance. When leading practice, policies and procedures can support us in ensuring that provision is an expression of the children and families we work with, ensure that our practices are compliant but also give us an opportunity to develop practice that is innovative.

Who owns the policies within the setting?

Have you ever thought about who owns the policies within your setting? Our answer would be that everyone who is involved or is part of the setting owns the policy. This means that managers, leaders, the children, their families, stakeholders and the community the setting serves, all have responsibility to ensure that the policies and procedures within the setting reflect the needs of everyone.

When a new member of staff joins a setting, they need to have a robust induction, and this includes having access to the policies and procedures of the setting. They must have a full understanding of what these mean in practice and as a leader you have the responsibility to ensure that this happens.

We often say to students that local polices need to have breath. By that we mean that they are living, meaningful and organic documents and should be an embodiment of actual practice. For local policy to have this type of meaning you need to ensure that you place yourself within the policy. The case study below explores this.

> ❝ **Case study – improving practice through regular policy review**
>
> Charlie had recently gained a position as a manager within a Family Hub. As part of his induction with the regional manager he had explored the policies within the setting. Charlie was aware that the mobile phone policy seemed to not have been reviewed since 2019. Last week a three-year-old had brought a phone into the setting and wanted to play games on this. Staff had agreed to this, and another child wanted to play with it – this led to the children arguing and the phone dropped to the ground and the screen was broken. Charlie decided that at the next staff meeting the mobile phone policy needed to be reviewed.
>
> - How might you prepare for this agenda item, is there any guidance or regulations that you may need to reflect?
> - Who might need to be consulted about any changes to this policy?

- How might you be able to ensure that staff are able to contribute to this policy development?
- How would you be able to consult with and give agency to the children's voices within this policy?
- Are there any other policies that might be connected to this change/development?

Key government policies and education inequalities

Societal and educational inequalities are deeply intertwined, with each perpetuating and reinforcing the other. Societal inequalities, such as disparities in income, housing, race, gender, and geographic location, often dictate access to quality education, creating significant barriers for marginalised communities. In turn, educational inequalities – manifested through underfunded schools, unequal access to resources, and systemic biases – limit opportunities for upward mobility, perpetuating cycles of poverty and exclusion. This relationship creates a feedback loop where those from disadvantaged backgrounds are less likely to access the education needed to challenge societal inequities, while societal structures continue to undermine efforts to achieve equitable educational systems. Addressing this link requires systemic reforms that tackle both societal inequities and the structural barriers within education.

The Joseph Rowntree Foundation (2022) stated that *'even at a young age there is a gap in educational attainment for young people by parental income level, and this continues throughout the different stages of a child's education'*. The Centre for Longitudinal Studies follows children over their life and found that, in the UK, children born in 2000 had lower attainment in cognitive tests in the early years if their parents had lower incomes. The gap in vocabulary development between children in the richest and poorest families (top and bottom 20% of incomes) was, on average, ten months at age three and 15 months at age five (CLS, 2017) (JRF, 2022, p89). Research shows that the impact of the Covid-19 pandemic has widened the attainment gap between the most and least disadvantaged pupils in the UK (Scottish Government, 2020). This is due to a range of factors including the digital divide, home learning environments and potentially deepening poverty during the pandemic.

Due to the nature of societal and educational inequalities as perpetuating each other across the life course, it is possible to see the significant role that quality ECEC can play in addressing these issues. The early years sector plays a crucial role in addressing societal and educational inequalities in the UK by laying a strong foundation for lifelong learning and development, particularly for children from disadvantaged backgrounds.

Research consistently shows that high-quality early education narrows developmental gaps and improves outcomes in language, literacy and social skills, helping to reduce the long-term effects of poverty and inequality. Recognising this, the UK government has prioritised increasing access to quality early education, with initiatives such as the introduction of 30 hours of government-funded childcare a week, over 38 weeks of the year, for children from nine months up to starting school. Interestingly, this funding is only available to eligible working parents who each earn over £9,518 (from April 2024) but less than £100,000 per year. This would suggest that the scheme seeks to encourage parents into work and may address inequalities caused by in-work poverty. However, children from families where parents cannot work will not be able to access this funding, perhaps perpetuating inequalities for the most disadvantaged children.

What is social policy?

Although it can be useful to focus on early years policy, we need to remember that Early Childhood Education and Care (ECEC) services do not exist in a vacuum but are inextricably linked to the other main social services provided for children and families as part of England's social policy. It is also important to remember that in relation to early childhood education and care, the devolved governments of Wales, Scotland and Northern Ireland, have responsibilities for their own early years services and policies. For example, each devolved government has its own safeguarding policy and legislation. Therefore, it is important that practice is understood within its own socio-political context.

Having defined policy above, Spicker (2014, p5) states that *social* policy is '*about welfare*'. Welfare is understood here in its widest sense as 'well-being', rather than the narrow meaning of benefits such as means-tested social security. Spicker (2014, p6) goes on to state that '*social policy is about people who lack well-being: people with particular problems or needs and the services which provide for them*'. These social services are the result of government policy on how to respond to people's needs and promote their welfare. These are mainly '*understood to include social security, housing, health, social work and education – the big five – along with others which raise similar issues such as employment, prison, legal services, community safety*' (Spicker, 2014, p1).

Social justice and social mobility

Before you begin this section, you will find it useful to write down your own views; this will help you later to form your own critical evaluation of the different perspectives and government policy.

Critical reflection – a just society

Write down your answers to the following questions and store them so that you can reflect back later.

In very basic terms, if we take social justice to mean a 'just society', that is a society which is fair to all individuals and groups:

- What is a fair society to you?

- What do you think governments should or should not do to create or allow a fair society?

- What rights should individuals have in your society?
- Who, if anyone, does your just society look after/protect, e.g. vulnerable individuals?
- If your society does protect individuals, how do you think it should be funded?

What is social justice?

Perhaps in your views you considered individuals having rights to participate in society. For example, being able to vote. You may have also thought about whether a person would have rights to access services and assets, such as housing, safe environments, education, health care, employment and a living wage, to live a dignified life in that society. You may have also considered whether the society would help the vulnerable and how this would be done in your just society.

There are a wide range of views of what makes a fair society and what counts as social justice. These are much-debated issues and how they should be implemented through policy and carried out in practice is also a complex matter. Examining further what is meant by a 'just society' requires us to consider the concepts of 'equality' and 'equity' (Table 3.1). Some people assume that these words have the same meaning, but closer consideration shows that the implications of either applying 'equality' or 'equity' can lead to different outcomes for people and for society.

The difference between equality and equity is also described as the difference between 'equality of opportunity' and 'equality of outcome'.

Table 3.1 *The differences between equality and equity*

Equal Opportunity (Equality)	Equality of Outcome (Equity)
Social Justice which puts the emphasis on 'equality of opportunity'.	Social justice which puts the emphasis on 'equality of outcome'.
Every person must be treated equally in all situations regardless of differences.	In education – the potential of every individual person to be realised.
For example,	For example,
Universal provision of primary education in the UK arguably gives every individual child the opportunity to do well in education.	Do all children start in the same position to make the best of primary education?
	Are there barriers/inequalities that make it difficult for some children to make the best of the opportunities provided by primary education?
	What support could be provided to promote more equal outcomes for primary children?

The above different perspectives on social justice (equality and equity) are linked to different schools of thought and theories such as those outlined in Table 3.2.

Table 3.2 *Different schools of thought regarding equality and equity.*

Equal Opportunity (Equality)	Equality of Outcome (Equity)
Social Justice which puts the emphasis on 'equality of opportunity'.	Social justice which puts the emphasis on 'equality of outcome'.
Every person must be treated equally in all situations regardless of differences.	Focus should be on ensuring that the potential of every individual person is realised.
Theorist: Robert Nozick (1974) *Anarchy, State and Utopia* **(1st ed.)**	**Theorist: John Rawls (1971)** *A Theory of Justice.*
Emphasis on individual responsibility	Emphasis on social co-operation
The role of the state/government is to protect individual rights, property, ownership and freedom of the individual to choose what to do with what they own.	The distribution of resources to benefit the least advantaged in society. This may mean unequal distribution – for example some individuals need more support than others.
The state/government does not use systems (no taxation, no benefits) to support vulnerable individuals because it is up to individuals to decide whether to help the vulnerable by giving them some of their resources, for example through charities.	Systems such as taxation should apply to the whole of society to enable the distribution of resources on the basis of an individual's needs with particular emphasis on the disadvantaged. (It is not left up to the individual to decide to help the vulnerable).

These different perspectives on social justice lead to different political beliefs and policies. In *general terms* the Right wing of the political spectrum tends to favour the form of social justice which emphasises individual responsibility and independence – for example, what can the individual do to escape unemployment and poverty and achieve success and how can opportunities be created to allow individuals to do this?

In *general terms* the Left wing of the political spectrum tends to favour the form of social justice which emphasises social co-operation and collective responsibility. This perspective is concerned with how systems in society affect individuals. For example, large-scale redundancies and closure of businesses in an area may make it very difficult to find employment. How can resources be redistributed to support individuals and families in times of need? However, in the last few decades there has been a blurring of these two positions by political parties.

A further debate is the argument about whether social justice and social mobility are opposite in their outcomes and whether the emphasis of social justice should be on social mobility. The government has a Social Mobility Commission (2025, np) which *'exists to create a United Kingdom where the circumstances of birth do not determine outcomes in life'*. The Social Mobility Commission's definition of social mobility is *'the link between a person's occupation or income and the occupation or income of their parents. Where there is a strong link, there is a lower level of social mobility. Where there is a weak link, there is a higher level of social mobility'.*

Conversely, there are arguments against social mobility as a strategy for social justice which are related to unavoidable disadvantages. What happens to the individuals who cannot climb the social ladder because of health conditions or other significant disadvantages? It is also worth recognising that social mobility can be downward. For example, a person is made redundant and then takes a lower – paid job.

Critical reflection – revisiting ideas

1. Review your original explanation of 'a fair society' and add any points you agree with from the sections in this chapter.

2. Reflect on whether your idea of a fair society has developed or been consolidated during the course of the chapter.

Policy into practice

As the practitioner you are uniquely positioned to impact how early years policy is experienced by the people you work with. Whilst policy intentions might be well-meaning, unless they are implemented appropriately, they may not have the impact they are supposed to. One key issue in this is that each child and family we work with is unique, yet policies, whether in education or otherwise, are designed to apply broadly, ensuring fairness and efficiency but often at the cost of personal nuance. This standardised approach may not always align with the diverse needs of individuals. This tension between the one-size-fits-all approach of early years policies and the deeply personal journey of each individual highlights the challenge that implementation poses and the crucial role that the early years practitioner plays in translating policy into practice.

The same or very similar policy will often feel very different within different settings due to the way that it is carried out and it is here that professional values become crucial. One key issue in implementation is to ensure that policy is accessible to everyone and to do this requires professional curiosity (see Chapter 7 for further details on this).

❝ Case study – making policy accessible

Steven has been bringing his two small children (two years old and nine months old) to the setting for a few weeks now. During the initial information gathering about the children, Steven made clear that the children's mother had fairly recently and quite suddenly passed away. Up until this point, the children had not been in childcare before and stayed home with mum. The staff in setting have done well to settle the children in and they seem, for the most part quite happy. Steven works five days a week. However, the children have been put in setting for three hours, two days a week on the days that Steven works in the office, and it is rarely the same person (often a friend) picking up to look after them for the afternoon.

- Having explored the above case study ask yourself why might the children be in setting only two of Steven's working days? What do you think is happening on the other days that Steven works?

- Given that Steven's family have never used childcare before, what policy might he be unaware of which could better support them?

- What might the impact be of Steven becoming more aware of the setting's policies which pertain to him?

In the above case study, it is possible to see that without professional curiosity and an open dialogue with families, policies can be inaccessible to some, which can marginalise them and exacerbate inequalities. Part of the role of the early years practitioner is to bridge the gap between the unique children and families in setting and the uniform nature of policy. By critically evaluating their own practice and advocating for sensitive implementation of policy, early years practitioners can explore ways to enhance inclusive and high-quality early education which better addresses societal and educational inequalities.

Chapter summary

This chapter explores how legislation, policy, and regulations in early childhood education and care are shaped by socio-political debates at local, national, and international levels. It examines the evolving priorities of governments and societies in addressing the needs of young children, particularly in relation to education, care and well-being. Additionally, this chapter encourages reflection on the role of leadership in early years settings, considering how the application of social policy influences the quality of provision.

Further reading

Children's book about UNCRC: UNICEF and Castle, C. (2002) *For Every Child*. Red Fox: Salsibury.

Website: Action for Children. Accessed at www.actionforchildren.org.uk/our-work-and-impact/policy-work-campaigns-and-research

Website: UNCRC UN Convention on Rights of a Child (UNCRC) – UNICEF UK.

References

Action for Children (2024) Where is child poverty increasing in the UK. Accessed at www.actionforchildren.org.uk/blog/where-is-child-poverty-increasing-in-the-uk/ on 29/01/25.

Beige, R. (2021) *Early Years Pedagogy in Practice: A Guide for Students and Practitioners*. London: Routledge.

Bronfenbrenner, U. (1979) *The Ecology of Human Development*. Cambridge, MA: Harvard University Press.

Cambridge Dictionary (2025) Custodian. Accessed at https://dictionary.cambridge.org/dictionary/english/custodianCentre for Longitudinal Studies (2017) Millennium Cohort Study Briefing 13: Intergenerational inequality in early years assessments. Available online at: https://cls.ucl.ac.uk/wp-content/uploads/2017/05/13_briefing_web.pdf

Children's Commissioner for England (2020) Best beginnings in the early years. Accessed at https://assets.childrenscommissioner.gov.uk/wpuploads/2020/07/cco-best-beginnings-in-the-early-years.pdf on 28/01/25.

Department for Education (2024) Early years foundation stage statutory framework for group and school-based providers. Accessed online at https://assets.publishing.service.gov.uk/media/65aa5e42ed27ca001327b2c7/EYFS_statutory_framework_for_group_and_school_based_providers.pdf

Department for Education and Department of Health (2014) Special educational needs and disability code of practice: 0 to 25 years. Accessed at www.gov.uk/government/publications/send-code-of-practice-0-to-25 on 29/01/2025.

Department for Education (2023) *Working Together to Safeguard Children*. London: Department for Education.

Her Majesty's Government (1989) *The Children Act*. London: HMG.

Her Majesty's Government (2010) *The Childhood Poverty Act*. London: HMG.

HM Treasury (2003) Every child matters. Accessed online at www.gov.uk/government/publications/every-child-matters.

Hodgkins, A., Malomo, M. and Solvason, C. (2024) Teaching Assistants, Respected Enough to Teach, but Not Enough to Be Paid Accordingly. *International Journal of Changes in Education*, Vol. 00(00) 1–9 [Preprint]. doi:10.47852/bonviewIJCE42024033.

Laming, W. H. (2003) *The Victoria Climbie Inquiry: Report of an Inquiry by Lord Laming* (Cm 5730). London: The Stationery Office.

Malomo, M. and Laurence. (2022) Finding yourself in safeguarding practice. In Richards, H. and Malomo, M. (eds) *Developing Your Professional Identity: A Guide for Working with Children and Families*. St Alban's: Critical Publishing.

National Audit Office (2001) *Modern Policy-Making: Ensuring Policies Deliver Value for Money*. London: NAO.

Paige–Smith, A. and Craft, A. (2011) Reflection and developing a community of practice. In Paige Smith, A. and Craft. A. (eds) *Developing Reflective Practice In The Early Years*. Berkshire: Open University Press.

Scottish Government (2020) Coronavirus (COVID-19): Impact on children, young people and families – evidence summary October 2020. Accessed at www.gov.scot/publications/report-covid-19-children-young-people-families-october-2020-evidence-summary

Social Mobility Commission (2025) What we do. Accessed at https://socialmobility.independent-commission.uk/about-us/what-we-do

Solvason, C., Sutton-Tsang, S., & Stobbs, N. (2025). Heading for burnout: The early years workforce in England post COVID-19. *Journal of Early Childhood Research*, 23(2), 137–149. https://doi.org/10.1177/1476718X241308402

Spicker, P. (2014) *Social Policy: Theory and Practice*. 3rd ed. Bristol: Policy Press.

The Children Act (1989) c.41 London: HMSO.

The Children Act (2004) c.31 London: HMSO.

The Childcare Act (2006) c.21 London: HMSO.

The Joseph Rowntree Foundation (2022) UK Poverty 2022: The essential guide to understanding poverty in the UK. Accessed at www.jrf.org.uk/report/uk-poverty-2022 on 22/1/2025.

The Joseph Rowntree Foundation (2024) No end in sight for living standards crisis: JRF's cost of living tracker winter 2024. Accessed at www.jrf.org.uk/cost-of-living/jrfs-cost-of-living-tracker-winter-2024 on 28/01/25.

UN General Assembly (1948) Universal Declaration of Human rights. Accessed at https://documents.un.org/doc/resolution/gen/nr0/043/88/pdf/nr004388.pdf on 29/01/25.

UNESCO (1994) *The Salamanca Statement and Framework for Action on Special Needs Education*. Adopted by the World Conference on Special Needs Education: Access and Quality. Salamanca, Spain: UNESCO.

UNICEF (2025) How we protect children's rights. Accessed at www.unicef.org.uk/what-we-do/un-convention-child-rights/ on 22/01/25.

United Nations (2025a) What are human rights? Accessed at www.ohchr.org/en/what-are-human-rights on 29/01/25.

United Nations (2025b) Sustainable development goals. Accessed at www.un.org/sustainabledevelopment/development-agenda/ on 28/01/25.

Wood, E., Kay, L. and Travers, J. (2023) Leadership in Early childhood education. In Nutbrown, C. (eds) *Early Childhood Education Current Realities and Future Possibilities*. London: Sage.

Westwood, J. (2017) Childhood in different cultures. In Powell, S. and Smith, K. (eds) *Early Childhood Studies,* 4th edition. London: Sage.

4 Leading practice to reflect current and emerging social policy

Emma Laurence

Building on Chapter 3, this chapter identifies effective individuals and teams as being essential to organising, evaluating and supporting work with young children and their families. It considers the role of leadership and management in supporting positive change for children and families. A range of theoretical frameworks and models of leadership will be explored throughout this chapter with opportunities to explore your own development as an emerging leader of practice.

Chapter objectives

This chapter:

- Gives an overview of the historical and contemporary understandings of leadership and its relationship with quality provision

- Identifies possible areas of focus for developing your own leader identity

- Encourage you to consider how your skills as an early years practitioner support you in your role as a leader and an agent of change.

Introduction

Many of my students are initially reluctant to identify themselves as 'a leader' despite the often-significant impact that they have on the quality of early years provision. This is particularly the case for those who do not occupy a formal leadership position in setting. Regardless of these more formal positions of authority, many in the early years sector are unwilling to consider themselves a leader. It has been speculated that this may be due to the nature of ECEC which is primarily characterised by warmth, nurture and patience. This is often at odds with typical understandings of professionalism and leadership which more often

DOI: 10.4324/9781041055358-7

reject the role of emotion work. Throughout this chapter I will argue that this reluctance is both misplaced and needs to be addressed. Both historically and more recently early years professionals are expected to show significant levels of autonomy and independence in practice and policy (Rodd 2013). Very quickly early years professionals develop significant leadership skills for meeting the demands of the contexts they work in. I therefore want you to read the remainder of this chapter safe in the knowledge that when I refer to early years leaders I am referring to all people who work in the early years. Regardless of your formal position, you are well positioned in developing your leader identity, and leaning into this aspect of your role will better support you in creating high-quality provision for the children and families you work with.

The term leadership '*has the quality of being familiar and commonplace. And yet, it is difficult to articulate or define in any precise way*' (Wilson and McCalman 2017, p152). Leadership can be a difficult field of literature to navigate as it is highly theorised and there is much discussion and debate between contrasting leadership constructs. Frustratingly, this can distance practitioners from identifying themselves as a leader in practice.

The expectations we have of leaders are often underpinned by traditional, gendered and hierarchical definitions which do not translate well to the types of leadership most often exercised in the early years. It is therefore important that we identify a definition of leadership with which early years professionals can resonate so that professionals can become more intentional in the ways that they influence practice and create quality provision. To do this, we must interrogate the traditional views which impact our internal compass regarding leadership. This chapter offers a brief historical context regarding the leadership literature as well as some more contemporary leadership constructs. As you read this, consider whether any of these historical perspectives still hold relevance today.

A brief history of leadership

Throughout history, the concept of leadership has captured the attention of people worldwide, filling our storybooks and structuring our society. In terms of research, the field of leadership is now so broad it is made up of a wide variety of different theoretical approaches and frameworks to explain this deeply complex phenomenon. In an extensive review of literature in 1991, Rost identified over 200 definitions of leadership published between 1900 and 1990. He provides a brief history of understanding over this time. Initial concepts of leadership align with what Thomas Carlyle (1841) calls 'the great man theory'. This concept of leadership suggests that a small number of people (men) have such innate qualities as superior intellect, exceptional strength, heroic courage or divine inspiration that they are propelled into positions of extraordinary leadership. Within this construct, leadership is largely concerned with domination and control (Moore, 1927). By the 1930s, notions of domination were being replaced by distinctions between influence, persuasion and coercion. At this point, personality traits became the focus at the centre of what leadership is (Stogdill, 1948).

By the middle of the century, leadership effectiveness continued to be largely defined as the ability to exercise influence over others. By now however, focus shifted away from natural traits towards specific behaviours which leaders adopt. By the 1960s there was a dramatic growth in interest in the field (both in terms of research and within popular texts). With this came a 'prolific stew' of definitions as the literature splintered into a range of disparate constructs. Until this point, leadership was continuing to be understood as behaviours which influence people towards shared goals (Seeman, 1960). However, in 1978, Burns introduced the notion of reciprocity, as leadership was beginning to be understood as a process between people rather than an act performed by a single person. Despite this explosion of literature, several themes persisted: leadership literature was largely concerned with influence by this point, but specifically non-coercive influence (Rost, 1991). Within mainstream literature leadership traits were brought to the fore again. This in turn, influenced public discourse around the topic. At roughly this time, there was also a movement towards defining leadership as a transformational process (Burns, 1978) concerned with inspiring people to be motivated towards organisational goals rather than simply punishing or rewarding them for their work.

Many of the concepts which grew in popularity within the 1990s will be explored more fully below. However, to summarise, there began to be discussion regarding the differences between what it is to lead and what it is to manage (Kotterman, 2006) and much of the focus within leadership literature shifted to look at the role of followers (Uhl-Bein et al., 2014) and with that came more relational understandings of leadership. Leadership also began to be recognised as inherently context dependent. That is, what makes for good leadership depends on what the situation requires. By the 21st century, the moral and ethical dimensions of leadership began being explored within literature (Brown and Trevino, 2006) as scholars began to recognise that leadership and power are inherently issues of ethics.

As we move into the knowledge era, and amidst the turbulence of our current context: navigating multiple environmental, financial and socio-political crises, leadership continues to be a high priority area of research. At the time of writing, searching the term 'leadership' in our University library yields 189,608 results within the last three years across a variety of fields, suggesting that there will continue to be a lack of consensus and shifts in thinking.

Stogdill (1974, p7) highlights that there are as many definitions of leadership as there are people attempting to define it; a point echoed throughout leadership literature. That means that if you surveyed 100 people, you would likely get 100 different answers to questions like 'what makes a good leader?' However, it is likely that everyone you asked would quite quickly be able to offer an answer. Northouse (2021) calls this our 'gut level grasp' of leadership as he identifies that despite there being no single definition, we all know what it means to us. To illustrate this to my students, I asked two of my children what a leader is and they offered a definition each:

> *You are really good at helping others when in trouble and help get them back on top.*
>
> *Nonie (nine years)*

> *Someone you follow and trust that shows you what needs to be done.*
>
> *Aurora (seven years)*

Critical reflection

In order for you to examine your own assumptions about leadership, write one sentence which captures your answer to the question, *What is a leader?* It might help you to think about leaders that you know either from your own experiences or more publicly. Try not to second guess yourself and just note down the first ideas that come to mind. What appear to be the values, qualities or characteristics most important to you?

Figure 4.1 *A brief history of leadership*

Whilst the above brief history (Figure 4.1) might suggest a journey of thought, the meaning we attribute to leadership, or who we consider to be leaders in our own lives, often does not align with the latest perspectives in literature. Instead, our understandings of leadership are perhaps developed in response to our current needs and context as well as definitions which resonate most with our individual experiences. This means that perspectives which are no longer accepted within academic literature may leave a legacy within the hearts and minds of the people we work with. This is evidenced by the fact that we have likely all heard the term 'natural-born leader'.

Critical reflection

Looking back at your definition of leadership, do you see any of the above constructs of leadership reflected in your own views? Which of these constructs best reflects your own initial ideas of leadership?

Leadership and quality

The differences between leadership and management will be discussed more thoroughly below. However, one distinction which is key to understanding the links between leadership and quality is that leadership, unlike management, is inherently focused on progression towards something. Being led by someone suggests a sense of direction, it is generally *to somewhere*. So, a key question for leaders must be, 'where to?' Central to leadership, then, is a vision of what is good so that we can then explore issues of 'how do we get there?' Within the early years sector, we are '*gripped by the notion of* **quality; quality improvements, quality experiences,** *and* **better-quality** *staff in order to build foundations* **for quality**' (Bailey and Solvason, 2019, p59). It seems obvious that we should strive for quality but what does this mean? When we consider quality education and care we all have different opinions about what that might look and feel like in practice. For example, whilst a psychologist might prioritise the significance of secure attachments and trusting relationships, a teacher may want to see a robust curriculum and meaningful learning opportunities. Dahlberg et al. (2013) go as far as saying that our persistent use of the term 'quality' despite no universal definition renders it meaningless. They liken it to words such as 'excellence', stating its general applicability is a reflection of its emptiness.

Despite this, issues of quality are of central importance to early years practitioners and, in particular, leaders. The lack of definition therefore cannot just mean that we cease trying to achieve high standards of education and care. As professionals, identifying your own priorities regarding what makes quality education and care is crucial in creating provision which aligns with your professional values.

Critical reflection

1. Imagine that you are the parent of a two-year-old son and you are looking for a day nursery for him. Write a list of what you would be looking for.

2. Now imagine that you are moving to a different town and are looking for a secondary school for your 13-year-old daughter with significant special educational needs.

What did you discover?

Whilst we may not be able to rely on a universal definition of quality to support us in this, there are elements which permeate the many attempts at one which are significant enough to provide a working understanding of quality. Alongside our own personal philosophies for early childhood education and care, much of our understanding of quality is shaped by policy, research and pedagogical trend. Perhaps one of the most significant determinants of what quality looks like in the early years sector in the UK is the Early Years Foundation Stage statutory framework. The stated aim of this government-issued document is to set out *'the standards that all early years providers must meet to ensure that children learn and develop well and are kept healthy and safe'* (DfE, 2024, p7). This forms the basis of much of the training, practice, evaluation and regulation of the sector and influences day-to-day practice in settings. In addition to these minimum standards of practice, it is increasingly being recognised that leadership is a key aspect of the quality of services available to children and their families and that quality improvement is a key function of early years leaders (Garvey et al., 2010, p128). Leaders require an understanding of the statutory obligations of their role as well as the more philosophical perspectives of the purpose of Early Childhood Education and Care in order to drive a shared vision of practice.

Critical reflection

We have identified that visions of quality ECEC can be quite varied. However, what would you consider to be the non-negotiables of high-quality provision for young children?

Make a list of five standards of quality provision. What do you think has shaped these views?

Contemporary leadership constructs

Leadership vs management

When we think about who the leader is in setting, our initial responses are often to think of the setting manager. Despite there often being significant overlap in practice regarding who is considered the leader or the manager of a setting, Rodd (2013) argues that there are some significant differences between the two roles. Table 4.1 outlines some of the distinctions made between leadership and management. She highlights that both are crucial roles and that both are required for a healthy organisation.

Table 4.1 Leadership vs management (adapted from Rodd, 2013)

LEADERS (Rodd, 2013)	MANAGERS (Rodd, 2013)
Focused on the future – the vision and aspirations for improvement	Focused on the present – getting things done and maintaining the status quo (stability)
Creation and review of policy	Implementation of policy in practice
Values of the setting	Facts
Philosophy	Action – what? by whom? by when?
Broad strategies	Specific tactics about how to deal with situations
Reflective on how things are done	Active – getting things done
Human resources	Material resources
Deliberation – thinking	Detail – practicalities
Why we do it	What we need to do

The table identifies that leaders are future-oriented, focusing on vision, values, and the philosophy behind actions. They prioritise creating and reviewing policies, reflecting on processes, and considering broad strategies and human resources. In contrast, managers concentrate on the present, emphasising stability and action. Their role involves implementing policies, managing practical details and using material resources. Leaders deliberate on 'why' things are done, whilst managers focus on 'what' needs to be done. It is possible to see that in early years settings both of these are crucial.

Transactional vs transformational

As has been highlighted, during the second half of the 20th century there was a shift towards more transformational types of leadership. Transformational leadership and transactional leadership represent two distinct approaches to guiding and motivating individuals. Transformational leadership focuses on inspiring and empowering others by fostering a shared vision, encouraging innovation, and emphasising personal growth and intrinsic motivation (Burns, 1978). Transformational leaders often build strong relationships, challenge the status quo, and align team efforts with long-term goals. In contrast, transactional leadership centres on maintaining order and achieving specific objectives through structured systems, clear roles, and the use of rewards and punishments. It is task-oriented and relies on performance-based exchanges to ensure compliance. While transformational leadership drives change, transactional leadership emphasises stability and efficiency.

Ethical leadership

Another key issue in leadership which has emerged in more recent decades has been the ethical and moral obligation of leaders. Ethical leadership is a style of leadership rooted in integrity, fairness and a commitment to doing what is right (Brown and Trevino, 2006). Ethical leaders prioritise transparency, honesty and respect in their interactions, fostering trust and credibility among their team. They lead by example, upholding high moral standards and ensuring their decisions align with ethical principles. Ethical leadership extends beyond personal conduct, as it is also about promoting a culture of accountability, inclusivity and fairness within the organisation. These leaders consider the broader impact of their actions on stakeholders, society and the environment, striving to create sustainable outcomes that benefit all. It is possible to see that within the early years ethical leadership is a crucial foundation in providing positive outcomes for the children, families and communities which we serve.

Catalytic leadership

Particularly important in the early years is the concept of catalytic leadership. This is a leadership construct which was created to directly combat the idea that leadership is only for those who are 'in charge' and the 'assumption that leadership is conjoined with authority and power' (McDowall Clark, 2012, p393). McDowall Clark argues that by their nature, the early years practitioner is a position of influence and that it is this influence that constitutes a leader and an agent of change. Within this construct, the early years practitioner acts as a catalyst for change by fostering progress through small, incremental steps. This approach emphasises recognising potential and opportunities for growth rather than imposing change from above. Catalytic leadership is characterised as a creative and dynamic process, focusing on adaptability and innovation rather than being defined by a fixed set of attitudes or behaviours required of leaders.

❝❝ Case study – 'Samuel's story of change'

Samuel started a voluntary placement at a primary school as part of the work placement requirement for the Foundation Degree in early years and was later employed as a Teaching and Support Assistant within the school. During the induction stage of his employment, he identified that the wording of the school's policies on bullying and equal opportunities used terminology which was (unintentionally) discriminatory towards LGBTQ+ individuals. In consultation with the Head Teacher and the PSE Lead the policies were revised to have a more inclusive and anti-discriminatory approach to LGBTQ+ children and families. Further discussion within the school led to the appointment of Leaders for each of the nine protected characteristics of the Equality Act (2010). Samuel also raised issues with the LGBTQ+ perspective presented in the curriculum materials and wrote to the Publisher to raise his concerns. This resulted in changes in the wording of the Publisher's curriculum documents and sources. In discussions with the Diocese, Head Teacher and PSHE Lead a reinvigorated inclusive approach to LGBTQ+ children and families and the other protected characteristics was embedded throughout the school. Samuel was also appointed as a member of the multi-academy staff council. Samuel's passion and deep understanding of the rights of the LGBTQ+ community enabled him to become a catalyst for change within his setting from the position of a teaching assistant. McDowell-Clark (2012, p391) proposed the concept of 'catalytic leadership' where the early years practitioner's 'ability to bring about and inspire change is not dependent on a position of power'. With appropriate diplomacy and knowledge within an empowering environment, agents of change can be 'movers and shakers' from any position within settings.

The above case study highlights an excellent example of catalytic leadership as Samuel has not been given the formal position of leader but has inspired significant positive change. Not all changes are so tangible that they form new policy, at times these may be something which on the face of it seems quite small, like where you stand at transition times so that you can welcome children and make yourself available to parents. It is the initiative, autonomous action and influence that these actions have on others which means that this constitutes a form of leadership.

Critical reflection

There are many reasons why someone may not have been able to do what Samuel has done. Put yourself in Samuel's shoes, as a student practitioner turned new teaching assistant in the school. You have noticed something which you think could be improved.

Consider, what does it take to have the conversations that Samuel had, and make the changes that were made? Draw a gingerbread person, on the inside of the gingerbread person identify the personal **skills**, **qualities** and **capabilities** that Samuel would need to draw from.

On the outside of the gingerbread person identify the conditions Samuel would need around him for this to be possible and for his ideas to become widespread changes. What kind of **environment** or **culture** would there need to be? What kind of **people**?

What has this exercise told you about the conditions and capacities required for leadership? How do these compare with your own skills and contexts? Being a leader requires us to consider not only how we can develop these inner capacities in ourselves but also how we can contribute to cultures which nurture these capacities in others so that ideas can be shared, and meaningful change can take place. Having completed the above exercise, is it possible to identify any strengths and areas for development for your own leadership development?

Change in the early years

Responding to policy change or reviewing how effectively a policy supports children and families (national or local policy), often leads to change. The change involved could be minor or major to a setting. For some staff/stakeholders change will be seen as an **opportunity.** For others the change may be viewed as unsettling, upsetting or a threat. Even though it is widely understood that we should seek to be continually improving practice, many of us who work with young children do so because it is something we consider to be incredibly important. Many of us put our all into what we do and so it is easy to see how any suggestion that our work is not good enough could be emotionally hard to take. If the negative responses remain however, they can sabotage the change and undermine the implementation of the policy. It is recognised in the early years sector that consistent change is one of the few constants we can rely upon. It is therefore crucial that leaders learn to manage change carefully and with compassion. A further exploration for how leaders can work with people to manage change is provided in Chapter 9. For now, it is worth considering your own relationship with change and how you might become more willing to reflect on your own practice and be open to changing it.

Adaptive leadership and the early years

Due to the ever-changing nature of the early years sector as well as the uncertain socio-political context in which we live, I would argue that the adaptive leadership construct is also appropriate here. Heifetz et al. (2009, p14) identify adaptive leadership as *'the practice of mobilising people to tackle tough challenges and thrive'*. Rather than being focused on improving any specific function of a setting, adaptive leadership is fundamentally concerned with the residual flexibility of an organisation in responding to the dynamic needs of the people they work with. Within an early years setting this might be the needs of the children, their families, the staff or the wider community. Crucially, due to its basis in psychotherapeutic understandings about overcoming challenge, the adaptive leadership approach emphasises the impact of relationships in managing engagement in the discomfort of uncertainty.

There are significant parallels between the role of the adaptive leader and the role of the early years practitioner (Table 4.2).

Table 4.2 *Parallels between early years practitioners and leaders (adapted from Whalley, 2008)*

Leader	Early years practitioner
Encourages people to try out new ideas and develops a culture where people are not inhibited by a fear of failure.	Encourages children to try new things and make mistakes in order to grow and learn.
Supports staff subtly and respectfully so that staff feel a sense of ownership over their own progress towards goals but also feel supported by their leader.	An ability to subtly intervene in order to support children's progress.
Builds trust amongst staff through consistency and authenticity.	Builds secure attachments based on trust through consistency.
Supports others to feel encouraged to make their own decisions and take ownership over their own practice.	Enables children to make their own choices in a way which is safe.
Values the experience and unique values and skillsets of each staff member.	Recognises the uniqueness of each child and the importance of their wider context.
Is concerned with their own development as well as supporting others.	Is reflective and seeks to improve practice.

It is my hope that identifying these parallels will provide you with confidence that you are well positioned to effectively lead practice. The skillset that you have and continue to develop as an early years practitioner does not only support you in nurturing children and their progress but also in nurturing the people and progress within the community around you.

Chapter summary

This chapter has highlighted the evolving understanding of leadership roles and their impact on driving excellence in practice. The chapter has encouraged you to reflect upon your own values for leadership, supporting you to develop your own leader identity. Finally, it has prompted you to consider how your existing skills and expertise enable you to act as an effective leader and agent of change, fostering continuous improvement and innovation within your setting.

Further reading

Campbell-Barr, V. and Leeson, C. (2016) *Quality and leadership in the early years: Research, theory and practice.* 1st ed. Los Angeles, SAGE.

Modise, M. et al. (eds.) (2023) *Global perspectives on leadership in early childhood education.* Helsinki: Helsinki University Press. DOI: https://doi.org/10.33134/HUP-20

References

Bailey, E. and Solvason, C. (2019) Embedding parents' perspectives in the discourse for quality education and care in the early years, *New Zealand International Research in Early Childhood Education,* 22(1), pp. 59–71.

Brown, M. E. and Treviño, L. K. (2006) Ethical leadership: A review and future directions, *The Leadership Quarterly,* 17(6), pp. 595–616.

Burns, J. M. (1978) *Leadership.* New York, Harper & Row.

Carlyle, T. (1841) *On heroes, hero-worship, and the heroic in history.* London, James Fraser.

Dahlberg, G., Moss, P. and Pence, A. R. (2013) *Beyond quality in early childhood education and care: languages of evaluation* (Third edn). Abingdon, Oxon, Routledge.

Department for Education (2024) *Early years foundation stage statutory framework for childminders.* Available at: https://assets.publishing.service.gov.uk/media/65aa5e29ed27ca001327b2c6/EYFS_statutory_framework_for_childminders.pdf (Accessed: 30 October 2024).

Equality Act (2010) c.15 Available at: www.legislation.gov.uk/ukpga/2010/15/contents

Garvey, D., Lancaster, A. and National Children's Bureau (2010) *Leadership for quality in early years and playwork: Supporting your team to achieve better outcomes for children and families.* London, NCB.

Heifetz, R. A., Grashow, A. and Linsky, M. (2009) *The practice of adaptive leadership: Tools and tactics for changing your organization and the world.* Cambridge, MA, Harvard Business Press.

Kotterman, J. (2006) Leadership versus Management: What's the Difference? *The Journal for Quality and Participation,* 29(2), pp. 13–17.

McDowall Clark, R (2012) 'I've never thought of myself as a leader but...': The Early Years Professional and catalytic leadership, *European Early Childhood Education Research Journal,* 20(3), pp. 391–401. doi: 10.1080/1350293X.2012.704762.

Moore, B. V. (1927) The May conference on leadership, *Personnel Journal*, 6(1), pp. 124.

Northouse, P. G. (2021). *Leadership: Theory & practice* (8th edn). London, SAGE.

Rodd, J. (2013) *Leadership in early childhood: The pathway to professionalism* (4th edn). Maidenhead, Berkshire, McGraw-Hill.

Rost, J. C. (1991) *Leadership for the twenty-first century*. New York, Praeger.

Seeman, M. (1960) *Social status and leadership: The case of the school executive*. Columbus, Ohio State University Press.

Stogdill, R. M. (1948) Personal factors associated with leadership, A survey of literature, *Journal of Personality*, 25, pp. 35–71.

Stogdill, R. M. (1974) *Handbook of leadership: A survey of theory and research*. New York, Free Press.

Uhl-Bien, M., Riggio, R., Lowe, K. and Carsten, M. (2014) Followership theory: A review and research agenda, *The Leadership Quarterly*, 25(1), pp. 83–104.

Whalley, M. (2008) *Leading practice in early years settings*. Exeter, Learning Matters.

Wilson, S. and McCalman, J. (2017) Re-imagining ethical leadership as leadership for the greater good, *European Management Journal*, 35, pp. 151–154.

Theme 3
The planner

Chapters Five and Six will support you in your duties as a planner for children.

Duty 1 Promote the health and well-being of all children, self-regulation and resilience through learning rich environments, opportunities for challenging play and a healthy attitude towards risk taking.	**Knowledge:** 1 2 3 4 6 7 8 9 11 14 15 16 17 18 19 20 21
	Skills: 1 2 4 6 10 15 16 17 18 19 21 22 23
	Behaviours: 1 2 3 4 5 6 8
Duty 3 Participate in and lead daily routines and practice, including children's personal care, play and maintaining the physical environment.	**Knowledge:** 1 2 3 4 7 9 10 11 15 17 20
	Skills: 3 4 6 7 8 9 10 17 19 23
	Behaviours: 3 4 5 6 7 8
Duty 5 To take the lead and provide support in disseminating best practice in the use of observation, assessments and planning to meet children's needs and extend their holistic development within the aspect or environment for which they are responsible.	**Knowledge:** 1 2 3 6 7 8 9 10 11 12 13 15 18 19 21
	Skills: 2 3 4 5 6 7 8 9 12 13 14 15 16 18 20 23
	Behaviours: 1 2 3 4 5 6 7 8 9

DOI: 10.4324/9781041055358-8

Duty 6 Promote, demonstrate and facilitate a clear understanding of diversity and equality to support all children, including those with additional needs, those of high ability, those with English as an additional language and those with disabilities. To be able to use and evaluate distinctive approaches which engage and support inclusivity of all children within their social and cultural context.	**Knowledge:** 1 2 3 4 5 6 7 8 11 13 14 15 16 17 18 19 20 21 22
	Skills: 1 2 3 4 5 6 8 10 11 12 13 15 16 18 19 20 21 22 23 25
	Behaviours: 1 2 3 4 5 6 7 8 9
Duty 9 Reflect and build on practice through ongoing professional enquiry and action research to contribute to the pedagogical approach of their setting. To be accountable for day-to-day practice, longer term planning, management and training within the specific aspect or environment for which they are responsible.	**Knowledge:** 2 3 4 6 7 8 9 10 11 12 13 15 16 17 18
	Skills: 1 2 3 4 5 6 7 9 10 14 15 18 19 21 23
	Behaviours: 1 2 3 4 5 6 7 8 9

5 It's child's play – playful curricula and spaces

Michelle Malomo

Introduction

This chapter will focus on developing your skills in implementing and developing practice that reflects a playful pedagogy in the current social policy context. Throughout the chapter, an emerging critical understanding of the inter-relationships between political, economic, cultural and ideological contexts in children's lives will also be explored. Your emerging thinking will be captured through reflective activities throughout the chapter to support development of practice within this area.

Chapter objectives

This chapter will:

- Consider what play is and how it has been given currency within childhood

- Explore and examine where play sits in the current social policy landscape

- Explore contemporary theorists and how these might present a new understanding of playful approaches

- Support the development of a 'blue sky' personal playful pedagogy.

What is play?

When I work with students to consider this question we tend to go around in circles in our thinking. As professionals we develop thinking about play that is entrenched both in our practice alongside being informed and controlled by accepted discourses and curriculum (DfE, 2024). Primarily the accepted discourse is that play is a vehicle for learning. In my experience,

DOI: 10.4324/9781041055358-9

adults can often be dismissive about the value of play. They have even said to me whilst in practice: 'your job is easy – all you do is play all day'. Even as I write this, I feel frustrated that the full value of play is dismissed. Early in my practice, I have attempted to justify the value and currency to play by saying 'play is learning'. Beigi (2021, p81) suggests that children learn most naturally from play. But if we see play only from this perspective, we limit its value and power within children's worlds. Brock, Jarvis and Olusoga (2018, p18) explore this notion and suggest that in the desire to understand its potential for learning, play becomes exploited and hijacked from children. I often suggest to students that when play is constrained in this manner, we limit our own understanding as to the potential power that play holds for children. Bottrill (2018, p25) offers an explanation stating that,

> Play is one of the most misunderstood concepts. In today's educational world it is also one of the most underrated. And yet it is the most vital component for development – the gift of play is the greatest thing we can ever possibly give a child. Unfortunately, the incessant clamour for measurement and adult world-dominated thinking overshadows the truly rich potential of play.

Interestingly, Lester (2019, p25) explains that despite having studied and worked with play for four decades, a definition of what play is remains elusive. He says that '*as adults we seem to be obsessed with trying to work out why we play, what it is and what it all means that perhaps we lose sight of the movements of play and the pleasure and joy that moments of play produce*'.

Later in this chapter we will see how a deeper understanding of the nature of play can unlock its power in our practice beyond learning and potential, empowering us to lead and inspire practice in this area.

Therefore, you will need to delve deeper in your quest for an understanding of the nature of play, in doing so you will discover there is much ambiguity about what play is. Sutton-Smith (1998) suggests we fall into 'silliness' as we grapple with its definition. In this chapter there will be moments of silliness but also maybe confusion in our seeking a fresh understanding of play. There may be a feeling of disturbance of your thinking, values and practice in considering this question. This is what Festinger (1957) calls *cognitive dissonance*. As you read this chapter you may feel a repositioning of your thinking which may in turn affect your practice.

However, when considering the question of what play is you may feel this is obvious. After all, we have all at some point been players and experienced play. Sicart (2014, p1) claims that '*play is a mode of being human*' so perhaps we should all be qualified to define it. Throughout history, great thinkers and theorists have explored what play is and what it is not. Reed and Brown (2000) conclude that play is tricky to define as it has to be felt rather than being done. This suggests that it may not be the same for everyone and is perhaps a mode of being *uniquely* human. Think about the children that you work with, each of them is an individual doing and experiencing childhood. If play is an expression of being human, it will look different for each child. This is why when we attempt to place play within a curriculum that is driven by goals, it becomes problematic. Play, it appears, has many facets and encapsulates many behaviours, activities (Bruce, 1991) and ways of being human. It is an individual expression and is not bound by a conclusive definition. Macdonald (2022) helps a deeper understanding of the correlation between understanding the nature of play and its value stating that,

> The challenge in defining and utilizing play to support children's development lies in the nature of play itself. If we understand that play is individual and unique for all children we may wonder how play can be planned for children through curriculum structure pedagogy and provision.
>
> Macdonald, 2022, p4

If play is an individual expression, then what might this mean for practice? Do current social policy and accepted discourses of practice make space for this uniqueness? Or could there be more playful ways to be with children? Below is a reflective activity that may support you in starting to define what play is through returning to your own childhood experiences of play.

Critical reflection – playful regression exercise

- Take a moment to think about yourself as a child at play. You may find it helpful to take a couple of deep breaths as you start to focus.

- Think about what you are doing. Where are you? Who is there with you? What can you smell and feel? How are you feeling about this memory?

- Note down the memory that you have been thinking about.

- What does this memory tell you about the nature of play and what it might be?

Explore and examine where play sits in the current social policy landscape

The UNCRC Convention on the Rights of the Child (1998) ratified the need for signatory countries to ensure that these rights are implemented within law. They also agreed to monitor and evaluate how effectively this is implemented. Article 31 of this convention states that children have the right to play. However, there has been confusion about the nature of what play might be. In 2013, the United Nations published a General Comment No 17 to explore what this might mean with the intention to provide clarity. In this comment there is a justification that the elements of Article 31 need to be protected to ensure that the unique and evolving nature of childhood is possible. This in turn ensures that children can develop holistically and be resilient (United Nations, 2013).

Further clarification around play was included within the comment stating:

> Research evidence highlights that playing is also central to children's spontaneous drive for development, and that it performs a significant role in the development of the brain, particularly in the early years. Play and recreation facilitate children's capacities to negotiate, regain emotional balance, resolve conflicts and

make decisions. Through their involvement in play and recreation, children learn by doing; they explore and experience the world around them; experiment with new ideas, roles and experiences and in so doing, learn to understand and construct their social position within the world.

United Nations, 2013, p4

Therefore, this clarification justifies the need for play within childhood. However, each country will implement this differently. More recently, the unprecedented events of the global pandemic influenced children's ability to play freely within communities and there is research that suggests that the pandemic limited children's quality of life with a detrimental effect on their well-being (Holt and Murray, 2021; All Party Parliamentary Group on a Fit and Healthy Childhood, 2021; Ford et al., 2021). However, Russell and Stenning (2023) offer an alternative perspective concerning the limitations of lockdown. They suggest that in lockdown children played within the conditions and according to their desires. Play occurred in streets, with families, and lockdown restrictions did not stop play occurring. This suggests that despite barriers to play, children will find a way to have this important need met.

Within the UK we do not at present have a national play strategy adopted by government. Each home nation does have organisations that lobby for play. These have been included in the further reading and resources within this chapter.

As professionals it is important that we explore different perspectives and understandings of the potential therapeutic benefits of play. These theoretical frameworks and perspectives primarily have been developed in the field of Playwork but have value for professionals in the early years.

Contemporary theorists: a new understanding of playful approaches – there is hope on the horizon!

At this stage in the chapter, it would be reasonable to say that we have not been able to define what play is. The question itself becomes rhetorical in nature. Even though we may not answer this fully, we will be able to reach our own conclusions and arguments through exposing ourselves to the thoughts of others. In section of the chapter we will throw a spotlight on some contemporary theorists who help us to articulate some of what is known about the characteristics and nature of play. Having explored these with students over time it has always been insightful to see the practice that emerges from this. Engagement with theory often empowers student practitioners to articulate what they see in the playful processes that occur every day rather than being fixated upon the outcomes of play – it liberates practice. Within the constraints of this chapter, we will not be able to explore all the thinking around the play process but will highlight theories that have commonly underpinned practice within the field of Playwork. Jarvis, Brock and Brown (2018, p82) describe Playwork as being *'rooted in an understanding that children learn and develop through their play'* but there are *'many instances where the process (of play) are interrupted or impaired'* (Jarvis, Brock and Brown 2018, p82). Having this understanding about where practice around the play process has grown is helpful before we consider these theories.

Psycholudics – the play cycle (Sturrock and Else, 1998)

Have you ever been to a conference that has inspired you? I imagine that this was the case for those who were the first readers of Sturrock and Else's (1998) conference paper 'The Playground as a therapeutic space: Playwork as Healing' (known as The Colorado Paper). Within this paper they suggested that playworkers could be potential healers. Unlike many of the theorists that have been explored to this point, they suggested that you *could* define play. They stated that the purpose of play is to be creative and suggest through play there is the potential to heal trauma, neurosis and psychic ill. They coined the term psycholudics to describe the process that play provoked. They saw play as a cycle, within which processes occur. Their work has been further developed by King and Newstead (2020). King and Newstead (2022, p175) undertook research to ascertain the use and understanding of psycholudics and suggested that '*a wider use of the Play Cycle theory in childcare may lead to a greater understanding of play as a process rather than an outcome*'. This theory gives us further descriptive language that is helpful for professionals when observing the child at play and to identify their role within the play cycle. The process of play is owned by the child and as such is intrinsically motivated. It begins from within the child. This is interesting as it suggests that for play to occur it starts from within and is not by adults directing the process.

The play cycle

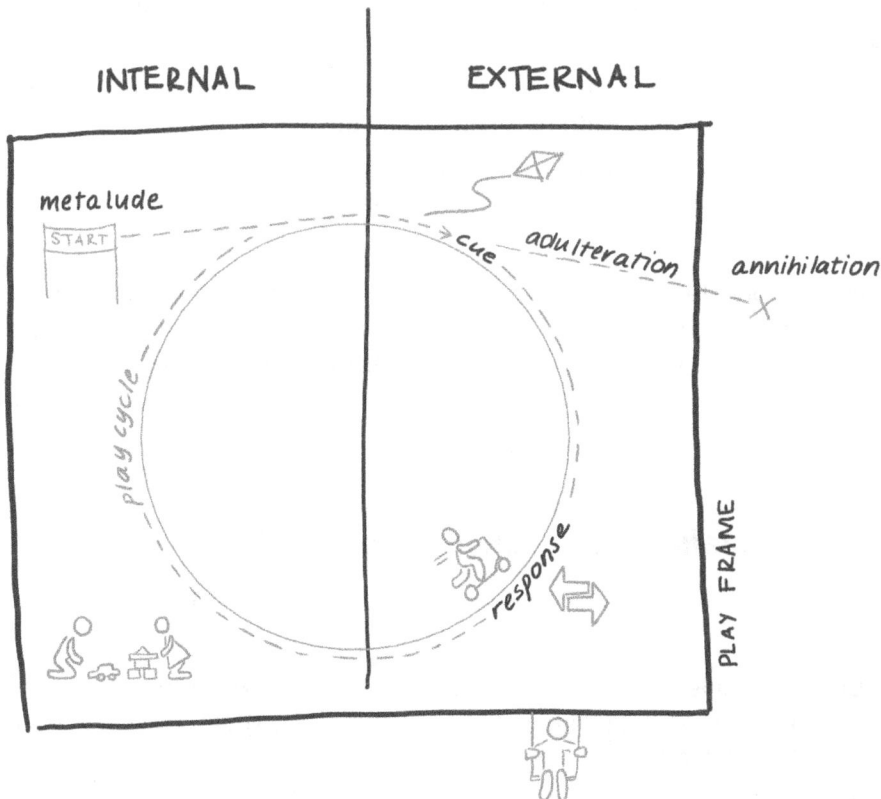

Figure 5.1 *The play cycle*

The play cycle is made up of different parts that help explain the process of play. If we gain an understanding of the process of play, we can in turn understand how to better support this. In turn this will mean that our approach is more sensitive. The parts of the play cycle are explored below and can also be seen in their simplest form in Figure 5.1.

Metalude – Play is intrinsically motivated and the metalude is the thought process that occurs before play starts. This will be individual in nature. As a professional at this part of the process you need to think, does the environment spark these thoughts for children?

Play cues and returns – once thoughts have been ignited, the player will send out a cue or an invitation to play. This may be to another person, to the environment or to part of themselves. It can take various forms including a verbal invitation, a gesture or stance. A **return** is the response that occurs when a cue is sent back from another person or the environment in response to the cue.

Play flow – this occurs when there's a response to a cue and a frame is created. When flow occurs, it can last seconds or weeks.

Playframe – this is initiated by the child to provide the context: the enclosure of play. It can change in shape and size. For example, Physical: mats, stones, rope, tyres, hedge, structure, designated area, fence; Narrative: storyline, music, rules and so forth; Emotional: when play is exploring a particular feeling, so the props, the action, the place and the story can keep changing because it's the experience of the feeling that holds it all together. Sometimes the adult will hold the frame to enable the play to continue; this may involve resourcing the play.

Annihilation – this occurs when play comes to an end. This can occur naturally. However, often adults and other children can annihilate the play cycle.

Adulteration – This is when adults control the play. They take the play away from the child when it does not belong to them and control the intentions.

Having explored psycholudics with professionals, they describe a new purpose in practice and become content standing at the edge of the play frame, only intervening in play when either invited, or to hold the frame. It freshens their observation practice, and they can describe what is occurring within the process rather than an obsession with the outcomes of children's play. It also supports the development of more therapeutic and insightful interventions into children's play.

Critical reflection – can play heal all ills?

- Having explored the theory of psycholudics, what is your role as an adult within the play cycle?

- Describe a time when you have adulterated or annihilated play within your practice. How might an understanding of the play cycle develop your sensitivity in interventions with children's play?

- Do you think that play can cure and is a process where healing occurs?

Taxonomy of Play types (Hughes, 1996)

I remember very clearly a video clip that I watched and still share with students where Bob Hughes describes why we need to play. But he begins with how he views children. He says they are *'lone organisms in a hostile planet in the middle of nowhere'*. You may be thinking that this is a strange way to think about children, but is it? He then goes on to explain that this is the reason why children need to play. In this theory, play is framed as a means to survival. This may seem foreign in your current thinking. However, there is value in exposing your thoughts to this way of thinking about play.

About 30 years ago I was very fortunate to be able to attend a lecture by Bob. After listening to him, my own thinking about play was challenged and developed through his explanation of different play types. I felt that I developed for the first time a rich language that empowered me to describe the play that I was seeing. Furthermore, it became clear to me that there is a misconception that play is always a joyous and a nice experience. Have you ever said to children, or has it been said to you – go and play nicely? Returning to the description of children as lone organisms, there is something primal about describing them in this manner. It is fitting then that there are types of play that, when played out, may not appear nice, but perhaps will become a very primal expression of being human within childhood.

Hughes (2012, p96) believes that without play we would not be here. Take a moment to think about the claim that is being made here. As a professional how do you feel about this? Exploring Hughes' thinking further he also suggests that there is an evolutionary power in play, and it is this that makes it so incredibly powerful. Through his Taxonomy of Play types, Hughes (1996) supports deeper discussion about play. Prior to this, professionals would describe what they saw as play even though the behaviours that were being seen differed in their nature and display. At present within the Taxonomy there are 16 play types, but Hughes recognises that there may be more and throughout history, different types of play may have been more prominent. Jarvis, Brock and Brown (2018) suggest that Hughes also saw play as a biological drive and that this reflected forms of play and patterns seen in our human ancestors, further explaining the primal nature of play. Jarvis, Brock and Brown (2018, p79) state that Hughes explains the ancestorial aspects of play in a contemporary context by seeing play in the following ways:

Animal – children interacting with the elements (earth, wind, fire and water).

Savage – cruel interaction with other species (have you ever cut up a worm?).

Nomad – ranging for mental mapping.

Pastoral – children taking care of things, (this can be explored through mastery play, gardening for example).

Tribal – for example, membership of gangs and clubs.

🗣️ **Critical reflection**

- Having read this section of the chapter take a moment and note your thinking.

- What do you think about the way in which Hughes describes children? Looking at each element of his description and reflecting particularly his description of a hostile planet, what sense can you make of this in your work with children?

- When you are in practice take a moment to see children playing – can you see the ancestorial nature in the behaviours, i.e. Animal, Savage, Nomad. Pastoral and Tribal.

The Taxonomy of Play types

Below is an overview of Hughes' Taxonomy (1996). Within this there is a description and what the type of play might look like. It is important to remember that whilst children are playing, the play that they display may overlap and it is possible that what you see may cover several play types.

Table 5.1 *Taxonomy of Play types (adapted from Hughes, 1996, and Rees-Edwards, 2022)*

Play type	Description	What might it look like?
Communication play	Play where children use words expressions, gestures to express themselves.	Babies babbling, singing, miming, telling jokes.
Creative play	Play where children explore arts and crafts. Supports children to solve problems, express themselves and be curious. No outcome in the form of product.	Junk modelling Loose parts play Picking glue off your fingers.
Deep play	Play where children explore and take risks. There may be a sense of being exposed to danger.	May involve scary play – being monsters Playing chicken or cherry knocking Playing funerals Climbing and jumping from trees.

Table 5.1 (*Cont.*)

Play type	Description	What might it look like?
Dramatic play	Play where children re-enact scenarios from what they may have experienced in really life, through stories or through media (television, film or social media).	For example, using a mobile phone and copying what they have heard an adult say. Often, they will take on the persona of a character. Can be on their own or with others.
Exploratory play	Play that involves children discovering properties of objects, toys and the environment happens when they manipulate these.	For babies this might mean mouthing objects. For children in the outdoors this could mean children having the freedom to explore the elements and environment.
Fantasy play	Play that is unlikely to happen in real life. They can take on different roles and explore boundaries. This play can use imagination and potentially creative thinking.	Super-hero play, flying to the moon.
Imaginative play	Again, this play provides an opportunity to explore the world and make sense of the world by using their imagination. However, this type of play explores situations that are more likely to happen to them. By playing with these events children can control the outcomes.	Playing teachers, doctors and nurses. Using toys to become characters in the scenarios.
Locomotor play	Play that encourages development in physical skills.	This might include hopping, jumping, riding a bike and playing with balls and large loose parts.
Mastery play	Repetitive play that enables children to master skills.	This might take some time as children may need to repeat that activity. There may be some risk involved as children master the skills.
Object play	This play involves children exploring, using and manipulating objects within their play. This play will facilitate fascination and curiosity with objects.	An example would be a child playing with a cardboard box – the possibilities are endless.

(continued)

Table 5.1 (*Cont.*)

Play type	Description	What might it look like?
Recapulative play	This play is complex and involves children exploring evolutionary behaviours. It is instinctive in nature.	For example, this play might involve children making dens and shelters. It will also involve children exploring the elements and natural resources. It may also involve children exploring stories, myths and languages.
Role play	This type of play involves children taking on roles within their play.	Children may explore roles that are familiar to them – playing teachers, shopkeepers as well as imitating family members or pets.
Rough and tumble play	This play involves playfighting rough and tumble – which might be seen as pushing others, climbing and rolling with others.	During this sort of play children are happy and appear to be enjoying this experience.
Social play	This play involves any activity or opportunity within play that involves interacting with others. It provides an opportunity for children to develop social skills that they can use.	This could be a game of peek-a-boo with a baby. It could involve play that develops social skills – i.e. turn taking.
Socio-dramatic play	This play can be solitary or involve others. It is linked to fantasy play. It can be based on, or it may involve elements of make believe. It is diverse in nature and reflects the individual child's experiences/needs.	This play may involve children expressing emotions and feelings that may be causing anxiety.
Symbolic play	This is play where children use objects actions and ideas to represent something else.	For example, using a broomstick as a form of transport.

Often when we look at pictures of children at play, we do not truly know what is happening in the brain of the child that we are observing. However, as practitioners it is exciting to see how children play in different environments. Below are three pictures (Figures 5.2, 5.3 and 5.4) that show children playing. Take a moment to consider Table 5.1 – what play types might be being played out here?

Figure 5.2 *Child playing in a tunnel (taken by Samantha Sutton-Tsang)*

Figure 5.3 *Child looking at a snail (taken by Emma Laurence)*

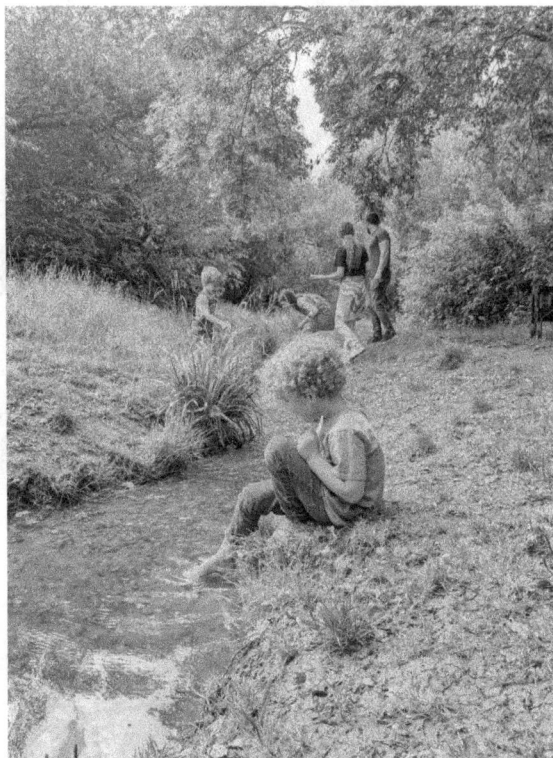

Figure 5.4   *Children playing near a stream (taken by Emma Laurence)*

⊙⊙ Critical reflection – applying the taxonomy to practice

- How might you use the Taxonomy of Play types within your own practice?
- Take time to observe children at play in practice. What play types can you see? What might this help you understand about the child?

Compound flexibility (Brown, 1989) and Nicholson's loose parts (1971)

So far in the exploration of contemporary theories we have not thought about the environment in which the child plays. The environment in which play occurs also holds the potential to maximise the development for the child (Brown, 1989).

Brown (2003) suggests that the whole play environment has powerful potential in affecting that child's development. He suggests that *'the degree of flexibility in the play environment has a direct effect on a child's opportunities for experimentation because it governs the level of control that the child is able to exercise'* (Brown, 2003, p56).

Having spaces where children can manipulate their environments ensures that there are possibilities to explore their needs and desires. This also supports adults to understand the potential possibilities within play spaces – both indoors and outdoors. Think about this for just a moment – what possibilities are there within your play space for children to shape their environments? If we apply Brown's theory of compound flexibility to our play spaces, we are maximising the opportunities for children's development. This theory also puts the child at the centre of this process and in turn raises their self-confidence and self-esteem. This then has the knock-on effect for them to explore the environment with the best conditions for holistic learning and development. Viewing the environment from this perspective enables us to constantly evaluate the opportunities and consider how flexible it is in enabling children to take control of the space. Nicholson's (1971) theory of loose parts also has value in supporting this approach. He suggests that professionals include 'loose parts' – movable artefacts that are placed within the environment – for the children to use in their exploration of their own playful needs. These can include a range of items and further ideas can be seen in further reading for this chapter.

Critical reflection – how flexible is our play space?

- Think of one of your key children. How does your current environment encourage flexibility and movement of resources to meet their needs?

- Do children truly experience freedom within their play within our setting?

- Look at your space in terms of loose parts – what can you do to increase the possibilities?

Developing a 'blue sky' personal playful pedagogy

As this chapter comes to its conclusion my hope is that by exploring the potential of playful experiences for children you have had a shift within your thinking beyond play as a vehicle for children to learn. Play has the potential to provide healing, a place where children can be well, and where they can explore their needs and desires. I hope that through exploring the theories and thoughts within this chapter you feel better equipped and inspired to develop and facilitate playful spaces with endless possibilities. This may mean that you share this newfound knowledge with others in your settings. The final critical reflection asks you to reflect and think about this within your practice.

Critical reflection – blue sky – playful pedagogy

- Take a moment to think about the theories that have been explored within this chapter – how have these changed or developed your thinking?

- What changes might you make within your setting to enable these theories to become part of your practice?

- It maybe that you feel in the past you have been stopped in making changes or constrained by accepted discourses. Flip this thinking by asking yourself, as I lead practice in this area – what is potentially stopping me? Once you have identified these factors think about how you can work around these.

- Think about one thing that you will do in the next six weeks to develop a more playful space within your setting.

Further reading

The *further reading supports you to explore the late thoughts and publication/research on play.*

Websites:

Play England www.playengland.org.uk/

Play Wales https://play.wales/

Play Scotland www.playscotland.org/

Play Board Northern Ireland www.playboard.org/

References

All Party Parliamentary Group on a Fit and Healthy Childhood (2021) The Covid Generation: A mental health pandemic in the making. www.mqmentalhealth.org/wp-content/uploads/THE-COVID-GENERATION-REPORT-April2021.pdf

Beigi, R. (2021) *Early years pedagogy in practice: A guide for students and practitioners.* London: Routledge.

Bottrill, G. (2018) *Can I go & play now? Rethinking the early years.* Los Angeles: SAGE.

Brock, A., Jarvis, P. and Olusoga, Y. (2018) *Perspectives on play: Learning for life.* Second edition. London: Routledge.

Brown, F. (1989) *Working with children: A playwork training pack.* Leeds: Children First.

Brown, F. (ed) (2003) *Playwork: Theory and practice.* Buckingham: Open University Press.

Bruce, T. (1991) *Time to play in early childhood education.* London: Hodder & Stoughton.

Department for Education (DfE) (2024) Early years foundation stage statutory framework for group and school-based providers. Available at: https://assets.publishing.service.gov.uk/media/65aa5e42ed27ca001327b2c7/EYFS_statutory_framework_for_group_and_school_based_providers.pdf (Accessed: 30 October 2024).

Festinger, L. (1957). *A theory of cognitive dissonance.* Stanford, CA: Stanford University Press.

Ford, T., John, A. and Gunnell, D. (2021) 'Mental health of children and young people during the pandemic', *BMJ*, 372, p. n614. doi: 10.1136/bmj.n614

Holt, L. and Murray, L. (2021) 'Children and Covid 19 in the UK', *Children's Geographies*, 20(4), pp. 487–494. doi: 10.1080/14733285.2021.1921699.

Hughes, B. (1996) *A playworkers taxonomy of play types*. London: Playlink.

Hughes, B. (2012) *Evolutionary playwork*, Second edition. London: Routledge.

Jarvis, P. Brock, A. and Brown, F. (2018) Three perspectives on play. In Brock Jarvis and Olusoga (eds), *Perspectives on play: Learning for life*. Third edition. London: Routledge.

King, P. and Newstead, S. (2020) 'Re-defining the Play Cycle: An empirical study of playworkers' understanding of playwork theory', *Journal of Early Childhood Research: ECR*, 18(1), pp. 99–111.

King, P. and Newstead, S. (2022) 'Childcare worker's understanding of the play cycle theory: Can a focus on "process not product" contribute to quality childcare experiences?' *Child Care in Practice*, 28(2), pp. 164–177. doi: 10.1080/13575279.2019.1680532

Lester, S. (2019) *Everyday playfulness: A new approach to children's play and adult responses to it*. London: Jessica Kingsley Publishers.

Macdonald, N. (2022) What is Play? In Waters-Davies, J. (ed.) *Introduction to play*. London: Sage.

Nicholson, S. (1971) 'How not to cheat children', *Landscape Architecture*, 62, pp. 33–34.

Reed, T. and Brown, M. (2000) 'The expression of care in the rough and tumble play of boys', *The Journal of Research in Childhood Education*, 15(1), 104–116.

Rees-Edwards, R. (2022) Types of play. In Waters- Davies, J. (ed) *Introduction to play*. London: Sage.

Russell, W. and Stenning, A. (2023) 'Kerbs and curbs, desire and damage: An affirmative account of children's play and being well during the COVID-19 pandemic', *Social & Cultural Geography*, 24(3–4), pp. 680–698.

Sicart, M. (2014) *Play matters*. First edition. Cambridge: MIT Press.

Sturrock, G. and Else, P. (1998) The playground as a therapeutic space: Playwork as healing. In Sturrock, G. and P. Else (eds) *Therapeutic playwork reader one*. Sheffield: Ludemos.

Sutton-Smith, B. (1998) *The ambiguity of play*. Cambridge: Harvard University Press. Available from: ProQuest Ebook Central. (Accessed: 8 October 2024).

UNCRC (1998) The United Nations Convention on the Rights of the Child. Available at: www.unicef.org.uk/wp-content/uploads/2016/08/unicef-convention-rights-child-uncrc.pdf (Accessed: 16 October 2024)

United Nations (2013) *General comment No. 17 (2013) on the right of the child to rest, leisure, play, recreational activities, cultural life and the arts (art. 31)*. Accessed at www.cypcs.org.uk/wpcypcs/wp-content/uploads/2021/02/General-Comment-17.pdf

6 Facilitating child-centred practice

Emma Laurence and Michelle Malomo

Having developed a play-centric pedagogy within Chapter 5, this chapter builds upon this and asks you to reimagine a child-centred and therapeutic approach to pedagogy and provision design. What would early childhood provision look like if it were bespoke for each child's uniqueness? This chapter forges a bridge between these reimaginations and real-world practice so that you can locate pockets of practice which embed these ideals.

Chapter objectives

This chapter:

- Offers an opportunity to engage in an imaginative reconstruction of a child-centred society

- Gives an overview of the historical and political contexts regarding child-centred pedagogy

- Identifies possible areas of focus for developing your own theory for child-centred practice.

Introduction

Following an exploration of the core values which underpin a playful pedagogy in Chapter 5, this chapter explores these values fully and considers more broadly how children are positioned in ECEC, particularly with regards to shaping practice, informing pedagogy and designing provision. It first explores the policy context regarding child-centred practice as well as some of the disparity between espoused practice and policy in action. It then delves deeper into the multiple terms which are often used interchangeably, such as 'child-centred', 'child-initiated', and 'the child's voice', to identify the impact that these seemingly small nuances

DOI: 10.4324/9781041055358-10

have on practice. We then explore some of the theoretical pioneers regarding child-centred and therapeutic approaches to pedagogy before looking at some of the contemporary pedagogies which descend from this work. The chapter ends by identifying the next steps in cultivating your own theory for practice, which we hope will inspire reflection well beyond the pages of this book. First though, this chapter adopts a playful approach to redesigning practice which seeks to take imagination seriously. This is adapted from the work of Ruth Levitas (2013) who, having spent decades devoted to sociology, noted that much of the work of sociologists seemed to offer criticism of existing ways of doing things rather than potential solutions or imaginative reconstructions of how things could be. Lester (2019) echoes these thoughts by suggesting that having the ability to question 'what if ' supports a way of thinking that releases us from the constraints of accepted ways of paradigms, being and beyond the often messiness of life. Levitas suggests using *utopia as method* in order to identify and express the '*deepest desires of our hearts and minds*', which she considers a '*necessary form of knowledge and of truth*' (Levitas, 2013, p3) particularly regarding human needs and human flourishing. For that reason, we begin this chapter with our own imaginative reconstruction of a child-centred society.

What if ... an imaginative reconstruction of a child-centred society

Imagine a world where children are the primary focus. The world looks different here, more alive. When you look outside, there are significantly more trees, the landscape rises and falls, and paths meander amongst wild flowers and shrubs alive with bird song. There are nooks and hideaway spots to get lost in around most corners as town planners have come to understand the significance that spaces like this have in promoting children's communication. Many roads are closed off to cars during daylight so that children can play safely in the streets. This means that most families find it easier to walk, run, cycle, and scoot to work or school. When working with children, town planners found that a key concern is whether the road surface is smooth enough for skateboards and rollerblades. People plan a longer travel time than before, so that they can make it to work successfully without stepping on the cracks or falling in the 'lava'. In schools and early years settings, planning meetings are conducted with and by children, whereby the upcoming calendar is explored as a source of inspiration of where minds may wander in the coming season and how best to support this. Children are also involved with determining how best to develop and exercise their skills and show off their understandings. This term, this has culminated in turning their school into a 'living museum' for the local community whereby people from the local area are transported back in time to tour the *Titanic*. This is a big day in the community calendar, and many local people attend, with others offering their help to the children in preparation for, or in the running of, the day.

Outside of school, there are greater levels of social cohesion and empathy in the community, and everyone plays a role in looking after the community's children. There is always something to get involved in such as storytelling events, local festivals, and community gatherings, which foster connections and strengthen relationships. With children at the centre of the community, adults have become more playful too. This weekend saw the local authority hide-and-seek champion crowned after a six-hour, 120-people tournament. Play is recognised as essential for mental and physical well-being. Healthcare systems integrate play therapy and recreational activities into treatment plans acknowledging the therapeutic benefits of exercising creativity and curiosity whilst engaging with people who are important to you. People don't need to be encouraged to engage in physical activities and outdoor play in order to maintain a healthy lifestyle as much of the year people spend time outside in communal spaces just moments from their homes. The workplace looks different too; there are not set operating hours and the workplace has become more free-flowing. There are spaces where families pop in to see their loved ones and children come along with their parents, making use of the recreational facilities or – where possible – getting involved with the job at hand. It has been found that the *'greater audacity to imagine'* (Svitak, 2010) that children exhibit has been something that adults have begun trying to emulate and exercise in themselves. So many areas of industry have thrived in new ways since adopting this approach. Science, engineering, technology, art, entertainment, and literature are all considered to have been subject to an explosion in innovation and investment. Priorities generally in society have shifted. At large, people seem to really be prioritising nurturing the fun, happiness, and social connections in their lives above all else.

⌨ Critical reflection

- Reflect honestly on what this utopian vision has made you feel. You may find that your instinct is to dismiss it as unrealistic. Or perhaps it inspires you?

- What if you could redesign society for children what would it look like?

- What do you consider are the benefits to vision building exercises like this?

What is child-centred practice

Early years practice will always reflect, to some degree, the discourses of what childhood is and should be, as well as ideas around human flourishing. Throughout history, ideas about the ways that children differ to adults and what this means for the way that we raise them have shifted dramatically. It is in relatively recent years that constructions of childhood have shifted towards a more rights-based, citizenship-oriented and participatory discourse and this has been a key driver in the development of the concept of child-centredness. However, Lester (2019, p60) identifies a propensity of westernised constructs of childhood in which they must 'retain their natural innocence and sense of wonder by being close to nature and it falls to adults to protect them from the violence and ugliness of contemporary society'. Child-centredness reflects the broader societal view that children are social actors and agents in their own lives and so should be afforded opportunities to exercise this.

Rather than providing a formulaic method for achieving child-centredness, child-centred practice is a philosophy or an approach to work with children and families, so there is no one way to develop child-centred provision and this looks different between settings. Additionally, there is no single definition of child-centredness and as Chung and Walsh (2000) state, *'the term balances on many layers of complex and sometimes contradictory meanings forged over the years by competing interest groups'* (p215). The term can be interpreted to mean learning driven by the child's interests, children's participation in decisions related to their lives, differentiating learning opportunities based upon needs or a puritan understanding whereby adults (as much as is possible) do not put any parameters on what children must do. Despite this, there is an assumed consensus regarding a definition which is evidenced by how universally the term is used in early years policy and literature. The following case study exemplifies this as a trainee teacher reflects on changes in her developing philosophy regarding child-centredness and the role of the adult.

❝❝ Case study – changing understanding of child-centredness

Having worked in early years settings for the beginning of my career, child-centred practice had been a central concept to my professional philosophy since I left school. I had always valued free play, unsolicited activity and throwing out all the planning because we found a particularly good spider web we needed to study. However, having begun my studies toward a BA (Hons) in Early Childhood, I began to realise that despite these values, the spaces for children to lead their own lives within my setting were still relatively small. For example, having been introduced to Hart's (1992) ladder of participation, I found that within individual sessions, children were perhaps occupying rung 6 which is identified as 'adult-initiated, shared decisions with young people' or perhaps even rung 7 which is described as 'youth-initiated and directed'. However, this only happened within parameters which I set, at specific 'free flow' times of the day, within an environment which I designed. In terms of their overall experience, children were not deciding to come to my setting, what hours they attended, how the space was designed, what meals they were served, what the planning looked like or leading the conversation about them with their parents. It dawned on me that there was nuance here and that perhaps I hadn't acknowledged that there was a broad spectrum of practice which could be defined as child-centred. This was compounded further in lectures when another student argued that child-centred practice suggests an invisible practitioner and nullifies their expertise. My knee jerk response was that this was false, but I began to realise that I often discussed the importance of the unique child but where did uniqueness of the adults in the room feature? It became apparent that my time on my degree was a rich opportunity for me to interrogate the finer points of my philosophy and identify my own definition of what child-centredness means to me and what the role of the adult was within this.

This provided a catalyst for reflection, and I adapted my theory of child-centred practice to align more closely to Langford's (2010) discussion of a democratic approach to learning. This democratic approach maintains a recognition of the child's agency and embeds this across as much decision-making in setting as is possible. It also allows for a greater appreciation of the identity of the professional as a dynamic, attentive and unique resource in creating quality care and education and in sensitively supporting children to play a role in this. This meant that the practitioners' role was better valued in my setting and, in doing so, practitioners became more creative in the ways we could support children to become partners in the setting. Some of the changes in practice included planning meetings with children where we would together look at the upcoming calendar and think about the opportunities we had for learning and what directions we may want to take this. We also involved children in developmental reviews with parents whereby we looked with children at their learning journal scrap books and discussed all the things we had learned and the things we were proud of and wanted to share with families. Children were also included in the evaluation and design of the environment in a number of ways. For example, we brought in a puppet who had never been in setting before and asked the children to show him around and tell him about all of their favourite things in setting.

On reflection, by taking the term 'child-centred' for granted and not exploring what this means for me, I had missed opportunities to align practice with my values. Creating my own definition of child-centredness has in turn developed a more multi-faceted approach to embedding this in my practice.

Critical reflection

- What is the potential impact of an unclear definition of child-centredness on practice?

- What does child-centredness look like in your setting? Does this align with your philosophy of child-centredness?

- Where do adults fit within your definition of child-centred practice?

The policy context

England's ECEC sector can be characterised by two key, competing agendas. Child-centredness, including a growing understanding of the fundamental need for meaningful relationships and rich engaging environments, is held in tension with ideas of school readiness, and neoliberal agendas which endorse standardisation and a one-size-fits-all approach. Children are at the centre of everything we do within early childhood education and care and yet are missing from almost all conversation about quality provision and best practice. The students we work with are often aware of this tension and express frustration about it as they often want to advocate for the agency of children but see aspects of practice which hinder this. Often by engaging with policy and identifying the aspects of it which align with their values students feel more confident in allowing children to take part in leading their own learning and justifying this within the existing policy context.

The shift towards child-centred approaches became legitimised in UK policy in 1967 through the Plowden Report. Though this report was focused primarily on primary schools, the central message of the report is that 'at the heart of the educational process lies the child' (Plowden, 1967, p9) and it advocated increased parental involvement, learning through discovery, and universal preschool education for the less privileged. Evidence of this growing movement of child-centredness in contemporary policy can be seen within the fields of education, social work, and international rights. In terms of education in the early years, the EYFS Statutory Framework *'sets the standards that all early years providers must meet to ensure that children learn and develop well and are kept healthy and safe'* (DfE, 2023a, p7). The document states that *'children learn by leading their own play'* (p17) and that *'practitioners must stimulate children's interests, responding to each child's emerging needs and guiding their development through warm, positive interactions coupled with secure routines for play and learning'* (p17). Supplementary government guidance for practitioners is available within the Development Matters document (DfE, 2023b) and this provides further endorsement of child-centred pedagogies (amongst a mix of approaches for teaching and learning). For example, the document states that *'young children's learning is often driven by their interests'* and that *'plans need to be flexible'*. Further endorsement for child-centred pedagogies is seen in the Birth to Five Matters guidance (Early Education Coalition, 2021) which has child-centred approaches throughout. This guidance has been written for the sector by those who work within the sector. This means that in order for you to plan effectively within the early years, you must consider first who you are planning for, what their interests are, what their current stage of development is, and what the most fitting provocation might be to engage those interests in a way that is accessible to the child. It also means that you must be ready to be surprised by the children you work with and change the plan at the last moment in order to follow new interests at the time that they emerge.

In social work and safeguarding practice, child-centredness is often represented in the prevalent use of the phrase 'the child's voice' and calls for this to be central to safeguarding and child protection practice. Creating a culture with what Buckler (2023, p110) describes as having 'children at its heart' is an essential part of practice. Listening to the voice of the child is a phrase which, on the face of it, poses a problem for children who have not yet learned to speak or who are non-verbal. However, this phrase does not simply refer to hearing what a child is saying but emphasises the need to understand the child's experiences, wants, and needs.

Underpinning all of the above policy is the United Nations Conventions on the Rights of the Child which recognises the roles of children as social, economic, political, civil, and cultural actors. The Convention sets out the minimum standards for protecting the rights of children and has become the most ratified human rights treaty in history (UNICEF, 2024). One hundred and ninety-six nations have ratified this convention across the world with the United States of America being the only country that has not. The UNCRC is made up of 54 articles. These articles are underpinned by the principles that the best interests of the child should be a primary consideration in all actions concerning children, and that the child has a right to express their views freely in all matters affecting the child, with those views being given due weight. The movement towards child-centred practice then, is an international one much bigger than any call for standardisation or school readiness. It is therefore important that policy is interpreted to support the individual needs of children and not the other way around.

Theoretical pioneers

The growing commitment to child-centred practice is not a new one and is understood by many to have emerged in the 19th century in response to developing concerns regarding the abusive treatment of many children. Throughout the 19th century, the work of campaigners such as Lord Shaftesbury and Charles Dickens was making child abuse and the protection of children a major social concern. Parliamentary reform began to follow from the 1880s with the development of The Prevention of Cruelty to, and Protection of, Children Act in 1889. For the first time, a statute existed to impose criminal penalties to deter mistreatment of children. The first half of the 20th century saw the establishment of a distinct phase of early education for children under the age of seven which echoed the purposes, practices, and pedagogies of the traditional model of primary schooling. At the time, this was characterised by formal methods of teaching whereby knowledge is transmitted by active experts to the passive child. Around the same time, growing understandings in education, philosophy, and later psychology and child development created an overall movement towards child-centred education. The aims and priorities for child-centred education placed great value on richly resourced environments, child-led, unsolicited activity and on practitioners being considered a human resource, working with children to afford freedom to explore, discover, and create for themselves.

Perhaps one of the most significant theoretical pioneers to underpin this shift in understandings of children was Jean Piaget (1896–1980) who transformed our understandings of children and development. Coming from the field of psychology, Piaget is considered by many to be one of the founding fathers of cognitive development which he describes as a progressive reorganisation of mental processes as a result of biological maturation and environmental experience. Essentially, he found that children think in remarkably different ways to adults and that independent exploration and discovery were important at all stages of cognitive development. Children's learning happens in stages in line with their level of biological maturity. Piaget has also come to influence child-centred teaching, in which teachers begin with the student's existing understandings and help them build on and develop these. Conversely, Vygotsky (1896–1934) – a contemporary of Piaget – argued that rather than being exclusively biologically determined, cognitive development depends heavily on social interaction. According to Vygotsky, children's learning occurs within a social context in cooperation with someone else. Though he was also a proponent of child-centred practice, his work emphasised the importance of meaningful relationships and positive social interactions in child development.

Whilst theorists such as Piaget, Froebel, Dewey, Rousseau, and others significantly impacted the way we understood the theory behind child development, Susan Isaacs (1885–1948) is considered by many to have had one of the most significant influences on practice today, perhaps doing 'more than anyone else to integrate the increasing theoretical knowledge of child psychology with practical methodology in both education and child rearing practices' (Smith, 1985, p17). Isaacs had a background in philosophy and psychology and trained as a psychoanalyst before becoming a lecturer in infant education at Darlington Training College. She later took a position at an experimental nursery called the Malting House Garden School. Her observations here informed much of her published works. Some of her key ideas were regarding the environment, the importance of play, and the role of the adult. Despite being over a century ago, the Malting House School environment might look very familiar to professionals in the sector today. She advocated for an environment which is richly resourced to stimulate learning through play. Similar to Montessori schools, the furnishings such as tables, chairs, and cupboards were positioned at a lower height. Mattresses and rugs were provided for peaceful activities and relaxation. The main room led directly to the garden, featuring amenities like a playhouse, sandpit, tool shed, gardening plots, and one of Britain's earliest climbing frames (Pound, 2005). There were very few constraints at the Malting House Garden School, giving children plenty of opportunity for unsolicited play and discovery. Her work identifies the role of the practitioner as making the environment comfortable, helping children to feel secure and at ease and providing them with optimal conditions for learning. She, like many before her, also considered it crucial to have an in-depth knowledge of each child which could be gained by observing children at play. To achieve this, Isaacs developed record cards to support staff in documenting their knowledge of each child to inform planning. Unlike a lot of research, Isaac's work was made accessible to practitioners and parents, and this bridged a gap between research and practice.

Existing pedagogical approaches

Child-centred practice is a central principle embedded in a number of contemporary pedagogical approaches. As you develop professionally, it will be useful to explore a number of different pedagogies in order to locate your own practice ideals. This will also support you in developing a network of like-minded practitioners. However, Brookfield (1995) warns us of the potential to be blown about by ever-changing pedagogical trends. It is therefore worth acknowledging that rather than trying to locate your practice within any single approach, practitioners should reflect upon the relationship between the key principles which underpin different pedagogies and the practices which exercise these. You can therefore develop provision which is tailored to your setting, the values which underpin it, and the children and families it serves. Far too many influential contemporary pedagogies exist than can be suitably examined in this book. However, the following three approaches hold child-centredness as a central priority.

In-the-moment planning

Though in-the-moment planning (Ephgrave, 2018) has garnered popularity in recent years, it is not a new practice and will feel very familiar to many practitioners. Relying upon children's natural drive to play and learn, in-the-moment planning does away with the traditional, long-winded observation, assessment and planning cycle and condenses this down to an intuitive immediate response to children's interests as they emerge. It requires adults to understand the levels of engagement (Laevers, 1994) and to work closely with the children and identify 'teachable moments' as children play. Practitioners then respond to these and extend their interest, by asking open-ended questions and identifying alternative ways to apply this interest elsewhere in the environment.

Curiosity approach

The curiosity approach (Hellyn and Bennett, 2019) draws on ideas from its philosophical predecessors such as Reggio Emilia, Montessori, Pikler, and Steiner and prioritises nurturing active learning. In-the-moment planning is a tool that proponents of the curiosity approach might employ but they will do this within environments which are neutrally decorated and without bright plastic and electronic toys. Instead, this environment would be filled with loose parts and natural materials which don't have a clear function. This is thought to support children's imagination and critical thinking skills. Much like with the other pedagogies mentioned here, the child will lead their own learning and adults will play a supporting role in this. Part of this role is creating engaging invitations and provocations for children.

Therapeutic approaches

Whilst the above two pedagogies perhaps emphasise the educational elements of ECEC, therapeutic approaches focus on the unique position that ECEC settings have in buffering children from the negative impacts of early childhood trauma. 'Therapeutic approaches' is an umbrella term which encompasses a huge range of trauma-informed practices integrated into education and care. The overarching principle of these is the recognition that trusting relationships have the potential to create resilience for children and families. Trust and security develop over time and require consistency, dependability, and meaningful connection. Therapeutic approaches to ECEC therefore prioritise attunement with children and the timely and sensitive response to their needs as they emerge.

Practical pockets of your vision of practice

Child-centred practice depends on who the children are. It is not a one-size-fits-all approach and requires reflexivity in order to develop provision which aligns with the shared vision of practitioners and the idiosyncratic needs of the community they serve. Theoretical understandings and specific pedagogies are simply tools in carving out what that practice might look like, but this process is an intuitive one, and just as Levitas (2013) suggests, imagination and heart are required to create quality ECEC provision in this regard. Having considered our imaginative reconstruction and explored the vision within policy, it is crucial that practitioners identify practicable actions which can be taken in order to create pockets of your utopian vision in your everyday work with children.

🗣️ **Critical reflection**

- In order to do this, reflect again on what your imaginative reconstruction of society would look like and ask yourself what the key elements of this are.

- Use these key elements you have identified as being crucial to your vision for child-centred practice as a means to reflect upon your practice as is. Score each of these key elements throughout the day and consider what factors are impacting this score. For example, if one of the key elements of the vision outlined in this chapter is 'meaningful relationships between children and adults', how could these relationships be better supported during the planning process? Or in the design of the environment? Is there a way to better include children in this process?

The practicable actions you identify to develop your own child-centred practice will depend upon your own hopes for the children you work with, as well as what those children demonstrate that they need from you.

Chapter summary

This chapter has identified that child-centredness is a prevalent approach across all manners of work with children and families, though different professionals may use different language for this, such as 'the child's best interests', 'the voice of the child', and 'individual needs and interests'. What these terms look like is open to interpretation and so it is crucial for you to reflect carefully, not only on what your own vision is for child-centred practice but also how you can consistently check this vision against the developing needs and desires of the children you work with.

Further reading

Levitas, R (2013) *Utopia as method: The imaginary reconstitution of society*. Basingstoke: Palgrave Macmillan.

Svitak, A (2010) *What adults can learn from children*. TED. [Online] available at: www.ted.com/talks/adora_svitak_what_adults_can_learn_from_kids (accessed 18 March 2024).

References

Brookfield, S (1995) *Becoming a critically reflective teacher*. San Francisco: Jossey-Bass.

Buckler, R (2023) *Developing child-centred practice for Safeguarding and Child protection*. London: Routledge.

Chung, S and Walsh, D (2000) 'Unpacking child-centredness: A history of meanings', *Journal of Curriculum Studies*, 32(2), pp 215–234.

Department for Education (2023a) *Early years foundation stage statutory framework for group and school-based providers*. London: HMSO.

Department for Education (2023b) *Development matters non-statutory curriculum guidance for the early years foundation stage*. London: HMSO.

Early Years Coalition (2021) *Birth to 5 matters: Non-statutory guidance for the Early Years Foundation Stage*. St Albans: Early Education. Available at: https://birthto5matters.org.uk/wp-content/uploads/2021/04/Birthto5Matters-download.pdf

Ephgrave, A (2018) *Planning in the moment with young children*. Oxfordshire: Routledge.

Hart, R (1992) *Children's participation: From Tokenism to Citizenship*. New York: UNICEF.

Hellyn, L and Bennett, S (2019) *From ordinary to extraordinary – The curiosity approach.* Birmingham: The Curiosity Approach.

Langford, R (2010) 'Critiquing child-centred pedagogy to bring children and early childhood educators into the centre of a Democratic pedagogy', *Contemporary Issues in Early Childhood*, 11(1), pp 113–127.

Laevers, F (1994) *Five levels of well-being.* Leuven: Leuven University Press.

Lester, S (2019) *Professional practice in supporting children's play A new approach to everyday playfulness.* London: Jessica Kingsley Publishers.

Levitas, R (2013) *Utopia as method: The imaginary reconstitution of society.* Basingstoke: Palgrave Macmillan.

Plowden, B et al. (1967) *Children and their primary schools: A report of the Central Advisory Council for Education (England). Vol. 1. The report.* London: HMSO.

Pound, L (2005) *How Children Learn.* Leamington Spa: Step Forward Publishing.

Smith, L (1985) *To Understand and to help: The life and work of Susan Isaacs(1885–1948).* Plainsborough: Associated University Presses.

Svitak, A (2010) *What adults can learn from children.* TED. [Online] Available at: www.ted.com/talks/adora_svitak_what_adults_can_learn_from_kids (accessed 18 March 2024).

UNICEF (2024) *Convention on the rights of the child.* [Online] Available at: www.unicef.org/child-rights-convention (accessed 18 March 2024).

Theme 4
The Advocate

Chapters Seven and Eight support you in your duties as an advocate for children.

Duty 4 To be an effective key person and advocate for the child, supporting the child's developmental, emotional and daily needs within a secure and caring relationship. To ensure the effectiveness of the key person approach across the aspect or environment for which they are responsible.	**Knowledge:** 1 2 3 4 6 7 8 9 10 11 12 13 14 15 16 17 19 20 21
	Skills: 1 2 3 4 5 6 7 8 9 10 11 12 15 16 17 18 19 20 21 22 23 25
	Behaviours: 1 2 3 4 5 6 7 8 9
Duty 6 Promote, demonstrate and facilitate a clear understanding of diversity and equality to support all children, including those with additional needs, those of high ability, those with English as an additional language and those with disabilities. To be able to use and evaluate distinctive approaches which engage and support inclusivity of all children within their social and cultural context.	**Knowledge:** 1 2 3 4 5 6 7 8 11 13 14 15 16 17 18 19 20 21 22
	Skills: 1 2 3 4 5 6 8 10 11 12 13 15 16 18 19 20 21 22 23 25
	Behaviours: 1 2 3 4 5 6 7 8 9

DOI: 10.4324/9781041055358-11

Duty 8 Demonstrate leaderful practice through the effective deployment of resources and practitioners keeping the child's voice and needs central to practice.	**Knowledge:** 1 2 3 4 8 9 10 11 12 13 15 16 17 18 19
	Skills: 2 3 5 10 14 15 17 18 21 22 23 25
	Behaviours: 1 2 3 5 6 7 8 9

7 Let's get it right – safeguarding

Samantha Sutton-Tsang and Sarah Phillips

This chapter explores the statutory guidance aimed at safeguarding children's welfare in the early years sector and the collaborative efforts to protect children from harm. It prompts a critical assessment of Munro's (2011) assertion that the focus should be on learning to do the right thing (protecting children) rather than merely following procedures correctly. Through references to thresholds for statutory intervention, current literature, and sector-specific regulatory and inspection frameworks, the chapter draws from a Designated Safeguarding Lead and a student's reflections on safeguarding in practice, encouraging practitioners to actively engage in creating cultures of vigilance within the sector to enhance their practice.

◎ Chapter objectives

This chapter will:

- Enable you to identify and apply the key legislative acts and statutory guidance to your safeguarding practice

- Support you to develop strategies to foster a culture of vigilance and professional curiosity within your practice

- Explore the child's voice and your role in advocating effectively for children to provide appropriate support and child protection.

Introduction

Safeguarding can be an area of practice which leaves professionals feeling uneasy and worried about getting things right. The responsibility to protect and promote the welfare of children is one which weighs heavy on the shoulders of all who care deeply about children

DOI: 10.4324/9781041055358-12

and their families. Throughout this chapter, we hope to support you in feeling confident in this aspect of your practice.

Safeguarding and legislative frameworks

Safeguarding is a crucial aspect of ensuring the well-being and protection of children and young people (DfE, 2024; HM Government, 2023). It involves providing the right help, at the right time, from the right people, employing a multi-layered and multi-disciplined approach (Frost, 2021). This approach considers various factors, such as the individual needs of each child, the timing of interventions, and the appropriate individuals or services to provide support. Importantly, safeguarding strategies must be tailored to each child and young person.

> *No single practitioner can have a full picture of a child's needs and circumstances. If children and families are to receive the right help at the right time, everyone who comes into contact with them has a role to play in identifying concerns, sharing information, and taking prompt action.*
>
> DfE, 2024, p7

Practitioners must understand key legislation and policies related to safeguarding children and young people. In England, the framework for child protection and safeguarding is covered by three main Acts:

• Children Act 1989

• Children Act 2004

• Children and Social Work Act 2017.

The Children Act 1989 sets out the legislative framework for child protection, emphasising the paramount importance of the child's welfare. It also outlines the expectations and requirements regarding duties of care to children, ensuring that their well-being is always the primary concern. The Children Act 2004 built on this by encouraging partnerships between agencies and increasing accountability for local authorities and partners in safeguarding children and promoting their welfare.

The Children and Social Work Act 2017 introduced several new provisions, including the establishment of the Child Safeguarding Practice Review Panel to review and report on cases. It also replaced Local Safeguarding Children's Boards with local safeguarding partners and mandating the review of each child death to identify relevant public health and safety issues.

Statutory guidance and multi-agency collaboration

Alongside key legislation, practitioners must adhere to current policies in the setting, statutory guidance and curriculum frameworks. Statutory guidance from the Department for

Education (DfE) outlines the responsibilities of organisations and agencies involved with children to aid, protect, and promote their welfare. The 2023 edition *of Working Together to Safeguard Children*, which supersedes the 2018 version, emphasises that '*safeguarding is everyone's responsibility*' with *Keeping Children Safe in Education* (DfE, 2024, p143) stating that, '*Safeguarding and promoting the welfare of children is everyone's responsibility. Everyone who comes into contact with children has an important role to play*'. It is important to acknowledge that this statutory guidance is subject to regular updates, with the most recent revisions as of February 2024. Consequently, it is advisable to consult online sources for any potential changes or updates to the guidance.

However, even with these guidelines, child deaths still occur, raising questions about the effectiveness of current safeguarding practices. Serious Case Reviews (SCRs), now often referred to as Child Safeguarding Practice Reviews (CSPRs), are undertaken when a child dies or is seriously harmed, and abuse or neglect are suspected. These reviews aim to identify lessons to improve safeguarding practices and prevent similar incidents from occurring in the future. The Wood report (DfE, 2016) critiqued the usefulness of SCRs and this led to a reformed system for the CSPR. The report's recommendations aimed to improve the effectiveness and efficiency of safeguarding practices and to create a more responsive and learning-focused system through improved multi-agency collaboration. Some of the key outcomes included the introduction of streamlined processes to determine if a more in-depth Local Child Safeguarding Practice Review is needed; the inclusion of local reviews to focus on specific localised incidents and national reviews to focus on broader issues across multiple areas. With there being a focus on learning and improvement, rather than identifying failures, CSPRs can help improve safeguarding practices. The improved collaboration between agencies under CSPRs highlights that safeguarding cannot be the responsibility of one person.

Gallagher and Sutton-Tsang (2017) explore the responsibilities of practitioners, indicating a potential risk: if safeguarding is deemed everyone's responsibility, there may be an assumption that someone else will report or address concerns when in fact we should all be actively contributing to the safeguarding process to ensure that we build a clear picture of a child's current situation and 'to be vigilant' in practice (p161).

Creating a culture of vigilance

A culture of vigilance in safeguarding fosters an environment where the safety and protection of children and vulnerable adults are paramount, ensuring that potential risks are swiftly identified and effectively managed. This requires all staff and stakeholders to feel empowered to take action, maintain an open mind, and work in a respectful environment with open communication.

❝ ❝ Case study – Seamus' reflection

Seamus, a student in their last year, studying the FdA early years and a Grade 2 Teaching Assistant working in a three-form entry school reflects on adopting a culture of vigilance in his practice and how an open mind can support your professional practice:

'Cultures of vigilance are often highlighted in Child Safeguarding Practice Reviews. For me, working in an environment close to where I live and having relationships with families connected to the school, it is often difficult to separate my assumptions from the actual home dynamics.

We never have a completely accurate picture from our interactions with a child or family. Keeping an open mind can help resolve issues, as it allows us to provide Early Help when needed and better assess the severity of disclosed situations. Being attentive, even with children who seem least likely to be vulnerable, can lead to positive outcomes.'

◔◑ Critical reflection

What could the impact be if Seamus did not challenge his assumptions about children's lives?

Have you ever noticed yourself making assumptions about the children you work with? How might this impact on your behaviours within the context of cultures of vigilance?

CSPRs (Staunton, 2016; Wonnacott, 2013) show that without a culture of vigilance, failures can occur, allowing harm to come to children. Recognising the uniqueness of each child, safeguarding must be customised to their specific needs. What works for one child or family may not work for another. Recognising this requires tailored, timely, and responsive support to prevent risks from escalating. Early intervention is crucial, involving appropriate people such as family, community resources, and specialised services. While most children receive adequate support from families and communities, enhancing these networks is key. Families might need additional support beyond mainstream services, making access to specialised services essential for addressing complex needs and providing personalised interventions.

Recognising the wider social contexts of a child means understanding that safeguarding is not just the responsibility of individual caregivers but a collective effort. Schools, healthcare providers, social services, and community organisations all play vital roles in creating a safety network (Gallagher and Sutton-Tsang, 2017). By fostering strong, interconnected support systems, we can ensure that every child has the opportunity to thrive in a safe and nurturing environment and a culture of vigilance enables practitioners to raise concerns with trained professionals and colleagues. This community of practice encourages professional challenge and curiosity to address unconscious biases and improve practice (McNellie, 2017; Murray, 2019).

Professional challenge and professional curiosity

Professional challenge is an integral aspect of robust safeguarding practice and effective multi-agency collaboration (Buckler, 2023). Decisions are based on the information available at the time, and it is recognised that differing perspectives among professionals from various agencies may arise, necessitating further examination. For instance, a teacher may have a different perspective than a social worker, owing to the distinct contexts and interactions each professional has with the same child, as well as their specialised training and expertise within their respective fields. Practitioners should therefore be open to scrutiny regarding their decision-making processes or chosen actions and must be supported to professionally challenge others regardless of their status (Darlington Safeguarding Partnership, 2021).

Professionals often prefer to believe that a child is safe, even when signs of abuse are apparent, leading to a dangerous form of denial (Davies and Ducket, 2016, p7). Often, we do not want to believe the worst is possible and sometimes practitioners may rationalise behaviour and be overly optimistic of a situation. This might mean accepting information from parents or carers at face value. This is what we call *Rule of Optimism* whereby professionals want to believe that all is well for a child (Reder et al, 1993). In order to be professionally curious, practitioners are required to rigorously examine all potential indicators of abuse or neglect to fully understand the child's lived experiences (Keeling and Goosey, 2021; NSPCC, 2021). By critically reflecting on the information presented, practitioners can achieve a clear understanding of the child's situation, free from parental influence and unconscious biases. Recognising that everyone carries a degree of unconscious bias shaped by personal experiences, background, and culture is crucial. Acknowledging these biases in interpreting facts allows practitioners to maintain an open mind, avoid assumptions and consider even the most challenging possibilities, and ultimately present an objective case. Professional curiosity is the ability and communication skills required to thoroughly investigate and comprehend the dynamics within a family. Rather than relying on assumptions or accepting information at face value (Brighton and Hove Local Safeguarding Children Board, 2017), this sometimes requires practitioners to challenge the status quo.

'Doing the right thing' versus 'Doing things right'

Munro's (2011) work emphasises the need to develop a deeper understanding of the complexities and uncertainties inherent in child protection practice. This emphasis has contributed significantly to discussions around ethical dilemmas in the field. Her research and writings advocate for approaches that prioritise reflective practice, critical thinking, and ethical decision-making to navigate these dilemmas effectively and she discusses the tension between 'Doing the right thing' and 'Doing things right'. These concepts highlight different aspects of decision-making and practice within child protection systems:

'Doing the right thing': This perspective emphasises the importance of focusing on the ultimate goal of child protection, which is ensuring the safety and well-being of children. 'Doing the right thing' involves prioritising the best interests of the child above all else, even if it means deviating from established procedures or protocols. It recognises that child protection work is inherently complex and that rigid adherence to rules or guidelines may not always result in the best outcomes for children.

'Doing things right': Conversely, this perspective emphasises the importance of adhering to established procedures, protocols, and standards of practice within child protection systems. It focuses on ensuring that interventions are carried out efficiently, effectively, and in accordance with legal and organisational requirements. 'Doing things right' prioritises consistency, accountability, and procedural fairness in child protection practice.

❝ Case study – Seamus' ethical dilemma

Men often feel more vulnerable working in early years settings for several reasons (Mistry and Sood, 2015). There are persistent stereotypes that this is a female profession and so men in these roles can face suspicion. Men may feel more constrained in their interactions with children due to fears of being judged or misunderstood leading to a reluctance to engage in nurturing roles. Here, Seamus reflects on the ethical dilemma of 'Doing the right thing' vs 'Doing things right' and the additional responsibility he feels as a male working in the early years sector:

'Munro's idea about doing things right or doing the right thing is a challenging concept for me. I personally find it hard when a child has fallen over and hurt themselves, is feeling unwell, or just needs a hug at times. Wanting to show my compassionate side but remaining professional. As a male in the early years, I believe I have a greater duty to protect myself within my role when it comes to children's personal care and this sensitive side of the job. We care very well for our children at our setting and like to ensure we treat all people fairly and I find it a challenge sometimes where "Doing the right thing" (heart) and Doing things right (brain) seem at odds with one another.'

The tension between 'doing the right thing' (heart) and 'doing things right' (brain) reflects the inherent challenges in child protection work, where practitioners must balance the need to act decisively to protect children with the need to follow established processes and procedures. Munro (2011) argues that while both perspectives are important, child protection systems often emphasise 'doing things right' at the expense of 'doing the right thing'. This can lead to bureaucratic barriers, delays in decision-making, and a focus on compliance rather than outcomes. This may cause professionals to experience anxiety or fear of repercussions if they deviate from established protocols. Additionally, it could undermine their professional judgement, resulting in a sense of disempowerment and frustration. The constant pressure to comply with procedures, coupled with the emotional toll of feeling unable to 'do the right thing', can contribute to burnout and job dissatisfaction.

Munro (Parliament House of Commons, 2011), in her evidence to the Education Committee, stated:

> One message is that the current system has quite inadvertently become focused on compliance with procedures and very defensive practice, so that people are more

concerned about whether they will be blamed than the impact on the child. They have ended up there for very good reason. I am not criticising them for it, but it is a fault in the way it is operating.

Munro (2011) advocates for a more balanced approach that recognises the complexities of child protection work and prioritises flexible, adaptive practice focused on achieving the best outcomes for children. This involves empowering practitioners to use their professional judgement and expertise to make decisions that are in the best interests of the child while still ensuring accountability and adherence to essential standards of practice. Through experience and collaboration, practitioners can develop a clearer understanding of how to effectively safeguard children and families.

Critical reflection

Reflecting on Munro's (2011) argument about the balance between 'doing the right thing' and 'doing things right', how can you, as a practitioner, navigate the tension between following established procedures and using your professional judgement to ensure the best outcomes for children, especially when these approaches seem to conflict?

Thinking back to Seamus' case study, how do you navigate the balance between showing compassion and maintaining professionalism, especially in situations where a child needs comfort or personal care? As a male in early years education, how would you manage the additional responsibility of protecting yourself while ensuring equitable and fair treatment for all children and reconciling the potential conflict between following protocols (brain) and acting on compassionate instincts (heart)?

66 Case study

Seamus shares his reflections on how he maintains a critically reflective and ethical approach in safeguarding practice:

'Critically reflecting is a sense of professional responsibility for improving the quality of provision for children and families. To maintain this, reflecting in the moment is something that often occurs without you realising. Reflection is an educational process where we learn valuable things about our practice (Bolton, 2010).

For me, in practice, taking an ethical approach means taking a non-judgemental approach, understanding that all children and families' experiences are different. This is vital when approaching concerns. As well as GDPR (Data Protection Act, 2018) we know the importance of protecting information that could reveal a child's identity and the serious harm that children and families could come to if this is not effectively upheld.

Safeguarding practice is underpinned by key pieces of legislation which makes it a requirement by law. Not following the correct steps of your setting's safeguarding policy or generally protecting individuals from harm, could mean that your practice is in breach of the law.

The importance of understanding and reflecting current policy in practice is something my setting takes seriously. Working in a large school and having such a diverse intake of children means it is important to understanding a wide range of strategies for safeguarding children and families.'

Seamus emphasises the importance of critical reflection in safeguarding, viewing it as a professional responsibility to enhance the quality of care for children and families. Seamus' reflections align with Munro's (2011) concepts of 'doing things right' versus 'doing the right thing' in several ways:

1. **Critical Reflection and Professional Responsibility:** Seamus' emphasis on continuous critical reflection aligns with 'doing the right thing', where the focus is on understanding and improving the quality of care for children and families. Reflecting in the moment and learning from experiences enables practitioners to make better, more informed decisions that prioritise the child's well-being over strict adherence to procedures.

2. **Non-Judgemental and Individualised Approach:** By advocating for a non-judgemental approach and recognising the unique experiences of each child and family, Seamus supports 'doing the right thing'. This perspective emphasises understanding and responding to individual needs rather than following a one-size-fits-all approach, which can often be a pitfall of 'doing things right'.

3. **Importance of GDPR and Protecting Information:** Seamus highlights the importance of safeguarding sensitive information in compliance with GDPR. This reflects 'doing things right' by following legal requirements and policies. However, it also ties into 'doing the right thing' by ensuring that children and families are protected from potential harm due to data breaches.

4. **Adherence to Legislation and Policies:** Seamus acknowledges that safeguarding practices are rooted in legislation and policies, which represents 'doing things right'. He recognises that failing to comply with these requirements can have legal implications, underscoring the necessity of following established procedures.

5. **Continuous Learning and Adaptation:** Seamus' commitment to regularly updating knowledge and understanding diverse strategies to support children aligns with both 'doing things right' and 'doing the right thing'. This approach ensures compliance with current best practices while also adapting to the specific needs of the children, thus balancing procedural adherence with ethical, child-centred care.

Seamus' reflection illustrates a balanced approach that incorporates both 'doing things right' by adhering to legal and procedural standards and 'doing the right thing' by critically reflecting, being non-judgemental, and prioritising the individual needs of children and families. This alignment with Munro's concepts highlights the importance of integrating ethical judgement with procedural compliance in safeguarding practice. His reflection also addresses the need to advocate for children through a child-centred approach.

Critical reflection

Thinking about your own safeguarding practice, reflect upon which of these five aspects of practice you feel most and least confident in.

Can you identify any actions which would support your development in this area?

Advocacy and the voice of the child

Within the context of the Children Act 1989 in England and Wales, it is imperative that children are included in the decision-making process. Professionals must consider the opinions of children when developing plans to promote their welfare (Buckler, 2023; Race and Frost, 2022). However, children's voices can sometimes be neglected, overshadowed by professionals adhering to *'adult-centric safeguarding processes'* (Race and Frost, 2022, p2). Race and Frost (2022) explore power dynamics within safeguarding practices, identifying 'protectionism' as a significant barrier to children's advocacy, where *'powerful adults restrict the lives and choices of children during safeguarding interventions'* (p2), thereby disempowering them and undermining their right to be heard. Article 12 of the United Nations Convention on the Rights of the Child (UNCRC) asserts that every child has the right to express their views, feelings, and wishes in all matters affecting them, and to have their views considered and taken seriously at all times, in contexts ranging from immigration proceedings, housing decisions and everyday home life (UNICEF, nd). Race and Frost (2022) emphasise that practitioners have the responsibility to advocate for children, recognising when 'protectionism' may override children's rights and ensuring the child's voice is heard and respected.

Working Together to Safeguard Children (HM Government, 2023) identifies that we have a shared responsibility to create a child-centred approach to safeguarding. Table 7.1 identifies what children have reported that they need for an effective safeguarding system and alongside this are key points for practitioners to implement in practice.

Table 7.1 *What children need for effective safeguarding and what practitioners can do in practice (adapted from HM Government, 2023, p12)*

What children need (HM Government, 2023, p12):	What practitioners can do in practice:
Vigilance: to have adults notice when things are troubling them	• Observe and Listen: Staff should be attentive to signs of distress or changes in behaviour. Regularly check in with children to gauge their emotional and physical well-being. • Encourage Open Communication: Create a safe space where children feel comfortable sharing their feelings and concerns. Use simple, age-appropriate language to engage in meaningful conversations. • Document Concerns: Maintain accurate records of any concerns or observations about a child's well-being. Share relevant information with appropriate colleagues or services as needed.
Understanding and action: to understand what is happening; to be heard and understood; and to have that understanding acted upon	• Respond to Concerns Promptly: When a child discloses a concern or shows signs of distress, act quickly to provide support and investigate the issue further. Ensure that their feelings are validated and addressed. • Involve the Child in Decisions: Where appropriate, involve children in decisions that affect them, explaining how their feedback will be used. This helps them feel heard and valued.
Stability: to be able to develop an ongoing stable relationship of trust with those helping them	• Build Strong Relationships: Foster consistent and trusting relationships between children and their families. Assign a key person to each child to provide continuity and stability. • Ensure Consistent Staffing: Minimise changes in staffing to provide children with stable and familiar figures in their lives. When changes are necessary, prepare children in advance and maintain consistent routines.
Respect: to be treated with the expectation that they are competent rather than not	• Value Children's Opinions: Show respect for children's thoughts and feelings by listening attentively and involving them in age-appropriate discussions about their care and learning. • Encourage Independence: Support children's growing independence and competence by providing opportunities for them to make choices and take on responsibilities suitable for their age.

Table 7.1 *(Cont.)*

What children need (HM Government, 2023, p12):	What practitioners can do in practice:
Information and engagement: to be informed about, and involved in procedures, decisions, concerns and plans	• Keep Families Informed: Regularly update parents and guardians about their child's progress, any concerns, and any changes in procedures or policies. Use newsletters, meetings, and digital platforms to maintain open communication. • Engage with Families: Involve families in setting goals for their children and in planning any interventions or support needed. Ensure they understand their role and how they can contribute to their child's well-being.
Explanation: to be informed of the outcome of assessments, and decisions and reasons when their views have not met with a positive response	• Provide Clear Information: When making decisions or changes that affect a child, explain the reasons behind them in a way that is understandable for their age. Offer feedback about the outcomes of any assessments or interventions. • Communicate Decisions: If a child's views or requests are not met, explain the reasons clearly and sensitively. Ensure they understand the rationale behind the decisions made.
Support: to be provided with support in their own right as well as a member of their family	• Offer Tailored Support: Provide additional support to children as needed, both in terms of their individual needs and as part of their family context. This may include accessing external services or offering extra help within the setting. • Support Families: Recognise that supporting children often involves supporting their families. Provide resources, guidance, and referrals to family support services as appropriate.
Advocacy: to be provided with advocacy to assist them in putting forward their views	• Act as an Advocate: Ensure that children's voices are heard in all relevant discussions and decisions. Support them in expressing their views and ensure that their needs are represented in planning and assessments. • Facilitate Access to Advocacy Services: Where needed, connect children and families with advocacy services that can help them articulate and pursue their rights and needs effectively.
Protection: to be protected against all forms of abuse, exploitation, and discrimination, and the right to special protection and help if a refugee	• Implement Safeguarding Measures: Adhere to safeguarding policies and procedures to protect children from abuse, exploitation, and discrimination. Regularly review and update these measures to ensure they are effective. • Special Protection for Vulnerable Children: For children who are refugees or in particularly vulnerable situations, ensure that they receive the additional support and protection they need. Collaborate with specialist services to address their specific needs.

Our next case study highlights the importance of effectively advocating the child's voice and provides an example of how practitioners can meet the needs of a child.

> ❝ **Case study**
>
> Claire, the Deputy Head Teacher and Designated Safeguarding Lead (DSL) at a large multicultural urban primary school, shares an advocacy example for a child with complex needs. Sara, a four-year-old Reception Class pupil, living with her mother, is contacted by her estranged father, who wants to take her to a Speech and Language Therapist after learning she is non-verbal. Sara's mother does not object and does not wish to have any contact with the father, but the school is concerned because Sara has not seen her father for 18 months and has no relationship with him.
>
> To ensure Sara's well-being, the school arranges for her father to collect her from the school office, with two key adults from her class accompanying her to monitor her reaction. They inform the father that if Sara shows any signs of distress, she will not be released into his care to prevent emotional harm. After careful observation, it is decided that Sara can go with her father to the appointment.
>
> This case study illustrates several key aspects of effective advocacy in an educational setting:
>
> 1. **Child-Centred Approach:** The school prioritises Sara's well-being and best interests, ensuring her needs and feelings are central to any decision made.
> 2. **Duty of Care:** The school demonstrates its responsibility to protect Sara from potential emotional harm, showing a commitment to safeguarding.
> 3. **Communication and Coordination:** Effective communication and coordination between the school, the father, and Sara's key adults ensure all parties are informed and involved in the decision-making process.
> 4. **Observation and Assessment:** The decision to allow Sara to go with her father is based on careful observation and assessment of her comfort and emotional state, highlighting the importance of evidence-based decisions in advocacy.
> 5. **Balancing Interests:** The school balances the father's interest in being involved in Sara's care with the need to protect Sara, showing the importance of managing competing interests in advocacy.
>
> Overall, the case study exemplifies how thoughtful, informed, and child-focused actions are essential components of effective advocacy in safeguarding children's welfare. This coincides with what children have highlighted they need to be effectively safeguarded, including the importance of relationships and valuing the child's voice. Fostering respectful and trusting relationships is a critical strategy in child advocacy (Buckler, 2023). According to the NSPCC (2024), a child's lack of input should trigger safeguarding concerns or encourage further professional investigation.

🗣️ **Critical reflection**

How can we, as safeguarding professionals, ensure that our practices not only comply with legal and procedural requirements but also genuinely prioritise the voices and best interests of the children we aim to protect?

Having engaged with the case study, can you see how Claire has ensured her practice has complied with legal and procedural requirements while also prioritising Sara's voice? Claire is an experienced practitioner and DSL and this may seem like a daunting decision to take for a developing practitioner. Thinking about your own developing practice, how can you prioritise the voices of children in your safeguarding practice without compromising your adherence to procedure?

Key lessons from CSPRs and NSPCC briefings

The NSPCC (2024) review provides a summary of key issues and lessons for enhancing practice concerning the child's voice. The review emphasises that professionals must facilitate the child's voice by cultivating relationships and establishing environments where children feel secure and confident in articulating their thoughts and experiences. The review also highlighted the importance of regularly seeing and engaging with children to better understand their views and feelings. It emphasised the need for consistency in seeking, hearing, and recording children's voices, especially for very young children and those with disabilities or complex communication needs. Professionals should develop the confidence and knowledge to communicate effectively with non-verbal children, moving beyond parental reports to focus on direct observations during routine contacts rather than focusing on 'incidents'. By actively seeking children's views rather than making assumptions, and by liaising with the wider family, and other adults who know the child, e.g. other professionals, you can gain a more accurate understanding of their lived experiences, triangulating the information that you gather from various situations and perspectives.

The NSPCC (2024) review goes on to highlight the importance of building stronger and trusting relationships with children to help professionals overcome barriers to understanding their lives more effectively. By encouraging families to attend health appointments, fostering one-to-one conversations with children, and making better use of home visits, professionals can better gather the child's voice and lived experience. Children might echo their parents' views; it is therefore important to ensure that children can speak independently of adults so that their disclosures are authentic. This allows for a clearer understanding of the child's perspective. Differentiating between the child's and parent's voices and seeking alternative ways to engage children can further support their ability to express themselves, even when they are discouraged by parents.

CSPRs provide critical insights and recommendations that help to shape better safeguarding policies and practices, ultimately aiming to protect children more effectively and prevent future tragedies. Below are some of the key messages that reoccur within CSPRs:

Listening to Children and Families: CSPRs emphasise the importance of listening to the voices of children and their families. They advocate for child-centred approaches where the child's welfare is paramount and endorse the need for the child's voice to be heard (Buckler, 2023).

Understanding of Family Dynamics: CSPRs provide insights into the complex dynamics within families that may contribute to abuse or neglect, highlighting the need for practitioners to understand family contexts and the factors that can affect children's well-being. It is important to not make assumptions and to avoid unconscious bias to make judgements on family situations.

Improvement in Multi-Agency Collaboration: CSPRs highlight the need for effective communication and collaboration among various agencies, identifying gaps and breakdowns that may have contributed to failures in protecting children. Timely and responsive communication and building professional relationships between agencies are essential (Lock, 2013; The Child Safeguarding Practice Review Panel, 2022; Wonnacott, 2013).

Early Intervention and Recognition: CSPRs often reveal missed opportunities for early intervention, emphasising the need for practitioners to recognise signs of abuse and neglect early on and take appropriate action promptly.

Assessment and Decision-Making: Deficiencies in assessment processes, such as failing to gather sufficient information or accurately assess risks, are frequently highlighted. CSPRs stress the importance of thorough, evidence-based assessments and improved decision-making processes and this can be support through training of staff to implement efficient assessment practices, along with enhanced communication between multi-agencies, families, and the child.

Training and Professional Development: CSPRs advocate for ongoing professional development to ensure that staff remain up to date with the latest safeguarding practices and policies, including the identification of disguised compliance, developing a culture of vigilance, and being confident to professionally challenge.

Policy and Procedural Changes: CSPRs often lead to changes in policies and procedures to ensure more robust safeguarding frameworks, including reporting protocols, case management procedures, and better support systems for at-risk children which enable routine follow-ups and not just putting in place intervention systems.

Learning Culture and Accountability: CSPRs promote a culture of learning and continuous improvement within organisations, encouraging a non-blame approach to understanding failures and focusing on systemic issues. Therefore, it is important to keep up to date with published reviews so that we can learn from them.

Resource Allocation: CSPRs shed light on resource issues, such as staffing levels, workload management, and access to services, calling for better resource allocation to ensure safeguarding teams have the capacity to perform their roles effectively.

Much of what is suggested above, for lessons learned from CSPRs and NSPCC reviews, is addressed within statutory guidance (DfE, 2024; HM Government, 2023) and curriculum frameworks which are regularly updated. Therefore, it is essential that practitioners know and understand the documentation to implement an effective safeguarding framework in practice.

Chapter summary

Having explored Seamus' reflections and Munro's (2011) framework on 'Doing the right thing' versus 'Doing things right' it is possible to recognise some of the challenges and ethical considerations faced by practitioners in safeguarding children and young people. Developing your leadership in safeguarding practice requires you to understand statutory guidance, critically reflect upon your assumptions and biases and to create communities of practice which prioritise the best interests of children.

Claire's example highlights the impact that confidence in one's own safeguarding practice can have. Her case study highlights that practitioners must aspire to strike a balance between adherence to procedures and prioritising the best interests of the child. She does this by fostering a culture of vigilance, professional curiosity, and advocacy to ensure children's voices are heard and their welfare is safeguarded. For you to develop your practice in this way, knowledge and understanding of current statutory frameworks and up-to-date learning from CSPRs will be essential. However, crucially, safeguarding practice does not happen in isolation from others and so creating and engaging with the communities of practice surrounding children and their families will be a key aspect of your role as a leader of practice. This is explored further in the next chapter.

Further reading

Frost (2021) provides a guide for professional to safeguard children and young people, including the historical context of safeguarding and child protection. A 'whole systems' approach is examined, offering practitioners support in practice.

Gallagher and Sutton-Tsang (2017) examine the responsibilities that we hold as practitioners and the level of expectation matched to the level of study for students on an Early Years degree, from 'Compliance with procedures' to 'Taking critical action to safeguarding children's well-being' to 'Becoming critically reflective practitioners', providing a framework for understanding professional's responsibilities within a network for safeguarding.

✑ References

Bolton, G (2010) *Reflective practice: Writing and professional development*. Thousand Oaks, CA: Sage.

Brighton and Hove Local Safeguarding Children Board (2017) *Working together to improve professional curiosity*. [Online] Available at: www.bhscp.org.uk/wp-content/uploads/sites/3/2019/11/Professional-Curiosity-Bulletin.pdf (accessed 17 July 2024).

Buckler, R (2023) *Developing child-centred practice for safeguarding and child protection: strategies for every early years setting*. 1st ed. London: Routledge.

Darlington Safeguarding Partnership (2021) *Professional challenge procedure and practice guidance (child and adult)*. [Online] Available at: www.darlington-safeguarding-partnership.co.uk/media/2024/professional-challenge-practice-guidance-feb-2021-dsp-12-final.pdf (accessed 17 July 2024).

Data Protection Act (2018) *c. 12*. [Online] Available at: www.legislation.gov.uk/ukpga/2018/12/contents/enacted (accessed 26 July 2024).

Davies, L and Duckett, N (2016) *Proactive child protection and social work*. London: Learning Matters/Sage.

Department for Education (2016) *Wood report: Review of the role and functions of the Local Safeguarding Children boards*. Available at: https://assets.publishing.service.gov.uk/media/5a80676fe5274a2e8ab4ff28/Alan_Wood_review.pdf (accessed 12 September 2024).

Department for Education (DfE) (2024) *Keeping children safe in education: Statutory guidance for schools and colleges*. [Online] Available at: https://assets.publishing.service.gov.uk/media/66d7301b9084b18b95709f75/Keeping_children_safe_in_education_2024.pdf

Frost, N (2021) *Safeguarding children and young people: A guide for professionals working together*. London: Sage Publications.

Gallagher, S and Sutton-Tsang, S (2017) Safeguarding: Understanding your responsibilities, in Musgrave, J, Savin-Baden, M, and Stobbs, N (eds) *Studying for your early years degree: Skills and knowledge for becoming an effective practitioner*. St Albans: Critical Publishing.

HM Government (2023) *Working together to safeguard children: A guide to multi-agency working to help protect and promote the welfare of children*. [Online] Available at: https://assets.publishing.service.gov.uk/media/65cb4349a7ded0000c79e4e1/Working_together_to_safeguard_children_2023_-_statutory_guidance.pdf (accessed 17 July 2024).

Keeling, J and Goosey, D (2021) *Safeguarding across the life span*. London: Sage Publications Ltd.

Lock, R (2013) *Coventry safeguarding children board serious case review: Re Daniel Pelka*. [Online] Available at: https://library.nspcc.org.uk/HeritageScripts/Hapi.dll/filetransfer/2013Coventry DanielPelkaOverview.pdf?filename=CC18C70DB7C8C3D49403BB94EB176F95207E5F662 35DCA89651F5ED2BA5DA9311A353B626FC11241A3DF9A45C446BB4D1ABAD04545542 F86BCD0195126CC3B3355977BB90D159C20EA09AB8B5D55192BEA9DB46F331CEBEE8 ACF9AC1744AA56434C44487&DataSetName=LIVEDATA (accessed 24 July 2024).

McNellie, J (2017) *A culture of safeguarding*. [Online] Available at: www.birmingham.gov.uk/downloads/file/6050/ofsted_asm_notes_spring_2017 (accessed 24 July 2024).

Mistry, M and Sood, K (2015) Why are there Still so Few Men within Early Years in Primary Schools: Views from Male Trainee Teachers and Male Leaders? *Education 3–13,* 43(2): 115–127. https://doi-org.apollo.worc.ac.uk/10.1080/03004279.2012.759607.

Munro, E (2011) *The Munro review of child protection: Final Report, A child-centred system.* [Online] Available at: https://assets.publishing.service.gov.uk/media/5a7b455ee5274a34770ea939/Munro-Review.pdf (accessed 17 July 2024).

Murray, M (2019) *Child safeguarding practice review: Overview report: Child Ab. Northamptonshire: Northamptonshire Safeguarding Children Partnership.* [Online] Available at: https://library.nspcc.org.uk/HeritageScripts/Hapi.dll/retrieve2?SetID=044C09FD-E0A3-4469-B0ED-C7B987C6123F&SearchTerm0=child%20Ab&SearchPrecision=10&SortOrder=Y1&Offset=1&Direction=%2E&Dispfmt=F&Dispfmt_b=B27&Dispfmt_f=F13&DataSetName=LIVEDATA (accessed 24 July 2024).

NSPCC Learning (2021) *Early years sector: Learning from case reviews.* [Online] Available at: https://learning.nspcc.org.uk/media/2704/learning-from-case-reviews-early-years-sector.pdf (accessed 20 July 2024).

NSPCC Learning (2024) *The voice of the child: Learning from case reviews.* [Online] Available at: https://learning.nspcc.org.uk/research-resources/learning-from-case-reviews/voice-child (accessed 17 July 2024).

Parliament House of Commons (2011) *Uncorrected Transcript of Oral Evidence to be published as HC 1312-i.* (Session 2010-12.) Available at: https://publications.parliament.uk/pa/cm201012/cmselect/cmeduc/uc1312-i/uc131201.htm (Accessed: 12 September 2024).

Race, T and Frost, N (2022) Hearing the Voice of the Child in Safeguarding Processes: Exploring Different Voices and Competing Narratives. *Child Abuse Review,* 31: 1–9. https://doi.org/10.1002/car.2779

Reder, P, Duncan, S and Gray, M (1993) *Beyond blame: Child abuse tragedies revisited.* London: Routledge

Staunton, A (2016) *Serious case review: CN11 'Bonnie': overview report.* [Online] Available at: https://library.nspcc.org.uk/HeritageScripts/Hapi.dll/retrieve2?SetID=D6D02469-A4B6-4F85-A0A4-7E35E2210EC2&SearchTerm0=bonnie&SearchPrecision=10&SortOrder=Y1&Offset=5&Direction=%2E&Dispfmt=F&Dispfmt_b=B27&Dispfmt_f=F13&DataSetName=LIVEDATA (accessed 24 July 2024).

The Child Safeguarding Practice Review Panel (2022) *Child Protection in England: National review into the murders of Arthur Labinjo-Hughes and Star Hobson.* [Online] Available at: https://assets.publishing.service.gov.uk/media/628e262d8fa8f556203eb4f8/ALH_SH_National_Review_26-5-22.pdf (accessed 24 July 2024).

Wonnacott, J (2013) *Serious case review under Chapter VIII 'Working Together to Safeguard Children' in respect of the Serious Injury of Case No.2010-11/3.* [Online] Available at: www.wigan.gov.uk/Docs/PDF/WSCB/Published-Overview-Report.pdf (accessed 24 July 2024).

UNICEF (no date) *A summary of the UN Convention on the rights of the child.* [Online] Available at: www.unicef.org.uk/wp-content/uploads/2019/10/UNCRC_summary-1_1.pdf (accessed 24 July 2024).

8 Childhood: it's their world – a global and sustainable approach

Alison Prowle and Janet Harvell

This chapter gives practitioners the opportunity to consider what it means to be a child, and a citizen of the world, from a global perspective. Contemporary theory and international/global approaches will be explored. There will be an opportunity to explore the impact that different cultures can have on children and their early childhood experiences and how different cultural practices challenge traditional (Western) theories of child development. You will be encouraged to develop an awareness of some of the challenges faced by many children globally, including the rights of refugees/displaced people. You will be encouraged to investigate how international approaches have influenced pedagogy and consider your own practice in light of developing understanding.

Chapter objectives

This chapter will:

- Consider what it means to be a child, and a citizen of the world, from a global perspective

- Explore how different cultural practices challenge traditional (Western) theories of child development

- Develop an awareness of some of the challenges faced by many children globally, including the rights of refugees/displaced people

- Investigate how international approaches have influenced pedagogy and practice.

DOI: 10.4324/9781041055358-13

Introduction

As discussed in Chapter 1 there is no typical childhood. When reflecting on this from a global perspective, it is particularly relevant when considering the increasingly diverse cultures experienced by children attending settings in the UK. The multicultural environments that we inhabit, and the diversity of the families that we interact with, reflect the importance of ensuring that we gain a holistic understanding of the children and families that we work with.

The importance of early childhood experiences and their impact on children's futures is recognised globally and, over the years, there has been a significant international focus on providing access to quality early childhood provision. This has been informed by Becker's (1964) Human Capital Theory (cited in CIPD, 2017), which recognises the impact of employee knowledge and education for business (and ultimately a country's) success. Consequently, the early years are seen as key to providing children with a strong foundation that will benefit them in adulthood, and *'has played a significant role in the development of current education and welfare policies'* (Harvell, 2013, p5). Both authors of this chapter have had significant experiences of working with and researching early childhood from a global perspective. Janet spent three years completing research into the early years curriculum and the role of the early years professional in the People's Republic of China, and both authors visited Dunkirk's Grande-Synthe Refugee Camp (France24, nd) twice as part of a personal research project. Alison went on to complete her Doctorate into the refugee experience. These experiences and research have had a significant impact on informing the chapter.

Global strategies

In recent years three key global strategies have been developed. These are Education for All (EFA), the Millennium Goals (MGs) and, more recently, the Sustainable Development Goals (SDGs). Launched in 1990, EFA was focused on achieving universal primary education by 2015 (UNESCO, 2015). However, 15 years later only one-third of 164 countries had achieved these goals and there was concern that the focus on literacy had diverted attention from other critical education areas such as quality, adult literacy and early childhood care (Ni Chonghaile, 2015). Simultaneously, the Millenium Goals which were in place between 2000 and 2015, focused primarily on the eradication of poverty, although this included two goals aligned with achieving universal primary education, the promotion of gender equality and empowerment of women (UN, 2015). These have now been superseded by the 17 Sustainable Development Goals (UN, nd) with a wider remit to reduce extreme poverty and inequality, whilst also recognising the critical need to protect our planet. Now, nine years later, there is some concern around current progress as the legacy from the Covid pandemic, economic crises, conflicts and climate change have detrimentally impacted achievement towards these and consequently progress has been delayed and, in some places, regressed. The previous discussion has identified some of the key global targets that governments have chosen to focus on. Globalisation, and the world's increasing interconnectedness, means that the early years practitioner should be aware of the impact of this when engaging with families within the setting. This is particularly significant when considering that childhood is a social construct, which is informed and created by children's unique culture (Montgomery, 2022).

The impact of conflict and climate change will be discussed later in the chapter.

Culture and gender equality

When considering culture, it is helpful to consider what we mean by the term. Although often incorrectly associated with 'race', any group of individuals can have, and develop, their own culture. Culture comprises the characteristics and knowledge of a particular group of people and can include difference in language, religion, food, social habits, music and arts. Diversity within the UK offers the potential to benefit from the richness of a range of cultural influences, especially within our local communities. This next section will explore the issues around culture and gender, stimulating a deeper understanding of what makes the children and families we work with who they are. Robert and Sarah LeVine (2019, p1) recognise that whilst such deep reflection supports professionals in recognising the diverse experiences that children bring with them, it also encourages the professional to 'question [their] own understanding of children's worlds'.

Although there will be many shared values, it is inevitable that there will be differences between cultures, and it is important for the early years professional to recognise and value these diversities. Some cultural practices such as different cuisines, faiths, festivals and language, are easily recognised, but there are many aspects of culture that are not as obvious. In 1976, Edward Hall identified the concept of the 'Cultural Iceberg'.

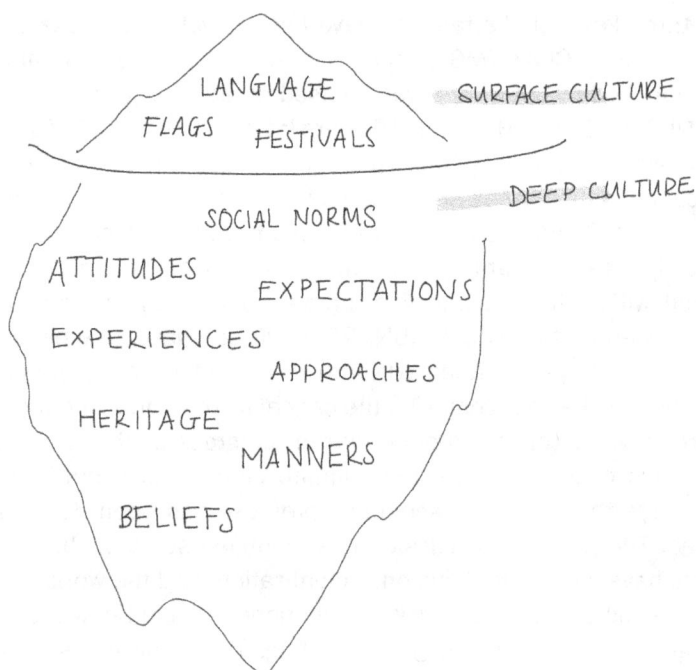

Figure 8.1 *Cultural Iceberg adapted from Hall (1976)*

This recognised that only 10% of a person's culture is visible (surface culture), with 90% of what informs a culture being hidden beneath the surface (deep culture) (BCCIE, 2024). This 'deep culture' reflects some of the attitudes, ideas, beliefs and communication styles that may not be so obvious. LeVine and LeVine (2019) discuss the importance of understanding such deep cultural influences as these will inform the way that parents engage with their children in their earliest years. For example, they explore the value that American families place on promoting early language and engaging in conversation (LeVine and LeVine 2019, p7), whilst Pascal Ferla (2019, p116) reflects that the focus on language in the early years is very much a Western value, and that in African cultures 'interactions with extended family are more significant'. In contrast, the experience of many Chinese children during the infamous one child policy era resulted in the 'Little Emperor syndrome', with only children being spoiled by both grandparents and parents who focused all their hopes and aspirations on one child; often referred to as the 4-2-1 generation (Harvell and Ren, 2019). One extreme example of this was observed during Janet's visits to China where a three-year-old child was still not walking independently because of being carried everywhere by her family. Similarly, staff often talked about poor social skills of the children, and the tensions with grandparents who were keen for their grandchildren to receive homework and attend additional study sessions; this was due to intense competition for entrance into selective schools, including primary, which was based on entrance test scores. This has become such a significant issue across education in China that the government recently introduced a range of policies to limit extra-curricular tuition in key subjects of Chinese, English and Maths, suspending *'online and offline tutoring for classes for children from kindergarten to 9th grade'* (Ye, 2021, cited in Harvell 2024, p127).

Other concerns may be related to sleep routines, food and mealtimes (to name a few), and it is important that settings provide opportunities for the families to share and explore this. I can recall one example from my early career when a young Muslim child who attended the setting refused to use the toilet. When speaking with his parents, we realised that at home he was used to using running water as part of the toilet routine and between us we identified that we could use a bottle of water to support his cultural needs. It worked!

Such differences demonstrate the importance of getting to know your children and families. Different cultural expectations informed by different values and priorities impact on the way that children are 'viewed' and the cultural capital they bring with them. The Early Years Alliance (2019, np) defines cultural capital as *'the essential knowledge that children need to prepare them for their future success … giving children the best possible start to their early education'*. These influence their interactions, behaviours and communications (deep culture). The greater your knowledge and understanding, the more you can empathise with, understand and support the range of children, families and colleagues that you will encounter.

The role of gender can also be significantly impacted by the dominant culture and is recognised within Sustainable Development Goal 5 which promotes the achievement of gender equality and the empowerment of all women and girls, recognising that *'gender equality is not only a fundamental human right, but a necessary foundation for a peaceful, prosperous and sustainable world'* (UN, 2023, np).

Although research by Dorius and Firebough in 2010 (cited in Robinson, 2024) concluded that there has been a decline in gender inequalities, current discourse recognises the significant detrimental impact that the Covid pandemic has had on the progress of many of the SDGs, including gender equality. As a result, it is now predicted that it will take 300 years to end child marriage (one in five females marry before their 18th birthday), 286 years to end discriminatory laws and 140 years before equality in leadership is achieved in the workplace (UN, 2023).

The previous data illustrate that gender equality in education continues to be a significant issue, with a focus on barriers to schooling for girls; indeed, three-quarters of children at risk of never going to school are girls. Consequently, UNESCO (2021) predicts that nine million girls aged six to 11 worldwide will never go to school, compared to approximately three million boys. Nevertheless, global progress towards gender parity in schools has progressed significantly over the last 25 years, with the enrolment of girls in primary and secondary education having increased by 180 million over this period, including 69 million in sub-Saharan Africa UNESCO (2021). With that said, it is important that we do not become blinkered to gender being just a feminine issue. Expectations for young men to earn an income can also lead to them dropping out of school, and many may never attend school as they are relied upon to help their families (UNESCO, 2021). Indeed, Chiu (2021) highlights a study into gender inequality in 14 low-income countries which found that boys were more likely to report hardships including physical neglect, violence and sexual abuse. Chiu (2021) goes on to criticise the current SDG indicators for ignoring men and boys. This also has an impact on men later in life as 'the only group where life expectancy has gone down is white men over 50, mainly due to self-directed violence and access to guns' (Chiu 2021, np). Although these issues are of real concern, the refugee situation and the impact of climate change on children are rapidly taking a key position in urgent challenges that need to be addressed by international policy.

Challenges facing children globally

At the same time, it is important to recognise that the developed countries also have their share of challenges. We live in a world that is fraught with inequalities. In high-income countries, some children have better healthcare, education and enjoy more opportunities than ever. However, even in affluent countries, a large proportion of children live in poverty and are faced with multiple adversity (Prowle and Hodgkins, 2020). In 2023, within the UK, 30% of children were deemed to be living in relative poverty, with 25% considered to be in absolute poverty, after housing costs (Brown, 2024). The relationship between poverty and wider adversity is complex and multifaceted (Prowle and Musgrave, 2018). A UK study identified that almost half of all children have experienced at least one Adverse Childhood Experience (ACE) and almost 9% have experienced four or more ACEs (Bellis et al. 2014) Examples of ACEs include:

• Physical, sexual or emotional abuse.

• Living with someone who abused drugs or alcohol.

• Exposure to domestic violence.

- Living with someone who has gone to prison.
- Living with someone with serious mental illness.
- Losing a parent through divorce, death or abandonment.

In turn, children who have experienced ACEs are at increased risk of poor physical and mental health, difficulties with social relationships and isolation. The number of ACEs a child has (Rankin and Regan, 2004), and the length of time the child remains in a challenging situation (Prowle and Musgrove, 2018), will determine how profoundly a child's long-term outcomes are affected.

However, when it comes to international comparisons, the inequalities become much greater. UNICEF (2024) has estimated that across the world, a billion children are 'multidimensionally poor', and lack clean water, safe shelter and nutritional food. In turn, poverty can lead to malnutrition, poor health and limited opportunities for future advancement. Millions of children, particularly in low-income countries, are unable to attend school due to factors such as poverty, conflict and discrimination. This limits their future opportunities and perpetuates cycles of poverty. Globally, children face numerous health challenges, including malnutrition, infectious diseases and lack of access to healthcare services (Clark et al. 2020). Vaccination coverage is also uneven, leading to otherwise preventable diseases. Many children are forced into labour, often in hazardous conditions, to help support their families. This interferes with their education and development and exposes them to physical and psychological harm (UNICEF, 2020). As mentioned previously, child marriage remains prevalent in some regions, leading to risky pregnancies, discontinuation of education and severely affecting girls' futures (Jan and Al Azzam, 2024). Recognising that the early years are foundational to children's later outcomes, practitioners are uniquely placed to advocate for all children everywhere to have access to environments and experiences that nurture their growth and potential.

The next sections focus upon two contemporary global challenges which impact disproportionately upon children; namely forced migration and climate change.

Child refugees

Child refugees represent one of the most vulnerable populations globally, facing immense challenges that affect their physical, emotional and psychological well-being. These children are often forced to flee their homes due to war or persecution, leaving behind all that is familiar to them. Abandoning homes, schools and family members, they are often forced to undertake hazardous journeys with risks of exploitation, abuse and trafficking. Around 41% of the world's 108 million refugees are under the age of 18, and an average of 385,000 children were born as refugees each year (Separated Child, 2024). The trauma experienced by child refugees can have long-lasting effects and without proper support, children struggle to rebuild their lives and integrate into new communities (Prowle, 2022). However, it should also be noted that refugee children can demonstrate remarkable resilience. Education can play a critical role in this process, providing not just knowledge but also a sense of hope for the future. Effective programmes should include psychosocial support, legal assistance and opportunities for integration, which help the children to heal and to adapt to their new environment (Harvell and Prowle, 2019). The following case study was drawn from the authors' work in a humanitarian camp in France in 2017. For ethical reasons, the case study does not reflect a real family, but is constructed from our discussions with numerous families at the camp.

❝❝ Case study – Ariya's story part 1

Ariya is six years old, and lives with her mother, father, eight-year-old brother Kiyan and little sister Henar (aged three), in a refugee camp in North France. The family have been in the camp for just over a year having fled Kurdish Iraq, where they were experiencing extreme violence and persecution.

Within the camp, their home is a small wooden hut. They have a tiny stove for cooking and heating and roll-up camping mats for beds. They have access to donated clothes but many of these are ill fitting. Sometimes there are donations of toys. Ariyah has a knitted 'pocket pal' which she was given by a camp volunteer. She loves this teddy and keeps it with her always. Since arriving at the camp, Kiyan has displayed challenging behaviour. His mother worries about how she can keep him safe when he is often running away from her and hiding. There have been reports of children going missing from another camp in North France. A usually confident little girl, Ariya has been suffering from nightmares and bedwetting. Both she and Henar have eczema and asthma.

Ariyah and Kiyan attend school at the camp for one hour a day, where they get to focus on reading, writing and maths. All three children also spend time at the children's centre where they enjoy a range of play and creative activities, provided by camp volunteers.

The family have made several unsuccessful attempts to travel to England where they have relatives. Ariyah describes how they were confronted with police with batons and barking dogs when trying to board a lorry. She is very traumatised by all that she has experienced.

Daily life in the camp is difficult. There are very limited facilities, frequent food shortages and regular police raids. Ariyah's parents are suffering from depression and anxiety. They worry about the safety of relatives who are still in Kurdistan. Despite this, the family remain hopeful that they will be able to settle in England and begin to build a new life for themselves.

🗣🗣 Critical reflection

- What are some of the adversities that the children have faced and how might these impact their well-being in the short and long term?

- Reflect upon the children's lives in relation to the United Nations Convention on the Rights of the Child (UNCRC, 1989). To what extent can they be supported to access their rights in this difficult environment?

- As a practitioner, what do you see as the needs and strengths of the family as they are revealed in this case study?

❝❝ Case study – Ariya's story part 2

Three months after this excerpt, Ariya and her family arrived in the UK, travelling by small boat. They immediately called the police and claimed asylum. Following a short period in Kent, the family have now been housed in the West Midlands. The children are attending a local primary school and Henar is in the day nursery provision on the same site. The school is based in a market town in which there is very little diversity.

Critical reflection

- What things might the children find strange in their new home in the UK? What will help them settle in?

- How could an attuned practitioner work with others in the school and beyond to support the family and to enable the children to begin to heal and rebuild their lives?

- What barriers may you encounter within this work, and how would you address them?

Climate change

It is strongly argued that children are disproportionately affected by climate change. Their physiological developmental and social vulnerabilities make them more susceptible to the adverse effects of changing climate compared to their adult counterparts (WHO, 2024). Children's bodies are still developing and are sensitive to environmental factors such as extreme heat, poor quality air and water pollution. Because their respiratory and immune systems are still maturing, children are more vulnerable to illnesses that are exacerbated by climate change, such as asthma, allergies and infectious diseases. Food insecurity caused by climate disruptions can lead to malnutrition, resulting in restricted growth and developmental delay.

Considering current trends, UNICEF (2021) extrapolates that by 2050, 820 million children could be experiencing heatwaves and droughts whilst 570 million children are exposed to flooding annually. Such disasters can often damage schools and homes, leading to prolonged educational disruptions to children's learning and development. The psychological toll of experiencing such events can result in long-term mental health challenges including anxiety and depression (Crandon et al., 2022). Children in low-income regions who already face significant hardships, are at greatest risk which exacerbates existing inequalities and jeopardises their future well-being and development. It is also worth remembering that children will inherit the long-term consequences of climate change, with environmental degradation and resource scarcity shaping their futures, limiting their opportunities and increasing challenges in their adult lives.

Climate change is a complex, pervasive and multifaceted problem that will require urgent and concerted effort from governments, industries and individuals in order to avoid the worst of its potential impacts. However, practitioners have a role to play in advocating for children's well-being and futures. The practice vignette below, shows how one UK infant school picked up the environmental mantle to become a beacon for hope and activism within their community.

❝ Case study – practice vignette

Victoria Voller is Headteacher of Shere Infant School in Hampshire and has experienced a growing concern about how best to support children to understand and respond to environmental issues. She has worked tirelessly to achieve an Eco School green flag and has promoted a culture of sustainability and eco activism across the school. Children have been encouraged to lobby decision-makers, whilst also adopting their own green practices at home and school. Twice a term, the children take part in *Fridays For Future* (a youth-led movement that began in 2018, after Thunberg and other young activists sat in front of the Swedish parliament to protest against the lack of action on the climate crisis). Here, children come off timetable, to focus entirely on climate issues. Victoria's philosophy is that small actions matter, and we all have a responsibility to do our bit to protect the planet.

When confronted by the enormity of challenges facing children across the world, it would be easy to become overwhelmed and inactive. However, this practice vignette shows how practitioners can model compassionate approaches, inspiring others to join in advocating for a more equitable and sustainable society.

Chapter summary

During this chapter you have been challenged to consider some of the different issues that children might experience from a more global perspective. This is particularly relevant when considering the impact that cultural diversity can have on children's upbringing and the importance for early years practitioners to better understand the effects of this 'Cultural Iceberg'. A significant element of cultural diversity will include the challenges faced when considering gender concerns. Although not solely a female issue, it is generally recognised that females are most disadvantaged when considering expectations and outcomes on a global scale. The chapter ended with some examples of refugee experiences, based upon the authors' experiences. This then led on to a discussion around climate change and the impact on children, whilst providing an example of how one headteacher is supporting the children in her school to become responsible climate activists. We hope that this chapter has encouraged you to examine childhood from a broader viewpoint and, to revisit the words of LeVine and LeVine (2019, p1), who encourage you to 'question [your] own understanding of [different] children's worlds'.

Further reading

Andrew, Y and Fane, J (2019) *The Sociology of Early Childhood. Young Children's Lives and Worlds.* London: Routledge. Chapter 2 *'Becoming ourselves in relationships'*. This explores the roles of relationships in the lives of children, and these relationships are ultimately informed by the culture that children exist within.

Montgomery, H (2022) *Different Cultures, Different Childhoods.* Available at: www.open.edu/openlearn/history-the-arts/history/different-cultures-different-childhoods (Accessed on 27 November 2024).

Sengupta, E and Blessinger, P (2018) *Refugee Education. Integration and Acceptance of Refugees in Mainstream Society.* Bingley: Emerald Publishing.

References

BCCIE (2024) *Hall's Cultural Iceberg.* Available at: https://bccie.bc.ca/wp-content/uploads/2020/09/cultural-iceberg.pdf (Accessed 1 August 2024)

Becker, G S (1964) *Human Capital: A Theoretical and Empirical Analysis, with Special Reference to Education.* New York, Colombia University Press.

Bellis, M, Lowey, H, Leckenby, N, Hughes, K and Harrison, D (2014) Adverse childhood experiences: Retrospective study to determine their impact on adult health behaviours and health outcomes in a UK population. *Journal of Public Health*, 36(1), pp. 81–91.

Brown, T (2024) *Child poverty: Statistics, causes and the UK's policy response.* Available at: https://lordslibrary.parliament.uk/child-poverty-statistics-causes-and-the-uks-policy-response/ (Accessed 13 August 2024).

Chiu, B (2021) *Gender inequality harms not only women and girls, but also men and boys.* Available at: www.forbes.com/sites/bonniechiu/2019/05/28/gender-inequality-harms-not-only-women-and-girls-but-also-men-and-boys/ (Accessed 1 August 2024).

CIPD (2017) *Human capital theory: Assessing the evidence for the value and importance of people to organisational success.* Available at: www.cipd.org/globalassets/media/knowledge/knowledge-hub/reports/human-capital-theory-assessing-the-evidence_tcm18-22292.pdf (Accessed 31 July 2024).

Clark, H, Coll-Seck, A, Banerjee, A, Peterson, S, Dalglish, S, Ameratunga, S, Balabanova, D, Bhan, M, Bhutta, Z, Borrazzo, J and Claeson, M (2020) A future for the world's children? A WHO–UNICEF–Lancet Commission. *The Lancet*, 395(10224), pp. 605–658.

Crandon, T, Scott, J, Charlson, F and Thomas, H (2022) A social–ecological perspective on climate anxiety in children and adolescents. *Nature Climate Change*, 12(2), pp. 123–131.

Early Years Alliance (2003–2019) *Cultural capital in the EIF: What you need to know*. Available at: www.eyalliance.org.uk/cultural-capital-eif-what-you-need-know#:~:text=The%20new%20EIF%20also%20introduces,start%20to%20their%20early%20education (Accessed 10 October 2024).

France24 (nd) Grande-Synthe *The humanitarian camp that France didn't want*. Available at: https://webdoc.france24.com/france-first-humanitarian-camp-grande-synthe/ (Accessed 10 October 2024).

Hall, E T (1976) *Beyond Culture*. Anchor Books, New York.

Harvell, J (2013) *The same ... or different? A comparative study of kindergarten policy and practices in China and England*. Available at: https://core.ac.uk/outputs/96772689/?source=2 (Accessed 1 August 2024).

Harvell, J (2024) Global perspectives on creativity. In Taylor, S. (eds) *Creativity in the Early Years. Engaging Children Aged 0–5*. London, Sage.

Harvell, J and Prowle, A (2019) Reflections on the Lived Experiences of Refugee Children in a French Refugee Camp. *BERA Research Intelligence – Special Edition*, (140), pp. 19–20. ISSN 0307-9023

Harvell, J and Ren, L (2019) It's a new dawn, it's a new day: Developing an early years workforce for a 21st century China. In Pence, A and Harvell, J (eds) *Pedagogies for Diverse Contexts (Thinking about Pedagogy in Early Childhood Education)*. London, Routledge.

Jan, N and Al Azzam, M (2024) Prevalence of child marriages and its socio-economic impacts. *Gwadar Social Sciences Review (University of Gwadar)*, 1(1), pp. 62–70.

LeVine, R and LeVine, S (2019) Precocious children: Cultural priming by parents and others. In Pence, A and Harvell, J (eds) *Pedagogies for Diverse Contexts (Thinking About Pedagogy in Early Childhood Education)*. London, Routledge.

Montgomery, H (2022) *Different cultures, different childhoods*. Available at: www.open.edu/openlearn/history-the-arts/history/different-cultures-different-childhoods (Accessed 29 July 2024).

Ni Chonghaile, C (2015) *Goals set at turn of century have been achieved by only one-third of countries, while just half have made universal primary education a reality, claims report*. In *The Guardian* 9 April 2015. Available at: www.theguardian.com/global-development/2015/apr/09/education-for-all-scheme-failed-meet-targets-unesco (Accessed 11 September 2022).

Pascal Ferla, J (2019) Cultural practices in childrearing in Tanzania and their potential in supporting responsive caregiving to young children. In Pence, A and Harvell, J (eds) *Pedagogies for Diverse Contexts (Thinking about Pedagogy in Early Childhood Education)*. London, Routledge.

Prowle, A (2022) *'Thank you for asking me about my story': An exploration of the perspectives of forced migrant parents, practitioners, and strategic actors in South Wales* (Doctoral dissertation, Cardiff University).

Prowle, A and Hodgkins, A (2020) *Making a Difference with Children and Families: Re-imagining the Role of the Practitioner*. London, Bloomsbury Publishing.

Prowle, A and Musgrave, J (2018) Utilising strengths in families and communities to support children's learning and wellbeing. In Cheeseman, S. and Walker, R (eds) *Pedagogies for Leading Practice* (pp. 125–141). Oxfordshire, Routledge.

Rankin, J and Regan, S (2004) Meeting complex needs in social care. *Housing, Care, and Support*, 7(3), pp.4–8.

Robinson, V (2024) *Gender inequalities: 'Past' issues and future possibilities*. Available at: www.bbvao penmind.com/en/articles/gender-inequalities-past-issues-and-future-possibilities (Accessed 29 July 2024).

Separated Child (2024) *Refugee facts*. Available at: https://separatedchild.org/our-work/refugee-facts/ (Accessed 8 August 2024).

UN (1989) *United Nations Convention on the rights of the child*. Available at: www.unicef.org.uk/wp-cont ent/uploads/2016/08/unicef-convention-rights-child-uncrc.pdf (Accessed 30 August 2024).

UN (2015) *The Millennium Development Goals Report 2015*. Available at: www.un.org/millenni umgoals/2015_MDG_Report/pdf/MDG%202015%20rev%20(July%201).pdf (Accessed 31 July 2024).

UN (2023) *Gender equality: Goal 5. In: The Sustainable Development Goals Report 2023*. Available at: www.un.org/sustainabledevelopment/gender-equality/ (Accessed 29 July 2024).

UN (nd) *The 17 goals*. Available at: https://sdgs.un.org/goals (Accessed 24 July 2024).

UNESCO (2015) *Education for all 2000-2015: Achievements and challenges*. Available at: https://en.unesco.org/gem-report/report/2015/education-all-2000-2015-achievements-and-challen ges (Accessed 31 July 2024).

UNESCO (2021) *Gender equality in education: digging beyond the obvious*. Available at: www.iiep.une sco.org/en/articles/gender-equality-education-digging-beyond-obvious

UNICEF (2020) *Child labour*. Available at: www.unicef.org/protection/child-labour (Accessed 3 August 2024).

UNICEF (2021) The climate crisis is a child rights crisis. Available at: www.unicef.org/media/105376/file/UNICEF-climate-crisis-child-rights-crisis.pdf (accessed on 10.6.25)

UNICEF (2024) Child poverty: Children are more likely to live in poverty than adults. They're also more vulnerable to its effects. Available at: www.unicef.org/social-policy/child-poverty (Accessed 12 August 2024).

World Health Organisation (WHO) (2024) *Children's Environmental Health*. Available at: www.who.int/health-topics/children-environmental-health#tab=tab_2 (Accessed 9 August 2024).

Theme 5
The collaborator

Chapters Nine and Ten will support you in your duties as a collaborator.

Duty 5 To take the lead and provide support in disseminating best practice in the use of observation, assessments and planning to meet children's needs and extend their holistic development within the aspect or environment for which they are responsible.	**Knowledge:** 1 2 3 6 7 8 9 10 11 12 13 15 18 19 21
	Skills: 1 2 3 4 5 6 7 8 9 12 13 14 15 16 18 20 23
	Behaviours: 1 2 3 4 5 6 7 8 9
Duty 9 Reflect and build on practice through ongoing professional enquiry and action research to contribute to the pedagogical approach of their setting. To be accountable for day-to-day practice, longer term planning, management and training within the specific aspect or environment for which they are responsible.	**Knowledge:** 2 3 4 6 7 8 9 10 11 12 13 15 16 17 18
	Skills: 1 2 3 4 5 6 7 9 10 14 15 18 19 21 23
	Behaviours: 1 2 3 4 5 6 7 8 9
Duty 10 Establish engaging, inclusive and collaborative relationships and participate in multiagency meetings. Enable and facilitate practitioners to develop professional relationships with parents, carers and multi-agencies to meet the individual needs of the children.	**Knowledge:** 1 2 3 5 7 8 14 15 16 17 18 19
	Skills: 2 4 11 13 17 18 20 21 22 23 24 25
	Behaviours: 1 2 3 5 6 9

DOI: 10.4324/9781041055358-14

Duty 11 Commit to becoming a reflective practitioner, enhancing skills and knowledge to improve pedagogical practice. Guide and support the development of the reflective practice of others.	**Knowledge:** 1 3 4 5 7 9 10 11 13 17 18 19 20
	Skills: 14 15 21
	Behaviours: 1 2 5 6 9
Duty 12 Initiate continuing professional development opportunities in response to identification of strengths and weaknesses both personally and within your team. Provide constructive feedback on points of practice on an informal day to day basis and contribute to formal performance management as necessary.	**Knowledge:** 11 17 18 19 20
	Skills: 15 16 21 22 23
	Behaviours: 2 3 5 6 9
Duty 15 Work in collaborative partnership with parents and carers in the planning, implementation and review of strategies in place to support children's experience, holistic development, learning and progress.	**Knowledge:** 2 3 4 7 8 10 13 14 15 16 21
	Skills: 1 4 5 6 8 9 11 12 14 18 19 23 24 25 26
	Behaviours: 1 3 4 7 8 9

9 Leading change, practice within organisations

Emma Laurence

Having identified yourself as a leader of practice within Chapters Three and Four, this chapter identifies the importance of the relationships within the team to support not only children and families but also one another in this line of work. Throughout this chapter models of teamwork, social capital and capacity building within organisations will be highlighted, as well as the impact of these in creating a shared vision for practice, making sense of policy and ultimately, driving quality improvement.

Chapter objectives

- To identify the need for collaboration and teamwork in leadership practice
- To explore the significance of a shared vision in driving improvement
- To identify the importance of social capital and psychological safety in creating meaningful change.

Introduction

In the world of early years education, the strength of the relationships within a team plays a vital role in shaping the experiences of children, families and professionals alike. A cohesive, supportive team not only fosters a nurturing environment for children but also ensures that professionals can rely on one another as they navigate the challenges and rewards of this field.

This chapter builds on the leadership understandings in Chapter 4 and delves into the significance of teamwork in early years settings. It explores how strong relationships within organisations can promote shared understanding and mutual support. We shift our thinking from leader development towards leader*ship* development, emphasising the space between

DOI: 10.4324/9781041055358-15

people who work together as being key to making the magic of EY practice happen. Theoretical models of teamwork, social capital, and capacity building will be examined, offering insights into how these concepts can be applied to develop collaborative practices. Through this lens, we will uncover strategies for building teams that not only support one another but also drive transformative outcomes for children and families.

The story we're told about leaders

As was discussed in Chapter 4, throughout history there has been a conscious shift away from the initial heroic notions of leadership which underpin the 'great man' theory (Carlyle, 1841). Despite this however, there are many aspects of this now debunked concept which linger on. In education and care, leaders are often still positioned as solitary figures with exceptional abilities who single-handedly drive success and overcome challenges. This view tends to emphasise authority, individual decision-making, and personal charisma, portraying leaders as saviours or visionaries capable of transforming outcomes through sheer determination (Tourish, 2019). While this perspective might be inspiring, it overlooks the collaborative and relational nature of leadership in modern educare settings. It risks creating unsustainable expectations for leaders, fostering dependency rather than empowerment among teams and marginalising the contributions of others. In the context of early years education and care, such a model is particularly ill-suited, as it fails to acknowledge the importance of shared leadership, collective capacity building, and the intricate web of relationships that underpin quality practice.

Throughout the last number of years, the sector continues to be challenged by socio-political turbulence and there appear to be two contrasting narratives regarding leaders in education and the early years. These stories describe the '*services of a saint, a workaholic with no family commitments or at any rate someone with superhuman qualities*' (Orchard, 2002, p159) and at the same time a workforce that are pretty much on their knees, emotionally exhausted, suffering chronic stress and high rates of burnout, which result in a retention and recruitment crisis. Whilst it seems impossible that these two narratives can co-exist, it is my view that they are in fact intrinsically linked. When we super-humanise leaders, we also dehumanise them and do not anticipate that they should suffer normal human fallibility.

The challenges facing the sector are not to be underestimated, out of challenge often come stories of hope and opportunities to learn about how we might nurture our adaptive capacities and create powerful communities in the face of adversity. Central to this however, is that our success as a species is so often attributed to how inherently social we are. We have all seen those goosebump-inducing videos where strangers come together to do the impossible and when you look closely, most stories of hope involve people relying on each other. Be it the gentle and persistent support of one meaningful relationship or an inspirational mass movement, people need people. It is therefore clear that whilst many resources continue to be squeezed, the most significant (and often overlooked) resource we have available in tackling these issues and in nurturing the resilience of the workforce is the humanity within it. It is crucial that we seek to challenge the superhuman narratives which prioritise holding individual leaders single-handedly responsible for all outcomes and instead seek to create communities of practice which nurture each other as well as the children and families they serve.

Leader development and leader*ship* development

In Chapter 4 we identified the early years practitioner as inherently holding a position of leadership. You were encouraged to consider your own skills and attitudes as an emerging leader and how these might be developed. We also noted that leadership is now understood to not exclusively reside within high-calibre individuals but to instead constitute an interaction which happens in the spaces between people who create shared momentum in the direction of improvement. However, despite this shift in understanding, most of what we see in terms of leadership development focuses on teachable skills which an individual can adopt in order to become more assertive, more decisive, or all around more effective in getting others to do what they want. That is, it often reflects the individualistic trait approach to leadership (Cullen-Lester et al., 2017) and fails to acknowledge its relational nature as an interactive process. Whilst individual skills and behaviours are important to nurture, there is an underlying assumption here that others in setting are passive objects devoid of their own ideas. This assumption deeply undermines the potential that multiple perspectives offer as well as the development of cultures which mutually nourish the capacity of all individuals.

In order to do this, there are key distinctions to be made between leader development and leader*ship* development, so that both can be considered in a comprehensive programme to nurture communities of practice. Leader development emphasises enhancing the individual skills, competencies, and self-awareness of a person in a leadership role. It is centred on personal growth, such as improving decision-making, emotional intelligence, and communication abilities. In contrast, leader*ship* development focuses on the collective capacity of a group or organisation to lead effectively. It involves building systems, fostering collaboration, and aligning strategies to ensure that teams or networks work together to achieve common goals. By balancing leader development with leadership development, early years settings can empower individuals while ensuring the entire team works cohesively to support children's learning and well-being.

This means that thinking within leadership development needs to shift to consider not only 'leaders' but also followers, dyads, and larger collectives within an organisation (Cullen-Lester et al., 2017). Leadership development from this collective perspective is about developing the social capital within systems: promoting cooperation, mutual respect, and trust between actors as central to system efficacy (Day and O'Connor, 2003, p 22). O'Connor and Quinn (2004) consider the promotion of the quality of these connections to be a key feature of leadership development. Where Chapter 4 supported you in your own journey of development as a leader, this chapter will now consider how you can contribute to the development of social capital and collective leadership in communities within which you work.

Leadership and a shared vision

A shared vision is a cornerstone of excellence in early childhood education and care (ECEC). It provides a unifying framework that guides educators, external professionals, families, and stakeholders in their collective efforts to support the holistic development of young children. By establishing a shared vision, ECEC settings create a sense of purpose and direction, ensuring that all actions and decisions align with common goals that prioritise children's well-being, learning, and growth.

In the dynamic and collaborative environment of early childhood education, a shared vision fosters consistency and coherence. It ensures that all members of the community understand and commit to the same values and objectives. For instance, a shared vision may emphasise the importance of play-based learning, inclusion, and fostering a love for lifelong learning. When everyone – from educators to management – operates within this framework, it minimises confusion and promotes consistent practices, even in diverse or complex settings. This coherence not only benefits staff but also enhances the experiences of children and families, who experience a seamless and aligned approach to care and education.

A shared vision also empowers and motivates staff. When early years practitioners understand and believe in the collective goals of their setting, they are more likely to feel a sense of purpose and satisfaction in their roles. This shared sense of purpose can inspire collaboration, innovation, and a commitment to professional growth. For example, early years practitioners may feel encouraged to share ideas, support one another, and engage in reflective practices that advance the quality of their provision. The shared vision acts as a compass, reminding practitioners of the broader impact of their work and fostering a sense of belonging and community.

Another critical benefit of a shared vision is its role in strengthening relationships with families and the wider community. Families are key partners in a child's learning journey, and a shared vision creates a foundation for meaningful collaboration. When families understand and align with the values and goals of the ECEC setting, they are more likely to engage actively in their child's education and development. Clear communication of the shared vision – through policies and programmes but also through everyday interactions – helps build trust and mutual respect between families and early years professionals. This alignment can extend to community partnerships, ensuring that local resources and services support the overarching goals of the ECEC setting.

In practice, developing and maintaining a shared vision requires intentional effort. Leaders play a crucial role in facilitating discussions and encouraging input from all stakeholders. This collaborative process ensures that the vision reflects diverse perspectives and remains relevant to the needs of the community. Regular reflection and review are also essential to adapt the vision as children, families, and societal expectations evolve. By fostering an inclusive process, ECEC settings can ensure that the shared vision remains a living, dynamic guide for action.

However, a shared vision is more than just a mission statement; it is a commitment to a mutual moral purpose. In the ECEC sector a shared vision provides the clarity and cohesion needed to create meaningful, positive outcomes for children, families, and communities.

❝ Case study – telling a new story

Having started her new role as a Headteacher to an underperforming primary school setting, Lisa noticed that many of the families were disengaged, and the staff appeared to feel anxious and unmotivated about their roles. Through initial discussions it became clear that they felt they weren't valued and that their work was making little difference to anyone except their own families, who they didn't see enough of. Lisa felt that the story of this school had become lost and that without it there was very little beyond the brick walls and the timetable that was holding people together. She began by hosting a collaborative session with all of the staff entitled 'My wish for this school', where they began to map out what their vision was for the new chapter that the school was embarking on. She felt it was important that this vision belonged to everyone, so she invited everyone to this meeting, the cleaners, the lunchtime staff, the lollipop lady, the groundskeeper as well as all the teaching and support staff. She made it clear that she wanted every person to have a voice in the direction of the school. Having gathered these ideas, the team then got to work on identifying five key values which underpinned this vision, these were: Community, Strengths, Safe, Generous, and Ambitious. Once they had identified their vision and values the next step was to embody this, to help others to see it and to make it something that the entire community could believe in. One of the ways that Lisa did this was through the weekly school newsletter. In week 1 of the new term they identified the school vision and values and invited children, their families and school staff to attend the school on an autumn Saturday to help repaint the corridors. Instead of using the school budget for painters and decorators, she used a small amount to buy paints and order pizzas, and used the strength and generosity of the community to enhance the space for their children. Whilst there is some slightly shabby edging in in places, the following newsletter told the story of a corridor full of music and chatter as a community came together to create a beautiful space for their children. The opportunity created new connections and gave families a new sense of ownership over the children's school. Lisa has since had offers from parents to paint the fences outside and to create a community garden with the children.

This case study highlights that it is not enough to develop a mission statement for the setting website, a shared vision has to be constantly negotiated, renegotiated, and embodied by all members of staff. Lisa has co-constructed a vision of provision with her professional community and then has created the opportunity to exercise that vision. She then uses this event as evidence to promote the vision further. This shared sense of purpose creates a unifying identity for the community as its members have a quantifiable role to play which is clearly valued.

Teamwork and collaboration

Teamwork and collaboration are integral to success in education and the early years, where a collective approach is essential for providing high-quality education and care. Effective teamwork ensures that early years practitioners can share insights, strategies, and responsibilities, creating a supportive environment for both staff and children. This allows practitioners to pool their diverse skills and perspectives, fostering innovative solutions to challenges and enriching the learning experience for children. Strong teamwork also promotes consistency in practices, ensuring that children experience a seamless provision and develop a sense of trust in their environment.

For the last number of decades legislation and policy increasingly emphasised the need for increased collaboration, driven by the varying rationales of holistic support and cost-effective, efficient provision. By working together and maintaining open communication, early years practitioners can build a positive and cohesive culture around children and their families. There are of course significant challenges to collaboration in the early years which should not be overlooked. These include limited resources in terms of time, money and staffing, communication issues, role confusion, and differing professional priorities as well as more interpersonal difficulties. Some of these issues are more difficult to overcome than others. However, by developing this aspect of your practice you will not just be able to better support in-setting teamwork, but this will also provide you with transferrable skills for working in partnership with parents, families, or external professionals.

⌬ Critical reflection

Think about the teams you have been a part of. These could be in your workplace, in your cohort in college or university, or even in your family.

Pick one of these teams and create a diagram which represents this team. What shape does your diagram take? What connections does each person have? Where do you fit in your team? Keep this drawing, as we will reflect again on this later in this chapter.

The terms teamwork, collaboration, and partnerships are often used somewhat interchangeably without much distinction drawn. Whilst some scholars (for example Carnwell and Carson, 2009) argue that there are significant differences between the terms which have implications for what they look like in practice, each team, partnership, or community of practice is idiosyncratic in response to its members and their context. With that said, the term collaboration generally describes a way of working with others which can be applied to a wide range of both formal and informal situations. It is non-hierarchical and values experience, contextualised understanding, and expertise over formal roles or qualification. Whereas the terms partnership and teams tend to refer to more formally recognised groups which may be subject to hierarchies, power imbalances, or external accountability measures. Teams and partnerships can therefore vary enormously in terms of their ability to collaborate meaningfully.

Group formation

In 1965, Bruce Tuckman developed a four-stage model of group formation or team development (Figure 9.1). He called the four stages: Forming, Storming, Norming, and Performing. These stages have stood the test of time and are still considered relevant today. You may be thinking that this theory does not apply to your team in setting because you formed as a team a long time ago. However, you will still find this theory useful because Tuckman's theory explains how the group dynamics and performance of the team can regularly change. As you probably know from experience, a team can be working together smoothly and then someone says or does something which upsets the teamwork.

Figure 9.1   *Tuckman's (1965) stages of group development*

Forming

Individual members meet for the first time as a group. There is likely to be anxiety about meeting new people, expectations, and how to fit into the group. Individuals may feel uncertain about their position in the group and/or the task and will look to the leader for direction and guidance related to decision-making. Trust may start to be built.

Storming

Individuals begin to feel more confident of their position in the group and the task in hand. A number of individuals will put forward their opinions which may cause disagreement and conflict. Sub-groups may start to form at this stage.

Norming

The group begins to form a consensus about how they operate and what they are doing. Differences are talked through to achieve the best for everyone – win–win. Trust and relationships start to develop further as people begin to feel clearer about their position or role in the group. Mutual respect underpins the group's processes.

Performing

The group becomes a team working together for the common good and common goal. Discussion and decision-making become easier as the level of trust increases and relationships develop. This is the stage where the most work is achieved or completed. The team trust each other enough for some decisions to be delegated to sub-teams or individuals.

However, even well-established teams can quickly return to the storming stage should a strong disagreement occur, or other factors which might disrupt the team spirit. Groups can also return to the Forming Stage if new members join the team.

Belbin's team roles

Belbin's (1993) research showed that the most successful teams were made up of a diverse mix of behaviours. He makes the comparison with sports teams, highlighting that one excellent goalkeeper is invaluable but a team of 11 of them would likely not do very well. He identifies nine clusters of behaviour needed to facilitate team performance – the nine team roles.

Each role reveals a unique approach to successful teamwork and interpersonal relations, shaping the way an individual contributes to and behaves within a team. The nine team roles are identified in Table 9.1, adapted from Belbin and Brown (2022).

Table 9.1 Belbin's team roles (adapted from Belbin and Brown, 2022)

Role	Strengths	Weakness	Don't be surprised if
Plant Tends to be highly creative and good at solving problems in unconventional ways.	Creative, imaginative, free-thinking, generates ideas and solves difficult problems.	Might ignore incidentals and may be too preoccupied to communicate effectively.	They could be absent-minded or forgetful.
Resource Investigator Uses their inquisitive nature to find ideas to bring back to the team.	Outgoing, enthusiastic. Explores opportunities and develops contacts.	Might be over-optimistic, and can lose interest once the initial enthusiasm has passed.	They might forget to follow up on a lead.
Coordinator Needed to focus on the team's objectives, draw out team members and delegate work appropriately.	Mature, confident, identifies talent. Clarifies goals.	Can be seen as manipulative and might offload their own share of the work.	They might over-delegate, leaving themselves little work to do.

Table 9.1 (Cont.)

Role	Strengths	Weakness	Don't be surprised if
Shaper Provides the necessary drive to ensure that the team keeps moving and does not lose focus or momentum.	Challenging, dynamic, thrives on pressure. Has the drive and courage to overcome obstacles.	Can be prone to provocation, and may sometimes offend people's feelings.	They could risk becoming aggressive and bad-humoured in their attempts to get things done.
Monitor Evaluator Provides a logical eye, making impartial judgements where required and weighs up the team's options in a dispassionate way.	Thoughtful, strategic and discerning. Sees all options and judges accurately.	Sometimes lacks the drive and ability to inspire others and can be overly critical.	They could be slow to come to decisions.
Team worker Helps the team to gel, using their versatility to identify the work required and complete it on behalf of the team.	Cooperative, perceptive and diplomatic. Listens and averts friction.	Can be indecisive in crunch situations and tends to avoid confrontation.	They might be hesitant to make unpopular decisions.
Implementor Needed to plan a workable strategy and carry it out as efficiently as possible.	Practical, reliable, efficient. Turns ideas into actions and organises work that needs to be done.	Can be a bit inflexible and slow to respond to new possibilities.	They might be slow to relinquish their plans in favour of positive changes.
Completer finisher Most effectively used at the end of tasks to polish and scrutinise the work for errors, subjecting it to the highest standards of quality control.	Painstaking, conscientious, anxious. Searches out errors. Polishes and perfects.	Can be inclined to worry unduly, and reluctant to delegate.	They could be accused of taking their perfectionism to extremes.
Specialist Brings in-depth knowledge of a key area to the team.	Single-minded, self-starting and dedicated. They provide specialist knowledge and skills.	Tends to contribute on a narrow front and can dwell on the technicalities.	They overload you with information.

Social capital, psychological safety, and teams

Many of us will have experienced workplaces and social settings which make us feel as though we should put our guard up. The result of this can be individuals protecting vested interests and a fear of failure. This can not only hinder creativity and innovation but can also allow problems to go unchecked or become exacerbated. It can mean that people work in isolation, not understanding each other's roles and not able to garner support or benefit from a community of practice. As has been highlighted, a key difference between leader development and leader*ship* development is the promotion of cooperation, mutual respect, and trust between people: collectively understood as social capital.

Research shows that social capital helps people to emotionally regulate, manage stress, and remain resilient in the face of adversity (Holmes et al., 2020; Van Bavel et al., 2020). Szreter and Woolcock (2004) identify three dimensions of social capital which support us in understanding the multi-dimensional nature of our social worlds. These include:

- **bonding social capital** between 'people like us' who are 'in it together' (Claridge, 2018, p2)

- **bridging social capital** 'between people who know that they are not alike' (Szreter and Woolcock, 2004, p655), and

- **linking social capital** between people who are 'interacting across explicit, formal or institutionalised power or authority gradients in society' (Szreter and Woolcock, 2004, p655).

It is generally understood that all three types of social capital are required for effective adaptivity and sustainability of a system/organisation. The extent to which capital is bridging or bonding is not static and depends upon the way that actors are relating to each other in a given interaction. Are we multiple different but equal social actors who are working together – bridging? Or are we all part of one shared setting identity – bonding? It is most likely that there are elements of both of these in many of the interactions we have in setting. Conversely, some settings may suffer a weak sense of shared identity due to differences in values or ways of working. This might mean there is very little bonding social capital. Within the education sector, an example of linking social capital might be between the manager and the people they manage or the setting and the Department for Education or Ofsted.

The following two school profiles illustrate the potential for quite stark differences in the resources available to education and care settings in terms of social capital.

❝❝ Case study example – social capital in education settings

School A is a small church school in a rural area. The Headteacher is also the DSL, SENCo and subject lead for English, IT and Music. The senior leadership team is made up of the Headteacher, a Deputy Headteacher who is also the year 2 class teacher and the Assistant Headteacher who teaches year 4. The Headteacher has the Local Authority Headteacher briefings to keep them informed of changes. Hundreds of headteachers attend these; they are conducted online with cameras and microphones off. There is also the board of governors who the Headteacher reports to and the diocese which prioritises the church–school relationship. The Headteacher has found these relationships to feel more scrutinising than supportive in nature. The Headteacher did meet another Headteacher at DSL training and seemed to have a good rapport but this was over a year ago and they haven't spoken since.

School B is also a small school but is part of a Multi-Academy Trust and then (MAT) which has schools across the local area, there are regular moderation and standardisation meetings with the other schools in the MAT as well as joint CPD training, the Headteacher here has got to know a number of headteachers from the other schools but some of them seem to hold their cards very closely to their chest so much of their conversation is polite, with some vaguely competitive undertones. There are also the cluster group meetings that the Headteacher has attended for seven years now. These are made up of headteachers from a range of schools who are across the same local authority and facilitated by the local university. Every half term the headteachers from these schools spend a day together exploring an area of practice or research and applying these to their own contexts. The headteachers have lunch together and there is an open and comfortable atmosphere. It's been the same headteachers in the group for the last seven years and they have strong and trusting relationships. More recently they have been hosting each other at their schools and exploring an area of practice which the headteachers would like support with. The host school decides the agenda, the activities, and the support that they would appreciate from the others and there is a forensic and supportive exploration of this area of practice and what the next steps may be for this school.

Contextualising this, it is perhaps unsurprising that social capital has such an impact on adaptive capacity. When both of these settings face significant policy change for example, it is possible to see how siloed ways of working can hinder the flow of resources and ideas as well as shared sense-making of what the policy changes will look like in practice. This is an issue that can be further exacerbated within the EY sector whereby settings are often very small, with few staff and very little infrastructure to support collaboration or even to gain external perspectives. Many childminders for example can work almost exclusively alone and many seek out informal professional associations in order to tackle the isolation of this. The significance of this investment into socio-professional networks is difficult to overstate. Regardless of team size though, there are actions which can be taken to promote social capital in work with children and families.

Importantly, Putnam (2001) emphasises that 'capital' is not merely defined by the number of relationships one has, but by the trust and reciprocity within them. Simply knowing someone is different from genuinely supporting them and trusting they would do the same in return. This mutual exchange strengthens relationships, making them a vital source of resilience and support during difficult times. Reciprocity within these connections allows individuals to rely on each other as a sounding board, a confidant, a source of knowledge and experience, and a gateway to valuable resources. It is possible to see how a lack of trust would exacerbate the potential for early years practitioners to work in siloed ways. This is made even more challenging within the context of constant change and improvements which might be considered a threat to current ways of working, or an offence against existing practice. Developing this trust and social capital is therefore crucial in order to effectively manage change.

Similarly, Harvard Business School professor Amy Edmondson, coined the term 'psychological safety' (1999, p354) which she defines as '*a shared belief that the team is safe for interpersonal risk taking*'.

> *The term is meant to suggest neither a careless sense of permissiveness, nor an unrelentingly positive affect but, rather, a sense of confidence that the team will not embarrass, reject, or punish someone for speaking up. This confidence stems from mutual respect and trust among team members.*
>
> *Edmondson, 1999, p354*

The key characteristics of psychological safe environments (Edmondson, 1999, p382) are:

- Mistakes are learning opportunities for the team and are not held against a specific person.

- Members of the team are able to bring up problems and tough issues.

- People on this team accept others for being different.

- It is safe to take a risk on this team.

- It is acceptable to ask other members of this team for help.

- No one on the team would deliberately act in a way that undermines another team member's efforts.

- The unique skills and talents of team members are valued and utilised.

As an early years practitioner you can lead practice in this area by being openly reflective about your practice and what you are working on, being up front about mistakes, and non-judgemental about the mistakes of others. Psychological safety takes time to develop but by being consistent in your compassion, acceptance, and transparency with those around you, you can positively contribute to this culture and in doing so increase the capacity to be flexible in response to the varied needs of stakeholders and to be able to adapt to the ever changing landscape of the early years sector.

Chapter summary

This chapter has identified that effective leadership relies on collaboration and teamwork so that an environment where individuals work together towards common goals can be fostered. It also identified that a shared vision is crucial in driving improvement, as it unites team members and provides direction for meaningful progress. Lastly, it encouraged reflection regarding social capital and the development of trust, strong relationships, and psychological safety. The chapter outlined some of the features of a workplace culture which prioritises these elements as well as some of the benefits of ensuring individuals feel valued and empowered to contribute ideas without fear. Understandings gained here can support practitioners in contributing to an inclusive and resilient culture that supports innovation and lasting change.

Further reading

Edmondson, A. (2018) *The Fearless Organization: Creating Psychological Safety in the Workplace for Learning, Innovation, and Growth*. Wiley.

Website: Read more about Belbin's team roles at www.belbin.com/about/belbin-team-roles.

References

Belbin, R.M. (1993) *Team Roles at Work*. Oxford, Butterworth-Heinemann.

Belbin, R.M. and Brown, V. (2022) *Team Roles at Work* (3rd ed.). Routledge. https://doi.org/10.4324/9781003163152

Carlyle, T. (1841) *On Heroes, Hero-Worship, and the Heroic in History*. London, James Fraser.

Carnwell, R. and Carson, A. (2009) Understanding Partnerships and Collaboration. In *Working in partnership from theory to practice*. Available from: www.researchgate.net/publication/265408621_Understanding_partnerships_and_collaboration

Claridge, T. (2018) *Introduction to Social Capital Theory*. [Online] Available from: www.socialcapitalresearch.com/wp-content/uploads/edd/2018/08/Introduction-to-Social-Capital-Theory.pdf?x85685

Cullen-Lester, K.L., Maupin, C.K. and Carter, D.R. (2017) Incorporating social networks into leadership development: A conceptual model and evaluation of research and practice, *The Leadership Quarterly, 28*(1), pp. 130–152.

Day, D.V. and O'Connor, P. (2003) Leadership development: Understanding the process. In S.E. Murphy and R.E. Riggio (Eds.), *The Future of Leadership Development*, pp. 11–28. New York, Psychology Press.

Edmondson, A. (1999) Psychological safety and learning behavior in work teams. *Administrative Science Quarterly, 44*(2), 350–383. https://doi.org/10.2307/2666999

Holmes, E., O'Connor, R., Perry, V.H., Tracey, I., Wessely, S. and Bullmore, E. (2020) Multidisciplinary research priorities for the COVID-19 pandemic: A call for action for mental health science, *The Lancet Psychiatry, 7*(6), 547–560.

O'Connor, P. and Quinn, L. (2004) Organizational capacity for leadership. In C. McCauley and E. Van Velsor (Eds.), *The Center for Creative Leadership Handbook of Leadership Development* (2nd ed), pp. 417–437. San Francisco, CA, Jossey-Bass.

Orchard, J. (2002) Will the Real Superhero Stand Up? A critical review of the National Standards for Headteachers in England, *International Journal of Children's Spirituality, 7*(2), pp. 159–169.

Putnam, R.D. (2001) *Bowling Alone: The Collapse and Revival of American Community*. New York, Simon and Schuster.

Szreter, S. and Woolcock, M. (2004) Health by association? Social capital, social theory, and the political economy of public health, *International Journal of Epidemiology, 33*(4), 650–667.

Tourish, D. (2019) Is complexity leadership theory complex enough? A critical appraisal, some modifications and suggestions for further research, *Organization Studies, 40*(2), 219–238. https://doi.org/10.1177/0170840618789207

Tuckman, B.W. (1965) Developmental sequence in small groups, *Psychological Bulletin, 63*(6), 384–399.

Van Bavel, J., Baicker, K., Boggio, P., Capraro, V., Cichoka, A. and Willer, R. (2020) Using social and behavioural science to support COVID-19 pandemic response, *Nature Human Behaviour, 4*(5), 460–471.

10 Collaboration – the power of multi-agency working

Michelle Malomo

This chapter will focus on the collaborative work that occurs within the arena of multi-agency working. The use of a theoretical framework of strength-based working and approaches when working within these multi-agency teams will be in focus. It will encourage practitioners to move away from approaches which focus on problems and difficulties, and instead look for strengths that empower and support families. Within the chapter an understanding of the theoretical and policy frameworks which influence professional collaboration will be considered as well as the influence of serious case reviews (SCRs). It examines how integrated working requires effective leadership at all levels. The chapter encourages practitioners to think about the key features, benefits and challenges of integrated working to support families who need extra support. An important aspect of the chapter is the critical appraisal of the role of leadership in joint working for children, young people, parents/carers and families. Within this chapter you will be encouraged to critically reflect upon your own practice, dispositions, and skills in relation to joint working and leadership.

Chapter objectives

In this chapter we:

- Will consider the challenges and benefits of multi-agency working
- Develop an understanding of strength-based approaches
- Support you in understanding the importance of leadership when working in a multi-agency team
- Have an opportunity for practitioners to consider their own practice within this area and where they may need to develop their skills and behaviours within this area.

DOI: 10.4324/9781041055358-16

The challenges and benefits of multi-agency working

When starting to write this chapter I recalled my own thoughts and feelings when the findings of the Laming report (2003) concerning the death of Victoria Climbié were published. Etched in my memory are the accounts of how she had been failed by professionals, the body maps that showed the number of times she had been abused and the picture of her young face smiling. I remember thinking why has this happened? What can society do to prevent this happening to other children? But, sadly in recent weeks further stories of children killed have made headline news. Each child's story highlights failures and missed opportunities by professionals that worked with the families. Malomo and Laurence (2022) acknowledge that unfortunately it is these enquires into the harm and death of children that inform changes in legislation and often the learning that can be gained from positive practice is not explored. The SCRs approach to reflection and learning from practice (although needed) appears to be a model where mistakes are the focus. Therefore, within this chapter there is the desire to build on the ideas presented in Chapter 7, with the intention of getting it right when we work in multi-agency teams. This will involve considering how a strength-based approach could offer a solution when reconsidering and developing practice in multi-agency teams.

Attempting to define what multi-agency working is supports an understanding of what knowledge, skills and behaviours are needed to ensure that this type of working together is effective and enables there to be a vision of best practice. Walker (2018) suggests that multi-agency working is potentially full of complexity, tensions and pitfalls. Considering the findings of SCRs the ineffective nature of working together is highlighted as one of the reasons that children and their families have been failed. However, the DfE (2023, p24) clearly states that for multi-agency working to be effective it must have a clear and shared vision concerning the best outcomes for children. Agencies and organisations must hold each other accountable and offer challenge were needed. Alongside this there is a strong emphasis where the *'voice of children and families combined with the knowledge of experienced practitioners and insights from data'*, will enable *'a greater understanding of the areas of strength and/ or improvement within arrangements and practice'* (DfE, 2023, p24). Placing the voices of children and their families at the heart of practice supports a shift in emphasis where children are the heart of interventions. This supports them to have agency and ensures that their voices are heard by everyone that surrounds them professionally. Bringing different agencies/organisations/professionals together often means that there are differences in approaches and ethos which can influence how they might work with families. This is where a shared vision is essential when working with children and their families. This ensures that all professionals are clear in their shared values and approaches. The need for this is highlighted in findings from numerous SCRs. A further effective feature described by the DfE (2023, p24) is the need for information to be communicated, analysed and shared effectively. Therefore, effective communication is essential to ensure successful collaborative working. Dickens et al. (2023) suggest that communication and courage are essential components of effective work with children and their families. This is an essential component of professional curiosity and is a skill and behaviour that seems essential to develop.

Dickens et al. (2023) state that SCRs consistently have suggested that three themes have emerged: poor quality of assessments, shortcomings in inter-agency working and information sharing, and not knowing the children and understanding their experiences. Alongside this, a lack of 'professional curiosity' and insufficient 'challenge' on the part of child protection practitioners are also cited as further reasons as to why children have been harmed and sadly killed. If this is a consistent finding within reviews it suggests that the system is broken and maybe we need to think about practice changing and developing to address these findings. As we move through this chapter, best practice theories will be explored to support the development of understanding that could inform practice within this area.

Critical reflection

Having read the opening section of this chapter:

What do you think are the challenges when working in a multi-agency team?

What are the attributes and characteristics of a good multi-agency team?

Reflect upon your own experience

What skills do you think you could bring to this type of team?

What knowledge, skills and behaviours do you feel you might need to develop?

Developing an understanding of strength-based approaches

The contemporary landscape of safeguarding in England has been influenced by the need to hold someone accountable for mistakes that have been made when trying to safeguard children. There have been numerous SCRs associated with named children. The purpose of SCRs seems to have been to apportion blame for what went wrong and where accountability has been central to government policy. Frost (2021, p32) suggests that this is both 'negative and damaging' and fails to recognise much of the success of multi-agency working. The government wanted to be seen to be accountable and commissioned two significant reviews: Munro (2011) and Wood (HM Government 2016). In Chapter 7 the Munro report has been explored and the importance of the findings and, if fully implemented, the difference that this could make to practice. It might be useful just to have a brief re-read of this chapter.

Reading the findings of SCRs, although necessary, can be difficult and challenging to digest. It also can be taxing to think about how as individuals you can have any influence on developing practice. However, it is important to maintain hope as further approaches are explored within this chapter. Building on the best practice theories for teamwork explored in Chapter 9, your contribution could make a significant difference. This is especially important when the relationship and knowledge of the family that you bring could give a unique insight as to the needs of the family. Having thought about why multi-agency working has been problematic and considering the recommendations of the DfE (2023), it is essential that professionals find their voices within multi-agency teams and that courage is developed. Alongside this, The Early Intervention Foundation (2020) suggests that having interventions that are based on well-researched approaches ensures that practice when working with children and their families is intentional, inclusive and provides shared ways of thinking for a multi-agency team.

Finding your professional voice

Many years ago, whilst in practice I remember attending my very first Team around the Family (TAF) meeting. At the time I was a principal of a private nursery school and was new to working collaboratively as part of this type of team. As I entered the room I was filled with fear and a gigantic dose of 'imposter syndrome' filled my body. Home (2024, np) describes imposter syndrome as *'a feeling of inadequacy that persists despite evidence of success'*. I knew the family and worked with them on a daily basis, but I remember thinking why am I here? I even let the notion that I am only an early years practitioner creep into my thinking! This is a thought that I have often heard expressed by those in the sector. However, once sat around the table with other professionals I realised that they didn't have the day-to-day relationship with the family that we had within the setting. I listened and everything seemed very clinical and lacked the empathetic stance that really knowing a family can bring. With a sharp intake of breath and a good dose of courage I found my professional voice. I shared my insight into the family – this in turn led to me working in play-based therapy sessions with the family. This outcome went on to support the family and build on the strengths that they had. Having professional courage is essential to ensure that we communicate what we know, and alongside this it is necessary to have the professional curiosity to ask questions as we work with the child and their family.

Before you consider the critical reflection below, take time to look at your settings safeguarding/collaborative working policies. How do these policies support practitioners to find their voices when supporting children and their families?

◯◯ Critical reflection – finding your professional voice

In what ways do you feel you could develop your professional voice?

When working with children and their families are you able to be curious? How might you act upon this within practice?

Within your workplace is there an opportunity to explore within your team how you support children and families within your setting? To move practice forward in this area could you raise this within a team meeting and consider how policy may need to be reviewed to support practice in this area?

A shared vision

It is important that when working within multi-agency teams there is from the outset shared values and an ethos that recognises the value of each team member's professional stance. But central to this must be a placing of the children and their families at the heart of all interventions. They must be given not only a voice but also empowered to have agency over what happens to them.

Over time and throughout diverse disciplines globally, having a strength-based approach has been well documented, e.g. Lopez and Louis (2009), SCIE (2015), Gottlieb (2013), Gottlieb et al. (2022), Department of Early Education Care and Development (2012), and DHSC (2019). Each of these interpretations has been developed through differing disciplines, however there is the commonality of placing individuals at the heart of the change and ensuring that changes within a family are sustainable and developing a resilient spirit. If the landscape of multi-agency working was full of blue sky experiences the challenge of taking this approach would be simpler. However, it can be challenging to look for strengths. As professionals we may find it challenging to look beyond the problems that the children and their families are encountering, and we might want to rush in and fix things. There will be situations and environments that will cause challenges and as professionals multi-agency teams must navigate what is needed and possible as they work with the family. But the reality is that often the sustainability of interventions is driven by lack of funding and limited resources due to social policy restrictions. Alongside this the impact and understanding of what resilience is can limit perceived success. Malomo (2022) suggests that we all encounter challenges in life and resilience involves the ability to process these occurrences and then move to a new place in our being, rather than the concept of bouncing back to who and where we were. The reality is that the adversities in life change us and this will be true for the families that we work with. Having an empathetic approach and supporting a resilient spirit seem key to the sustainability of lasting and meaningful changes within families.

When considering a strength-based approach the work of Hodgkins and Prowle (2023, p 20) is helpful and offers a model that can be implemented in practice. In explaining their approach to strength-based work they state that it is essential to start by perceiving the work with each family as a glass half full of possibilities and potential. They then explain their thinking through the analogy of a daisy (see Figure 10.1).

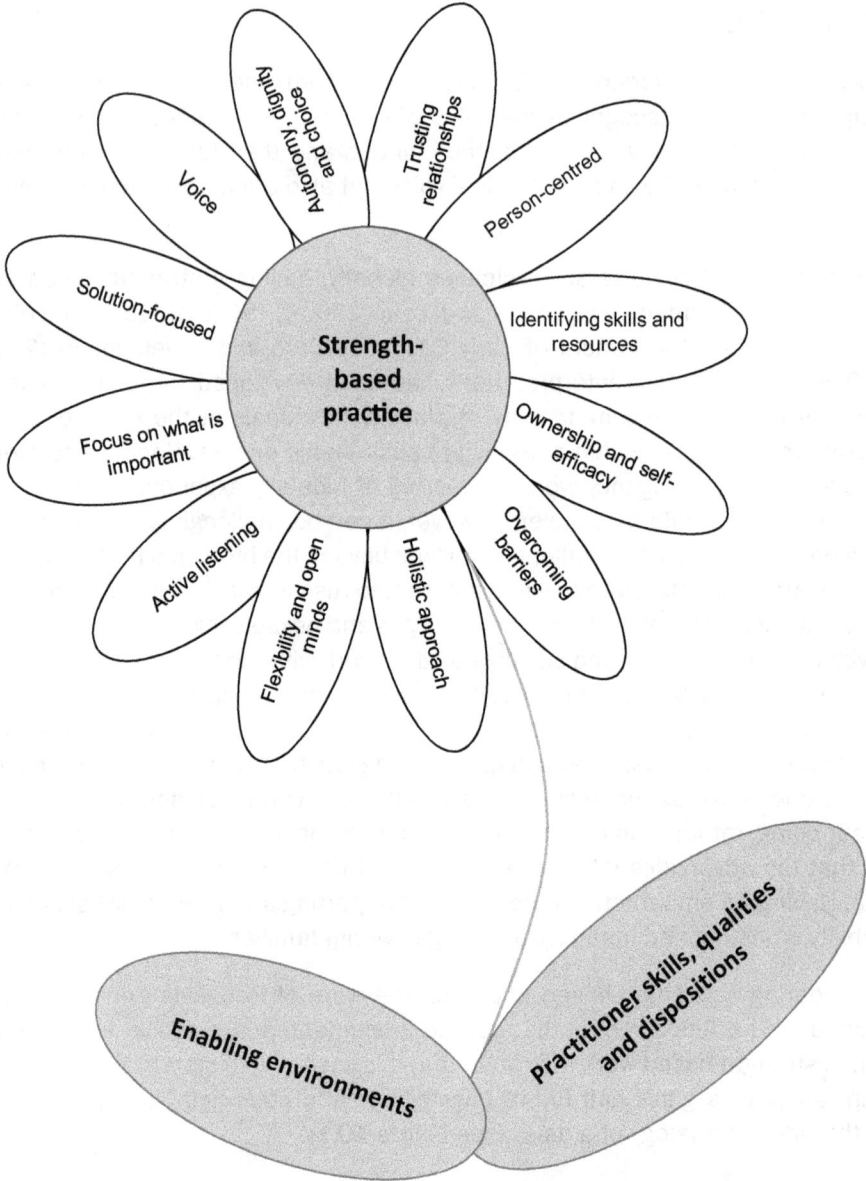

Figure 10.1 *Strength-based practice daisy from: Strength-based Practice with Children and Families, Edition 1, p7 by Angela Hodgkins and Alison Prowle, Copyright 2023 by Routledge. Reproduced by permission of Taylor & Francis Group*

This analogy clearly highlights how focusing on areas with a strength-based approach can have an impact on changes for children and their families. Hodgkins and Prowle (2023) do acknowledge that there must be an authentic approach when focusing on strengths and it is important that when challenges are faced there is honesty within this. This will build trust as you work with children and their families.

At the heart of their thoughts is the acknowledgement that enabling environments (both physical spaces and emotional) and practitioner skills, qualities and dispositions are crucial to affect sustainable changes when working in a TAF. They suggest that the practitioner's ability to form trusting and meaningful relationships brings about the collaboration that is needed to work effectively with children and their families. Each of the petals highlights crucial skills, dispositions and behaviours that will support a strength-based approach being the focus of the work of a TAF. Each one of the petals is a crucial element to enabling work to operate from a strength-based practice approach. These include Trusting relationships; Solution-focused; A focus on what is important; Voice; Autonomy, dignity and choice; Person-centred approach, identifying strengths, skills and assets; Ownership and self-efficacy; Resilience and overcoming barriers; Holistic approach; Flexibility and open-mindedness; Active and empathetic listening; Unconditional positive regard; and Optimism and hope. It may be helpful to explore and understand this theory further. Check out the recommendations within the further reading section of this chapter that support a deeper understanding of this approach in practice. To help you think about how you could apply strength-based practice the case study of the Agbani family is intended to support an exploration of this.

❝❝ Case study – the Agbani family

The Agbani family, from Nigeria, have been in the UK for three years. Oladipo (Dad, 42) had originally entered the country on a student visa and at the time he was able to bring his spouse Funmi (38) and their three children Joel 12, Emmanuel 8 and Ruth 2 1/2 with him. Funmi is currently pregnant with their fourth child. Oladipo has now applied for an extension to his visa to take up a position teaching in a school following successfully gaining his master's degree in education. Under the terms of the visa Funmi can work but has been unable to do so due to her poor health in pregnancy. Oladipo can only work a maximum of 20 hours until the visa extension has been granted. The family are in Manchester and have accessed support through the local Family Hub. When Ruth had her two-year-old check at the Family Hub it was noticed that she had a speech and language delay. Funmi has been reluctant to access further support and has been suffering with high blood pressure throughout her pregnancy. She recently came to the Family Hub outreach drop-in session openly upset and wanting to know if she could access the food bank as the family are still awaiting the outcome of Oladipo's visa application and are struggling to buy enough food.

You are a practitioner working at the Family Hub as a family support worker. You have been asked by the manager to work with Funmi and the family.

Having read the case study and using Hodgkins and Prowle's strength-based daisy model as a guide, work through the petals.

In which areas can you see strengths that could support this family? How might you use the petals to shape your own approaches and practice with this family?

With the information that you have about the family, what are you professionally curious about?

How would you approach supporting this family?

How might other professionals and agencies be able to help this family?

The importance of leadership when working in a multi-agency team

I have become aware, over time, that some EY practitioners are reluctant leaders and do not want to carry the label of a leader. In Chapter 4, the reluctance of many EY practitioners to consider themselves as leaders was explored. Over a number of years whilst teaching a multi-agency working module, I have seen very experienced and talented practitioners struggle to see themselves as a leader of practice. They have preconceived notions of what leadership is and many struggle when working with children, families and other professionals to recognise their own ability and to see their own strengths in practice. Repeatedly however, as they explore the content of this module and find their professional voices, they are more than capable of seeking out strengths within families, leading them to make sustainable changes and supporting them to develop resilient spirits.

The reality of practice is that families come in a variety of guises, and could be experiencing multiple adversities in a landscape of ever-changing social policy. Therefore, leadership too may take various forms. It might mean leading on researching what resources could support the child and their family, it might mean sharing and communicating what you know of the family's strengths. Leadership in the context of multi-agency working needs to be intrinsically motivated and fuelled by a passion and intent to get practice right. Clark and Murray (2012, p29) state that,

> self-leadership needs to be orientated by a worthwhile purpose greater than the individual to be constructive. It requires an inner direction to sustain self-motivation and moral purpose, providing agency to action for a greater goal. We prefer the term 'inner leadership' as it prompts self-reliance and self-organization to tackle problems or obstacles and persist with individual effort

This is the type of leadership that seems to emerge from practice. It has an intention to make meaningful and purposeful changes alongside families and this is what I see when I work alongside EY practitioners. Therefore, there is a need for practitioners to examine the necessity to have a reflective stance and take time to shift their mindset when it comes to leadership in multi-agency working.

⬤⬤ Critical reflection – the reluctant leader

What feelings do you have when you hear the term leader?

Read and reflect upon your thoughts of the above quote from Clark and Murray. How might the model of inner leadership empower you in multi-agency teams?

How are you leading practice within your day-to-day work?

Developing my knowledge skills and behaviours in collaborative working

As we come to the conclusion of this chapter it is important to take some time to apply and personalise what has been explored. As you have been reading the chapter have there been any light bulb moments where you have been able to recognise where you have strengths and where you may need to develop your own understanding as you develop your practice within this area? The title of this chapter suggests that work in this arena is powerful and can make a real difference to the lives of the children and families that we work with. However, I hope that it has become apparent that it can also empower and equip you with new skills as you lead practice within this area. Therefore, the final section of this chapter is a critical reflection on the development of your own skills.

⬤⬤ Critical reflection – developing my own knowledge skills and behaviours as I collaborate with others

Having worked through the chapter what new knowledge have you gleaned and how might this inform your developing practice?

Where do you feel you have strengths in this area of work?

Is there anything within this chapter that you feel could influence the practice within your setting? How could you share this and discuss this with others within your team?

What skills and behaviours would you like to develop to support you when working in multi-agency teams? Who might support you in this quest?

▤ Chapter summary

This chapter has explored the benefits and challenges of multi-agency working, highlighting the positive impact that good practice can have on children and their families. It has also examined current social policy expectations and emphasised a strength-based practice approach, demonstrating how this method can support children and their families in thriving.

Additionally, the chapter has underscored the significance of leadership, even in small areas, and how such efforts can contribute to meaningful change. Lastly, it has encouraged practitioners to reflect on their own development within this field, fostering continuous growth and improvement.

Further reading

This is an interesting video that looks at the impact of having a theoretical framework that can support a shared vision when working with children and their families.

Early Intervention Foundation (2020) www.youtube.com/watch?v=zZEvwA4_ifc&t=2s

Hodgkins, A. and Prowle, A. (2023) *Strength-based practice with children and families*. St Albans: Critical Publishing. Chapter 1 outlines the approach to strength-based practice explored earlier within this chapter.

References

Clark, R. M. and Murray, J. (2012) *Reconceptualizing leadership in the early years*. 1st edn. Maidenhead: Open University Press.

Department of Education (2023) *Working Together to Safeguard Children A guide to multi-agency working to help, protect and promote the welfare of children*. [online] Available at: https://assets.publishing.service.gov.uk/media/669e7501ab418ab055592a7b/Working_together_to_safeguard_children_2023.pdf (accessed 14 Jan 2025).

Department of Education and Early Childhood Development (2012) *Strength-based Approach*. [online] Available at: www.education.vic.gov.au/documents/childhood/professionals/learning/strengthbappr.pdf (accessed 14 Jan 2025).

Department of Health and Social Care (2019) *Strengths-based Approach: Practice Framework and Practice Handbook*. [online] Available at: https://assets.publishing.service.gov.uk/government/uploads/system/uploads/attachment_data/file/778134/stengths-based-approach-practice-framework-and-handbook.pdf (accessed 13 Jan 2025).

Dickens, J., Cook, L., Cossar, C., Okpokiri, C., Taylor, J. and Garstang, J. (2023) Re-envisaging professional curiosity and challenge: Messages for child protection practice from reviews of serious cases in England. *Children and Youth Services Review*, 152, https://doi.org/10.1016/j.childyouth.2023.107081

Early Intervention Foundation (2020) Developing a good theory of change:10 steps for evaluation success in early intervention. [online] Available at: https://www.youtube.com/watch?v=zZEvwA4_ifc&t=2s (accessed 4 Aug 2025).

Frost, N. (2021) *Safeguarding children and young people: A guide for professionals working together*. London: Sage.

Gottlieb, L. (2013) *Strengths-based nursing care: Health and healing for person and family*. New York: Springer Publishing.

Gottlieb, R. L., Vaca, C. E., Paredes, R., Mera, J., Webb, B. J., Perez, G., et al. (2022) Early Remdesivir to prevent progression to severe Covid-19 in outpatients. *New England Journal of Medicine*, 386(4): 305–15.

Hodgkins, A. and Prowle, A. (2023) *Strength-based practice with children and families*. St Albans: Critical Publishing.

Home, J. (2024) *Imposture Syndrome*. [online] Available at: www.bma.org.uk/advice-and-support/your-wellbeing/insight-and-advice/first-times-in-medicine/imposter-syndrome#:~:text=Imposter%20syndrome%20is%20described%20as,a%20significant%20contributor%20to%20burnout (accessed 08 Jan 2025).

HM Government (2016) *Wood Report Sector expert review of new multi-agency safeguarding arrangements*. [online] Available at: https://assets.publishing.service.gov.uk/government/uploads/system/uploads/attachment_data/file/987928/Wood_Review_of_multi-agency_safeguarding_arrangements_2021.pdf (accessed Jan 2025).

Laming, L. H. (2003) *The Victoria Climbié Inquiry Report*, Cm. 5370, London: TSO. [online] Available at: www.gov.uk/government/publications/the-victoria-climbie-inquiry-report-of-an-inquiry-by-lord-laming

Lopez, S. J. and Louis, M. C. (2009) The principles of strengths-based education. *Journal of College and Character*, 10: 1–8.

Malomo, M. (2022) Resilience. In Richards, H. and Malomo, M. (eds) *Developing your professional identity: A guide for working with children and families*. 1st edn. St Albans: Critical Publishing.

Malomo, M. and Laurence, E. (2022) Finding your place in safeguarding. In Richards, H. and Malomo, M. (eds) *Developing your professional identity: A guide for working with children and families*. 1st edn. St Albans: Critical Publishing.

Munro, E. (2011) *The Munro Review of Child Protection: Final Report, A child-centred system*. [Online] Available at: https://assets.publishing.service.gov.uk/media/5a7b455ee5274a34770ea939/Munro-Review.pdf (accessed 14 Jan 2025).

Social Care Institute for Excellence (SCIE) (2015) Care Act: Guidance on Strengths-based Approaches. [online] Available at: www.scie.org.uk/strengths-based-approaches (accessed 14 Jan 2025).

Walker, G. (2018) *Working together for children – A critical introduction to Multi-Agency working*, 2nd edn. London: Bloomsbury Academic Press.

Theme 6
The innovator

Chapter 11 will support you in your duties as an innovator.

Duty 8 Demonstrate leaderful practice through the effective deployment of resources and practitioners keeping the child's voice and needs central to practice.	**Knowledge:** 1 2 3 4 8 9 10 11 12 13 15 16 17 18 19
	Skills: 2 3 5 10 14 15 17 18 21 22 23 25
	Behaviours: 1 2 3 5 6 7 8 9
Duty 9 Reflect and build on practice through ongoing professional enquiry and action research to contribute to the pedagogical approach of their setting. To be accountable for day-to-day practice, longer term planning, management and training within the specific aspect or environment for which they are responsible.	**Knowledge:** 2 3 4 6 7 8 9 10 11 12 13 15 16 17 18
	Skills: 1 2 3 4 5 6 7 9 10 14 15 18 19 21 23
	Behaviours: 1 2 3 4 5 6 7 8 9

DOI: 10.4324/9781041055358-17

Duty 11 Commit to becoming a reflective practitioner, enhancing skills and knowledge to improve pedagogical practice. Guide and support the development of the reflective practice of others.	**Knowledge:** 1 3 4 5 7 9 10 11 13 17 18 19 20
	Skills: 14 15 21
	Behaviours: 1 2 5 6 9
Duty 16 To lead and manage across the area, aspect or environment for which they are responsible for.	**Knowledge:** 1 2 5 7 16 17 19 20 21
	Skills: 2 4 10 11 13 14 15 16 18 20 21 22 23 24 25 26
	Behaviours: 1 2 3 5 6 8 9

11 Innovative, appreciative, and impactful research for practice

Samantha Sutton-Tsang

This chapter identifies significant links between research and quality improvement. By taking an appreciative approach, it aims to support practitioners in evaluating practice and initiating small changes within their settings, based upon engagement with theory and research. It empowers practitioners to understand practice/work-based enquiry. Within this chapter, there is a strong emphasis on improving quality and ensuring that conducting research is purposeful either to the setting, to children's experiences or your own professional development.

🎯 Chapter objectives

This chapter will:

- Present the links between research and quality improvement
- Discuss Appreciative Inquiry as an approach for collaborative and purposeful research with stakeholders
- Analyse the purpose of a literature review
- Distinguish between suitable research paradigms for early years research
- Highlight the importance of reflecting on practice and research to inform progress
- Examine how a Community of Practice can support research and quality improvement.

Introduction

Research and quality improvement are often viewed as distinct endeavours, but they are deeply intertwined in the context of educational and professional practice. This chapter

DOI: 10.4324/9781041055358-18

seeks to highlight the significant connections between research and quality improvement, adopting an appreciative approach to support practitioners. By engaging with theory and research, practitioners can critically evaluate their practices and implement small, meaningful changes within their settings. This approach not only enhances the quality of the setting but also enriches children's experiences and contributes to professional development.

Drawing from examples of student research projects conducted at Level 5 on an FdA early years course (0–8 years), and emphasising the benefits of purposeful research, this chapter aims to empower practitioners to conduct work-based inquiries that are directly relevant to their settings and professional growth. Within this chapter, the terms practitioners and researcher will be used interchangeably since the student researcher will often be a practitioner in the setting.

Understanding research and quality improvement

Carrying out a research project for the first time can be an exciting and overwhelming process. Having a solid foundation to build your research on is key to success, therefore understanding the research process is vital. Research is a systematic investigation aimed at discovering new knowledge or understanding existing knowledge more deeply. It involves rigorous methodologies and can be theoretical or applied to practice (Nolan et al, 2013). In contrast, quality improvement (QI) focuses on enhancing processes, services, or outcomes through iterative changes (Reed, 2012). It is rooted in practical applications and often utilises data to inform decision-making. The intersection of research and QI lies in the shared goal of advancing knowledge and practice. Research provides the evidence base and theoretical frameworks that inform QI initiatives, while QI offers a practical application for research findings. When practitioners engage in research-informed QI, they bridge the gap between theory and practice, leading to more effective and sustainable improvements (Walker and Solvason, 2014).

When conducting research in practice, it is important to find a purpose that will benefit the setting, colleagues, and your own practice. The most beneficial type of research is that which leads to ongoing practice developments and can coincide with quality improvement. Reed and Canning (2012, p9) state that, 'Quality improvement is a continuous process rather than a single event'. It involves assessing various aspects of practice to better support and enhance the well-being and development of children and their families. This process encompasses the entire early years setting and is about more than the inspection process. Crucially, it involves self-evaluation to identify opportunities for improvement. This requires listening to the perspectives of stakeholders in the setting, including the children, and recognising key areas for enhancement. It is important at this point to highlight that ethical practice should be embedded throughout the research process and not just a procedural requirement of it. Careful consideration should be given to the research focus and whether it would be ethically sound to conduct research within your setting with colleagues, children and the families that you work with. Once a topic has been agreed by a supervisor, when undertaking research within the context of Higher Education studies, it is imperative that you comply with the ethical policies established by the awarding body.

Adopting Appreciative Inquiry in practice

While many of us picture researchers as experts who enter specific settings to address practical problems, in reality, practitioners engage informally in research on a daily basis as part of quality improvement to their practice. To maximise the impact of research on quality improvement, it is essential that research is purposeful and relevant to the setting (Walker and Solvason, 2014). This involves aligning research goals with the needs of the setting, the experiences of children, and the professional development objectives of practitioners. By co-constructing research with the setting, it is possible to support the existing shared goals and purpose.

An approach that I encourage my students to adopt is Appreciative Inquiry (AI). Originally developed '*to reveal, often overlooked positive aspects of experiences; to generate new theory and to anticipate a new reality*' (Clouder and King, 2015, p2), Appreciate Inquiry was a term developed by Cooperider and Srivastva (1987) and is a strengths-based, collaborative method for organisational change. Appreciative Inquiry emphasises what works well and why, to build on these strengths (Shuayb et al., 2009). Unlike traditional problem-solving approaches that focus on deficiencies, AI highlights positive aspects, creating a motivating and empowering environment for practitioners (Cooperider and Srivastva, 1987). When practitioner research uses an appreciative approach, it centres on existing strengths and identifies growth areas, fostering a strengths-based mindset and adding value to the setting (Bellinger and Elliott, 2011). Improvements should primarily enhance professional development and the environments in which practitioners operate, thereby promoting high-quality early years practice (Walker and Solvason, 2014, p2). This fully participative approach, involving stakeholders such as colleagues, children, and families, can help identify strengths in practice to be celebrated and built upon. Appreciative Inquiry's positive approach focuses on identifying and building on 'best practices' within a setting. This method is effective for collaborative work with employers and colleagues, as it starts with recognising good practices rather than pinpointing problems, distinguishing it from other research approaches (Shuayb et al., 2009).

Rather than unearthing a universal truth, the ultimate aim of research is to foster positive outcomes, and to 'bring about good' (Bloor, 2010). Research should be contextually relevant, addressing the specific needs and challenges of the setting. Contextual relevance ensures that the findings are applicable and can be readily implemented. Practitioners should consider the unique characteristics of their setting, such as the demographics of the children, the resources available, and the cultural context, when designing and conducting research. Appreciative Inquiry acknowledges that all knowledge is interconnected and collaboratively constructed. (Bellinger and Elliott, 2011, p712). Appreciative Inquiry draws upon the deep personal experiences of participants within the context of a specific topic, making familiarity with the subject matter essential for both researchers and participants. In partnership, the participants and the researcher's contributions help generate data and collaboratively construct knowledge, supporting the research process. Through a collaborative approach involving stakeholders and utilising interactive data collection methods such as focus groups and interviews, researchers and participants can jointly identify best practices, consider potential changes, and implement these changes within the setting (Shuayb et al., 2009).

Therefore, the focus of Appreciative Inquiry remains on the process of research rather than a definitive end product (Bellinger and Elliott, 2011) and for it to be successful, practitioner researchers must collaborate with stakeholders (Cooperider and Srivastva, 1987). Work-based inquiry empowers practitioners to take ownership of their professional development and the quality improvement process. By engaging in inquiry, practitioners develop critical thinking skills, enhance their understanding of practice, and contribute to the knowledge base of their field. A starting point to enhancing your knowledge base is conducting a literature review on your chosen topic.

Literature review

Successful research begins with a thorough literature review. This is essential in early years research and serves a critical purpose. Cohen, Manion, and Morrison (2011) state that a literature review involves a comprehensive analysis of existing studies and publications related to a specific topic, helping to clarify key concepts, establish the credibility of the research, and provide a contextual background while identifying gaps in your current knowledge. Walker and Solvason (2014, p47) encourage researchers to maintain an open mind and challenge any preconceived notions about their research by conducting a detailed and thorough literature review.

One primary purpose of a literature review is to establish the context for the research. It situates the current study within the broader field of early years education and care, highlighting the historical development of the topic and the progression of theoretical perspectives. By reviewing past research, the researcher can demonstrate how their work fits into the existing body of knowledge, ensuring that the study is relevant and timely. This contextualisation also helps in articulating the rationale for the research, making it clear why the study is needed and what it aims to contribute.

A thorough literature review allows the researcher to identify gaps in the existing knowledge. In early years research, this is particularly crucial as it ensures that the study addresses unmet needs or unexplored areas. By pinpointing these gaps, researchers can justify the significance of their work, arguing for its potential to advance understanding or improve practice. This process also helps in refining the research questions and objectives, ensuring they are both focused and meaningful.

Walker and Solvason (2014) evaluate the importance of the literature review by providing an exemplar of how to conduct one for an early years project. They identify the importance of reflecting on the process since the literature review plays a crucial role in informing the research design and methodology. By examining how previous studies were conducted, researchers can learn about effective methods and potential pitfalls. This insight helps in selecting appropriate research designs, tools, and techniques, which are especially important in early years research where ethical considerations and developmental appropriateness are paramount. Additionally, understanding the strengths and limitations of past research can guide the development of robust and innovative methodologies.

In early years research, the literature review is fundamental in developing a theoretical framework. Your theoretical framework forms the foundation of the study, offering a structured perspective to examine the research problem. By engaging with existing theories and models, researchers can build upon established knowledge and contribute to theoretical advancements. This is particularly important in early childhood education, where developmental theories and educational models greatly influence practice and policy.

A literature review also provides the necessary supporting evidence to enhance the study's credibility and reliability. By citing relevant research, researchers can justify their hypotheses, arguments, and findings. This evidence-based approach is essential, where the study's implications can significantly impact educational practices and policies. Grounding the research in established knowledge not only adds to its validity but also ensures its potential for practical application. Moreover, engaging with a wide range of literature enhances critical thinking (Cohen, Manion, and Morrison, 2011).

❝ Case study – Holly and Sinead's experiences of conducting a research project as part of their FdA early years studies. *Holly writes the following in her research project:*

The literature review has provided a deeper knowledge and understanding of the differing factors, potential controversies and opinions that interlink with my research question. Researching the importance of early identification of a speech and language delay strengthened my knowledge of the important role that early years practitioners have in recognising and responding to speech and language. I can begin to analyse the chosen framework within the setting having researched the key themes related to my research question.

Sinead reflects on the literature review:

By reading the relevant literature, I am more aware of the theory behind parent partnerships. I have found ideas on how to implement strategies at the setting where I work. I have sometimes overlooked the fact that some of these concepts are already being implemented in my setting. I have found it interesting to revisit the legislation and pinpoint the areas that focus on parent partnership. I have found myself questioning how I could be building better partnerships with each family and thinking of new ideas to engage families.

Holly and Sinead's case studies demonstrate how a literature review can significantly inform and enhance the research process, from understanding the context and strengthening professional knowledge to guiding the application of theoretical frameworks. Literature reviews can also benefit current practice and promote further critical thinking. Engaging in research is a powerful form of professional development. It enhances practitioners' knowledge, skills, and understanding of their practice. By conducting research, practitioners can stay up to date with the latest developments in their field, critically evaluate their practices, and contribute to the advancement of knowledge and practice.

⌬ Critical reflection

Reflect on how early years practitioners can effectively use literature reviews to identify and address gaps in knowledge, ensuring their research is both relevant and impactful for advancing educational practices and policies?

Developing a methodology for your research

Having conducted a literature review, the researcher must decide on their methodology and the data collection techniques that they will adopt to gather data from participants. After reading your literature and similar studies conducted in your chosen field of research, you may collate ideas to inform your research methodology and data collection methods.

The literature review can significantly shape your methodology by providing insights from previous studies related to your research topic. It is crucial to consistently refer to your institution's ethics policy and to integrate Bloor's concept of utilising research for the greater good, as discussed earlier in this chapter. Consider the practicality of your setting by evaluating which data collection methods are likely to be more effectively received by the participants you plan to engage, and this will influence your research approach or methodology.

❝ ❞ Case study – Victoria's experience

Victoria reflects on choosing an appropriate research approach for her research project:

> There are a wide range of different research approaches that could have been used. Denscombe (2017, p24) states that 'there is no single pathway to good research: there are always options and alternatives'. However, I would argue that choosing an option that best fits the project is important. This is supported by Savin-Baden (2017, p145), who believes that the methodology 'frames your whole project and helps you to choose the right methods'.

What counts as best fit will depend on the paradigm surrounding the research. Below is a brief exploration of some of the paradigms in which underpin research.

Paradigms in research

A paradigm, as defined by Hughes (2010, p35 cited in Mukherji and Albon, 2018, p69), is a way of seeing the world that frames a research topic and influences how we think about it. The two opposing paradigms in research are interpretivism and positivism. It is important to understand how these paradigms might impact on our research design.

Interpretivist paradigm

The interpretivist paradigm acknowledges that a researcher's personal and professional values, culture, and background can shape what data is identified, recorded, and how it is interpreted. As Denscombe (2003, p268) identifies, '*the researcher's self is an integral part of the analysis*' of the data. This perspective contrasts with more objective approaches by emphasising the subjective nature of understanding human experiences.

Walker and Solvason (2014, p65) explain that an interpretivist approach accepts the absence of set answers, recognising that individuals hold their own views. Research in this paradigm focuses on uncovering these views rather than seeking a single 'correct' answer. Mukherji and Albon (2018, p87) further elaborate that interpretivist research is interested in the meanings people ascribe to their actions, acknowledging that there may be multiple explanations for behaviours and events. The goal within interpretivist research is to gain detailed insight into specific issues rather than to make broad generalisations.

The interpretivist paradigm aligns well with the principles of early years education, which emphasise:

* the unique child
* the child's voice
* stakeholder views
* social constructions of childhood
* reflecting on practice

This approach resonates with the early years sector's commitment to understanding each child's unique perspective and experiences. It moves away from the notion of a single, unchanging truth, a concept more aligned with the positivist paradigm (Mukherji and Albon, 2018, p87).

Adopting an interpretivist paradigm is consistent with Appreciative Inquiry, as the perspectives of individuals who fully comprehend and experience the real world are vital for the success of Appreciative Inquiry. It is essential to maintain a positive outlook, demonstrate unconditional positive regard, and exhibit both empathy and reflective capacity throughout the research process (Clouder and King, 2015, p13).

Positivist paradigm

In contrast, the positivist paradigm focuses on gathering quantitative data through scientific methods, primarily involving experiments. This approach seeks to discover objective truths that can be generalised across different contexts. However, as Jarvis and Opie (2014, p64) point out, experiments can be unsuitable for undergraduate research in early years settings due to various ethical issues.

Positivist research aims for objectivity and replicability, often using large-scale data collection to identify patterns and establish laws. While this can be valuable for certain types of inquiries, it may not capture the rich, contextualised understandings that are crucial in early childhood education.

Integrating paradigms in practice

While interpretivism and positivism represent different ways of understanding the world, both can offer valuable insights for quality improvement in early years settings. Practitioners can benefit from integrating elements of both paradigms, using quantitative data to identify trends and areas for improvement, and qualitative insights to understand the underlying reasons and meanings behind these trends. For instance, a practitioner might use quantitative assessments to track children's progress in literacy. Concurrently, they might conduct qualitative observations and interviews to understand how children engage with reading activities and what motivates them. This combined approach can provide a more comprehensive picture, informing targeted and effective quality improvement strategies.

Understanding and applying different research paradigms can significantly enhance the quality of practice in early years settings. The interpretivist paradigm, with its focus on multiple meanings and individual perspectives, aligns well with the sector's values and goals. It emphasises the importance of understanding each child's unique experiences and the views of all stakeholders. Meanwhile, the positivist paradigm offers tools for objective measurement and analysis, which can complement qualitative insights.

By adopting a balanced approach that draws on both paradigms, practitioners can conduct purposeful research that supports continuous improvement, enhances children's experiences, and fosters professional development. This integrated approach ensures that research is both meaningful and impactful, ultimately leading to higher-quality early years practice.

Reflection on practice

Reflecting on practice and research in early years education involves critically examining how research findings and theoretical insights influence practical approaches and vice versa. This reflective process helps practitioners evaluate the effectiveness of their methods, identify areas for improvement, and ensure that their practices are aligned with current research. It encourages continuous learning and adaptation, fostering a more responsive and evidence-based approach to early childhood education. By integrating research into practice and reflecting on the research process and its outcomes, practitioners can enhance their understanding, refine their strategies, and ultimately improve the quality of education and support provided to young children.

Appreciative Inquiry presents an approach for research that is well-suited for cultivating a culture of reflective learning (Bellinger and Elliott, 2011, p715) and a reflective journal kept during the research process can provide several benefits including:

- **Enhanced self-awareness:** A reflective journal helps researchers gain a deeper understanding of their own thought processes, biases, and assumptions. By regularly documenting their reflections, researchers can become more aware of how their perspectives influence the research, leading to more objective and balanced analysis supporting the validity of the research.

- **Improved problem-solving and critical thinking:** Reflective journalling allows researchers to document challenges, successes, and insights as they occur. This ongoing record helps identify patterns and recurring issues, facilitating more effective problem-solving and strategy adjustments throughout the research process. Regular reflection encourages critical analysis of research methods and results. By questioning and evaluating their own work, researchers can develop a more nuanced understanding of their findings and improve the rigour of their research.

- **Increased clarity and focus:** Writing reflections helps clarify research goals, hypotheses, and methodologies. By articulating thoughts and ideas, researchers can refine their focus, ensuring that their study remains aligned with its objectives and is responsive to emerging findings at each stage of the process.

- **Documentation of progress:** A reflective journal provides a detailed record of the research journey, including decisions made, changes in approach, and milestones achieved. This documentation is valuable for tracking progress, preparing reports, and evaluating the overall impact of the research.

- **Enhanced communication:** Reflective journals can be useful for communicating the research process and outcomes to others, particularly if you have agreed to disseminate findings to your participants.

- **Emotional support and resilience:** The process of writing about experiences, frustrations, and successes can provide emotional relief and resilience. Reflective writing in a journal helps researchers process their experiences, manage stress, and maintain motivation throughout the research journey.

Bellinger and Elliott (p719) suggest that reflecting on the research process requires the researcher to engage in reflexivity, allowing them to challenge their own assumptions and critically evaluate the information gathered.

⊙⊙ **Critical reflection**

Why don't you start your own reflective research journal by capturing how this chapter has made you feel about embarking on your own research journey?

Reflective practice and reflective writing contribute significantly to quality improvement in early years education by enabling practitioners to pinpoint areas for development, enhance self-awareness, and make informed, evidence-based decisions (Reed and Canning, 2012). These practices facilitate collaborative reflection, assist in setting and monitoring goals, and promote a culture of continuous improvement. Additionally, reflective writing aids in effective communication with stakeholders and provides a documented record of professional development. By incorporating reflective practices into their routine, practitioners cultivate an environment of ongoing enhancement, thereby advancing their professional development and enriching the educational experiences of young children.

Developing communities of practice

Communities of Practice (CoP) consist of individuals who share a common interest or profession and engage in collective learning to enhance their practice (Wenger, 1998). In early years education and care, the development of a CoP can greatly support research efforts and contribute to quality improvement (Reed and Sansoyer, 2012). Cooperider et al. (2003, as cited in Reed, 2007) argue that within Appreciative Inquiry, participants bring diverse perspectives and experiences from various levels within a setting, enriching the research with a broader range of viewpoints and thus elevating the CoP. These communities provide a structured environment for collaboration, knowledge exchange, and professional development, all of which are essential for improving educational practices and outcomes through the co-construction of knowledge. For researchers in early years settings, CoP can serve as a valuable support system, offering numerous benefits that enhance both their practice and professional development.

⊙⊙ **Critical reflection**

As you embark upon your own research study, consider how your Community of Practice can support your research design.

Embracing communities of practice to support research

Communities of practice can benefit early years researchers by:

1. **Fostering collaboration and knowledge sharing:** CoP enable practitioners to collaborate, exchange ideas, and review each other's work, fostering best practices and innovations that enhance research quality and relevance in early years settings.

2. **Providing access to expertise and resources:** CoP members, often experts with diverse specialisations, provide valuable advice, resources, and updates. Early years researchers can refine their approaches and tackle challenges effectively by leveraging this collective expertise. Online platforms like social media groups and LinkedIn further expand access to a broader range of expertise.

3. **Encouraging reflective practice:** Reflective practice is essential for quality improvement, and CoP offer a supportive space for discussing experiences, challenges, and successes. Regular peer interactions and feedback help practitioners critically reflect, identify improvements, and enhance their research practice, fostering professional growth.

4. **Facilitating professional development:** CoP may organise workshops, seminars, and training sessions on research and early years education. These opportunities help researchers build skills, stay current with trends, and enhance their research capabilities, advancing knowledge and practice in early years settings.

5. **Providing emotional and moral support:** Research in early years settings can be challenging, with researchers facing various pressures and uncertainties. CoP outside of the setting (e.g. within the course cohort) offer impartial emotional and moral support by providing a network of peers who understand the unique demands of the field. This support can help researchers navigate difficulties, maintain motivation, and foster resilience.

6. **Encouraging innovation and creativity:** Diverse perspectives within CoP stimulate creativity and innovation. By discussing different approaches and exploring new ideas, researchers can develop innovative solutions and methodologies, fostering a culture of experimentation and continuous improvement.

7. **Enhancing dissemination and impact:** CoP can aid in the dissemination of research findings by providing platforms for presenting and discussing results with a wider audience. Researchers receive constructive peer feedback, refining their work before publication. CoP networks also help spread findings effectively, enhancing their impact on practice and policy in early years settings.

8. **Building a strong professional network:** Participating in CoP helps researchers build a strong professional network, which can be invaluable for career development and future collaborations leading to new research opportunities, partnerships, and funding sources, supporting the growth and sustainability of research efforts in early years education.

CoP play a crucial role in early years settings practice. They facilitate professional development, offer emotional support, stimulate innovation, and enhance dissemination of best practices. By leveraging the collective knowledge and experience of their members, CoP significantly advance research and practice in early childhood education. Integrating CoP into early years practice supports research, drives quality improvement, and creates a dynamic environment where continuous enhancement and professional growth are key to achieving excellence in education and promoting the overall development of young children.

Disseminating research findings

Sharing research findings with research participants and stakeholders is an important aspect of professional development and can further enhance the Community of Practice. Dissemination can take various forms, such as publishing articles in academic journals, presenting at conferences, or sharing insights within your community of practice. By disseminating their research, practitioners contribute to the collective knowledge of their field and inspire others to engage in research and quality improvement.

> ❝ **Case study – Victoria's experience of disseminating findings**
>
> Victoria shares her reflections on disseminating the findings of her study:
>
> It is important that consideration is given to how the findings of this project are shared with the setting in which the research was undertaken. Mukherji and Albon (2018) outline how the dissemination of research findings is linked to the principle of giving back to the setting that allowed the research to take place. Walker and Solvason (2014) support this point by discussing that dissemination of results is closely linked to ethical practice. Moreover, the study approach recognises the need to share the findings as these may benefit others.

Disseminating research findings is more than just providing feedback and outcomes to participants. Researchers have an ethical duty to keep participants informed of the research process and this goes back to what the researcher outlines in their introduction to recruiting participants, fulfilling any obligations mentioned at this point and adhering to the Appreciative Inquiry approach to research.

🗒 Chapter summary

There are numerous and varied research methodologies available to practitioners for conducting research. This chapter underscores the critical relationship between research and quality improvement, highlighting the value of an appreciative approach that prioritises strengths and fosters collaboration. By engaging with theoretical frameworks and empirical research, practitioners are able to critically assess their practices, implement incremental changes, and elevate the overall quality of their settings. Appreciative Inquiry provides a framework for practitioners to identify effective practices within their setting and collaborate with stakeholders to build upon these strengths (Bellinger and Elliott, 2011, p720). This method not only enhances outcomes for children but also facilitates practitioners' professional development and development of good practice in the setting.

Research and quality improvement are not distinct undertakings but rather interrelated processes that, when integrated, contribute to more effective and sustainable improvements. By engaging in purposeful research that is contextually relevant and centred on children's and families' experiences, practitioners can ensure that their efforts are both meaningful and impactful. Through practice-based inquiry, reflective practice, and collaboration within a community of practice, practitioners are empowered to continually refine their approaches and make significant contributions to the field of early years education.

📚 Further reading

Mukherji, P and Albon, D (2018) *Research Methods in Early Childhood: An Introductory Guide.* London: SAGE.

Shuayb, M, Sharp, C, Judkins, M and Hetherington, M (2009) *Using Appreciative Inquiry in educational research: Possibilities and limitations.* [online] Available at: www.nfer.ac.uk/media/xz3pdlb3/aen01.pdf [accessed 19 August 2024]

Walker, R and Solvason, C (2014) *Success with Your Early Years Research Project.* London: SAGE.

🖋 References

Bellinger, A and Elliott, T (2011) What are you looking at? The potential of appreciative inquiry as a research approach for social work. *British Journal of Social Work*, 41: 708–725. Doi:10.1093/bjsw/bcr065

Bloor, M (2010) The Researcher's obligation to bring about good. *Qualitative Social Work: QSW: Research and Practice*, 9(1): 17–20. https://doi-org.apollo.worc.ac.uk/10.1177/1473325009355616

Clouder, D and King, V (2015) What works? A critique of Appreciative Inquiry as a research method/ology. In Huisman, J. and Tight, M. (eds) *Theory and Method in Higher Education Research, Vol.1: Theory and Method in Higher Education Research II*. Bingley, UK: Emerald Group Publishing Limited, pp. 169–190. http://dx.doi.org/10.1108/S2056-375220150000001008

Cohen, L, Manion, L, and Morrison, K (2011) *Research Methods in Education* (7th edition). Oxon: Routledge.

Cooperider, D and Srivastva, S (1987) *Appreciative Inquiry in organizational life.* [online] Available at: www.oio.nl/wp-content/uploads/APPRECIATIVE_INQUIRY_IN_Orgnizational_life.pdf [accessed 19 August 2024]

Denscombe, M (2003) *The Good Research Guide: For Small-scale Social Research Projects.* Berkshire: Open University Press.

Denscombe, M (2017) *The Good Research Guide: For Small-scale Social Research Projects* (6th edition). Berkshire: Open University Press.

Jarvis, P and Opie, C (2014) Introduction to Methodology. In Jarvis, P., George, J., Holland, W. Newman, S (eds) *Research in the Early Years: A Step-By-Step Guide.* Oxford: Routledge.

Mukherji, P and Albon, D (2018) *Research Methods in Early Childhood: An Introductory Guide.* London: SAGE.

Nolan, A, Macfarlane, K and Cartmel, J (2013) *Research in Early Childhood.* London: SAGE.

Reed, J (2007) *Appreciative Inquiry: Research for Change.* London: SAGE.

Reed, M (2012) What do we mean by quality and quality improvement? In Reed, M. and Canning, N. (eds) *Implementing Quality Improvement and Change in the Early Years.* London: SAGE, pp. 9–23.

Reed, M and Canning, N (2012) *Implementing Quality Improvement and Change in the Early Years*. London: SAGE.

Reed, M and Sansoyer, P (2012) Quality improvement integrated working. In Reed, M. and Canning, N. (eds) *Implementing Quality Improvement and Change in the Early Years*. London: SAGE, pp. 42–56.

Savin-Baden, M (2017) Doing your research project. In Musgrave, J., Savin-Baden, M., and Stobbs, N. (eds) *Studying for your Early Years Degree: Skills and Knowledge for Becoming an Effective Practitioners*. St Albans: Critical Publishing, pp. 183–196.

Shuayb, M, Sharp, C, Judkins, M and Hetherington, M (2009) *Using Appreciative Inquiry in educational research: Possibilities and limitations*. [online] Available at: www.nfer.ac.uk/media/xz3pdlb3/aen01.pdf (accessed 19 August 2024)

Walker, R and Solvason, C (2014) *Success with Your Early Years Research Project*. London: SAGE.

Wenger, E (1998) *Communities of Practice: Learning, Meaning and Identity*. Cambridge: Cambridge University Press.

Conclusion

This book has only been possible because of the generous contributions of our authors. Their knowledge and skill in articulating the lessons they have learned through a diverse range of experiences has created a rich resource in supporting you to think beyond the duties of practice to take ownership of the unique contribution you bring to practice. We are really grateful to all of our authors for the time, effort and expertise they have poured into this book.

As editors, this book has provided a rich learning experience for ourselves and afforded the opportunity to be challenged and nurtured by the thinking of our authors. As each chapter has been developed it is the strong ethos of hope-inspired practice which provides the golden thread throughout this book. Throughout each chapter critical reflections are pivotal in giving permission for you to see yourself in theoretical frameworks, research and social policy in relation to work with children and families. This means that the book has the potential to be a handbook for change alongside developing the next generation of leaders.

Through the consideration of the many roles that early years practitioners adopt, the conversation is moved beyond just the regulatory requirements, towards empowering the potential for change. Chapters One and Two supported an exploration of the role of the Educator/Developer. These chapters had a context sensitive approach to the holistic well-being and development of children. They also included practical and meaningful examples of how practice could be developed within these areas. Chapters Three and Four address the role of the Custodian in practice. Within these chapters you were supported in considering legislation, professional guidance and local policy initiatives and identifying your role as a Leader in ensuring that policies contribute to quality provision. Chapters Five and Six consider the role of being a Planner of provision. These chapters support you in creating provision which is child-centred and adopts a playful pedagogy. Chapters Seven and Eight focus on your role as an advocate for children. They support your understanding of children's rights from a global perspective and encourage you to develop your professional curiosity and advanced safeguard practice. Chapters Nine and Ten explore your role as a Collaborator and encourage you to nurture sustainable and effective teams both in setting and in a multi-agency context.

DOI: 10.4324/9781041055358-19

Finally, Chapter 11 challenges you to take up the role of an innovator of practice with the intention of making meaningful and sustainable changes.

As we come to the end of writing this book, social policy in the early years is set for some further changes with more places for children at the heart of current government thinking. Alongside this there will be a need for leaders to step up and develop practices that are above and beyond the requirements of social policy but create the best childhood experiences for every child. It is our hope that this book supports this vision.

Index

For Product Safety Concerns and Information please contact our EU
representative GPSR@taylorandfrancis.com
Taylor & Francis Verlag GmbH, Kaufingerstraße 24, 80331 München, Germany

* 9 7 8 1 9 1 6 9 2 5 7 8 6 *